WILLIAMS-SONOMA
GRILL
SCHOOL

ANDREW SCHLOSS & DAVID JOACHIM

PHOTOGRAPHY BY RAY KACHATORIAN

weldon**owen**

CONTENTS

INTRODUCTION 7

EQUIPMENT 11

TECHNIQUES 21

BURGERS 35

BEEF 51

PORK 69

CHICKEN, TURKEY & OTHER BIRDS 97

FISH & SHELLFISH 121

VEGETABLES 155

PIZZA 183

DESSERT 193

BRINES, RUBS & SAUCES 209

INDEX 234

Grilling with Class

"Whatever you do, do it well." —Walt Disney

Food + fire. Is there anything more basic than grilling? Is there anything more elemental in the ever-expanding world of the culinary arts? Alongside modern methods such as sous vide and rotary evaporation, grilling may even seem like mere child's play, a rudimentary cooking technique that anyone can do.

Why, then, is grilled food so often served burnt, dried out, and completely devoid of sophistication? The answer is simple: turning out perfectly grilled food requires skill and a fundamental understanding of how cooking works. All cooking methods involve the manipulation of time, temperature, and moisture, culinary building blocks born in the blistering crucible of live-fire cooking. To grill well is to comprehend the very foundations of good cookery. In other words, grilling a steak is a process that must be done well to prevent it from being well-done.

For us, the goal of grilling is to give food a deeply browned, smoky-tasting crust while maintaining a juicy, meltingly tender interior. If you know the dynamics of fire's effect on food, such gustatory pleasures are completely within your grasp. We've spent years learning about these dynamics while practicing, studying, and traveling throughout the world of outdoor cooking. We've discovered what works and what doesn't to achieve that elusive goal.

In this book, we lay out everything we've learned, including our best tips and recipes. These pages reveal the art and science of various techniques that ensure perfectly grilled food every time. The nitty-gritty appears right up front in two chapters focused on how different grills work and how to use them effectively for direct and indirect grilling, rotisserie grilling, low and slow barbecuing, cooking in the hot embers, wrapping food in leaves or aluminum foil, and grilling on planks. The remainder of the book is structured around easy-to-follow "lessons" followed by recipes that demonstrate the principles of each lesson. For example, the burger lesson explains that the best way to make a juicy grilled burger is to add water that was lost when the meat was ground. Once you know that, you can experiment with more imaginative liquids, like five-spice soy sauce, roasted-garlic Worcestershire sauce, and herb-infused red wine. You'll also find out that water or another liquid is the key to getting smoke to stick to food when barbecuing. Armed with that knowledge, you can play around with water pans, spritzes, mops, and bastes in varying flavor combinations to create your own signature brand of smoke-infused barbecue.

Throughout the book, we also share insights on things like wild versus farmed fish, wet versus dry brining, and baby back versus St. Louis–style ribs. You'll discover little nuggets on grilling everything from beef rib steaks and pork rib chops to pork belly, whole birds, shellfish, pizza, cake, and all manner of vegetables and fruits.

The recipes are written as templates of technique with an emphasis on global flavors. Alongside Classic Beef Burgers with Lots of Toppings (page 39), you'll find Sichuan Tuna Burgers with Pickled Ginger Relish (page 44) and Lamb Kofta Burgers in Flatbread with Za'atar Tzatziki (page 43). Classic Barbecued Chicken (page 101) shares the spotlight with Grilled Chicken Breasts in Berbere Sauce (page 113) and Grilled Five-Spice Duck Breasts with Hoisin Glaze (page 117). Use the recipes as springboards for your creations. The Extra Credit ideas should get your creative juices flowing. For example, if you grill burgers often, you may soon find yourself crafting elegant stuffings, embellishing with stylish garnishes and sauces, and elevating flavors with rubs and glazes.

Just avoid the temptation to convince yourself (or your guests) that burnt food tastes delicious. A little char is welcome. A lot of burn? Not so much. Even when preparing simple foods like boneless chicken breasts, the process of grilling should be done with skill and some class. Approach the grill with style and grace. Your guests will thank you for it.

Andrew Schloss   David Joachim

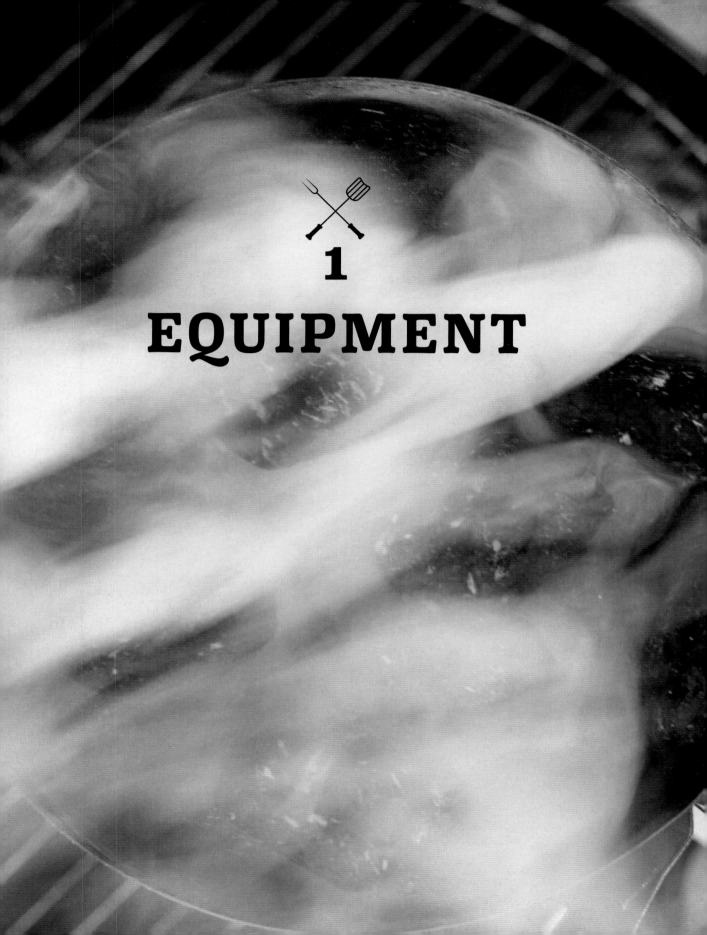

1
EQUIPMENT

TYPES OF GRILLS

You can grill without any equipment at all. A fire and a long stick are all you need to cook a steak. But most grillers appreciate their tools, and a well-built modern grill does make it easier to control heat and get consistently delicious results. When we talk about grills, we mean any physical structure designed to contain and control fire for the purpose of cooking food. Every grill has two basic parts: the firebox where the fire burns and the grilling grate on which the food cooks.

Three things distinguish most grills from one another: size, materials, and fuel source. The dimensions of the grilling grate and the cover height largely determine the available cooking space and the grilling techniques for which the grill is best suited. The grill can be constructed from any inflammable material, with steel, ceramic, and aluminum the most common, though fireplace grills are usually stone or brick. The density and the heat conductivity of the material partially determine the grill's overall cooking characteristics. Finally, the fuel source can be gas, charcoal, wood, or any combination.

When evaluating a grill, always consider all three factors. Also think about how often you grill and the amount of food you typically cook at any given time. The grill you buy should have ample cooking space for your average meal, but it's a good idea to go a little bigger than you think you will need. Having more space allows you to better manage flare-ups, and it gives you the opportunity to stretch your grilling chops, taking on more elaborate grill projects as your skills increase. Large roasts, like a whole turkey, a leg of lamb, or a prime rib, need a cooking area of at least 600 square inches (1524 sq cm) or 22 inches (56 cm) in diameter, preferably more. A larger grill allows you to cook both small and big foods.

The next thing to consider is the style of the grill, covered or uncovered, rotisserie-enabled or bare-bones hibachi. Here's a list of grill types ranging from simplest to most tricked out.

CAMPFIRE GRILL

This inexpensive grill rests over an open fire. It does not have a firebox. Instead, it has an adjustable-height iron or steel grill grate attached to a single stake or to two T-shaped legs that suspend the grate over the fire. Heat is controlled by the amount of coals you rake beneath the cooking grate and by adjusting the grate up or down. Campfire grills are suitable only for direct grilling methods. A fireplace grill (aka Tuscan grill) is similar, designed to fit into the constricted area of a fireplace. This type does not always have an adjustable grate, however, so you need to make sure the grate is elevated enough to be at least 4 inches (10 cm) above the coals of the fireplace.

ELECTRIC GRILL

A metal coil, rather than a flame, serves as the heat source for these inexpensive grills ($50 to $100). Otherwise, electric grills usually resemble hibachis and are designed for the same purpose: quickly cooking small amounts of thin, tender foods over direct heat. Some models have lids and can be used outdoors, but most are designed for simple indoor grilling. Heat is easily controlled with a knob that increases or decreases the flow of electricity.

HIBACHI

Here's where the all-important firebox comes into play. A hibachi looks like a deep, heavy-duty pan with a grill grate on top. The best models provide heat control with adjustable grill grates, air vents on the sides of the firebox, and a raised fire grate to allow oxygen to flow beneath the coals. Most hibachis are charcoal fired, but some modern versions are gas or electric. The cooking space is usually limited to 100 to 200 square inches (254 to 508 sq cm). A table grill (aka party grill) is a large version of a hibachi. It rests on tall legs at counter height and is used for grilling dozens of burgers or steaks for big grill parties.

KETTLE GRILL

This ball-shaped grill has become the standard of charcoal grilling in the United States. The Weber company originated the design and trademarked

it, but several other manufacturers make similar-shaped grills. The kettle grill improves on the hibachi base by adding a lid. With the lid closed, the kettle grill performs like an oven. Take the lid off and it performs like an hibachi-style grill. With the lid in place, waves of convecting heat surround the food, cooking it evenly from all sides, rather than just from underneath. And if you bank your coals on one side of the firebox and the food on the other (known as indirect grilling), you can gently grill roast large pieces of meat so they cook through without burning. Most kettle grills don't have adjustable-height grill grates, which means heat is controlled by the thickness of the coal bed and by the air vents on the bottom of the firebox and in the lid. Some models are also available with a gas-assist function that quickly ignites the charcoal with a burst of gas but still uses coals for cooking. The cooking area ranges from 14 to 24 inches (35 to 60 cm) in diameter.

PIT GRILL OR SMOKER

This grill type is expressly designed for smoking or barbecuing. The cooking chamber is often shaped like a horizontal barrel, as these cookers were originally made (and continue to be made) from steel barrels, with the firebox located in a separate chamber on one side. A chimney is attached to the lid on the opposite side from the firebox, thus creating a draft to draw smoke across the food. Some pit grills have an adjustable tray for charcoal placed under the food in the cooking chamber, allowing for both direct grilling and smoking via indirect heat. A typical steel barrel grill burns wood or charcoal. As with a kettle grill, heat levels are adjusted with lid and side air vents.

CERAMIC GRILL

Modeled on the traditional egg-shaped Japanese kamado oven, heavy-duty ceramic grills take advantage of the heat-retentive property of clay and a tight-fitting lid to roast food slowly at low temperatures (as low as 200°F/95°C). The design allows you to use very few coals to generate low heat for long periods. The airtight lid traps heat and moisture, creating exceptionally juicy roasts. Add wood and these cookers become efficient smokers. Ceramic grills usually have a cooking area of 10 to 20 inches (25 to 50 cm) in diameter, but vertical space allows you to add a grill grate below the main one.

GAS GRILL

Gas ignites instantly, emits a clean flame (no smoke or ashes), maintains a consistent yet variable temperature, and can be shut down easily. According to the Hearth, Patio, and Barbecue Association, these conveniences have made gas grills the most popular grills in the United States. Gas grills are typically constructed of durable steel from the firebox to the burners and include a hinged lid. The firebox bed contains a series of burners connected to a gas source and a system of heat diffusers, either metal plates, ceramic plates, or rocks, that sit above the burners. The burners are attached to temperature controls that regulate the flow of gas and oxygen into the burners. An ignition switch lights the burners, and there is usually a hole in the firebox for flame ignition should the ignition switch fail. The height of the grill grate, which is seldom adjustable, sits about 4 inches (10 cm) above the heat diffusers. Other features vary widely, creating a huge price range from about $250 to upward of $10,000. Our advice is to go for the basics and buy as much grill space as you can afford. Don't be swayed to pay extra for side burners, warming racks, and searing burners, all of which take up space and will be used infrequently.

BTUs

A BTU rating on a gas grill doesn't describe how hot the grill gets. (Most gas grills get no hotter than 600°F/315°C.) It is instead a measure of how much gas it takes per hour to fire up all of the burners. Larger grills require more BTUs per hour because they have more burners and a larger cooking area. A typical gas burner requires 9,000 to 12,000 BTUs per hour, so a small two-burner grill needs about 22,000 BTUs to fire up its burners to high each hour. But a large six-burner grill needs about 60,000 BTUs. Some very expensive grills are manufactured with burners that accept up to 25,000 BTUs per hour and will burn hotter than the average backyard gas grill. With that said, hotter is not necessarily better. Very few grill recipes benefit from incendiary heat.

TYPES OF FUELS

WOOD

Although most outdoor cooking in the United States is done over gas or charcoal, wood-fueled grills are still common in South America and Europe. Wood is an unpredictable fuel, riddled with hot spots and dead zones. A wood fire can flare up unexpectedly and then die away. But despite all of its technical challenges, nothing produces better and more nuanced flavor than grilling over wood. The original wood-burning grill was a campfire, though now several high-end grills are marketed as specifically designed for handling wood. When grilling over wood, always use seasoned hardwood like oak, alder, or maple. Fruitwoods such as apple or cherry; nut woods like hickory, pecan, and walnut; and olive wood and grapevines can add interesting aromas. Mesquite is a dense, fragrant hardwood that burns particularly hot.

CHARCOAL

Natural lump charcoal and briquettes are forms of preburned wood that are easier to ignite and keep burning than seasoned hardwood. To turn wood into lump charcoal, logs are buried in pits under sheets of metal and dirt. The logs are ignited and kept smoldering to burn off water, sap, and other volatile elements until what is left is pretty much pure carbon. The resulting charcoal ignites at roughly 500°F (260°C) and can get as hot as 700°F (370°C) once it really gets going. Some specialty wood charcoals burn at 800°F (425°C). As soon as it has ignited, carbon in the coals combines with available oxygen to produce carbon dioxide, which results in heat. The ratio of charcoal to oxygen is what determines how hot a charcoal fire will get. The air vents on the firebox and lid of a charcoal grill allow you to increase or decrease the flow of oxygen to speed up or slow down the combustion rate of the carbon and, consequently, to raise or reduce the heat.

Lump charcoal burns hotter and faster (by weight) than briquettes, which are pulverized and mixed with a binder, often starch, to help them hold their shape. The real measure of performance from lump or briquette charcoal is the density of the wood from which it is made. Hardwoods, like mesquite, oak, fruitwoods, and nut woods, burn hotter than soft woods, like pine. Unless specified, a bag of charcoal usually contains a mixture of hard and soft woods. Kingsford, the most popular brand of briquettes in the United States, adds some mineral char (from coal and limestone), which helps to raise and prolong the heat. When a recipe requires over 45 minutes of steady heat, briquettes tend to give more even results.

Charcoal can be ignited by using a fire starter (see page 18) or charcoal chimney (see page 18). We prefer a chimney because it lights coals quickly and doesn't add unwanted aromas from petrol starters. For the same reason, we never use petrol-soaked briquettes, sold as easy light or match light charcoal.

GAS

Gas, whether a tank of propane (LP gas) or a direct line of natural gas, is delivered to the grill burners through a main fuel hose. After opening the valve at the fuel source, the temperature knobs on the grill adjust the amount of fuel that reaches the burners. Most gas grills use a spark ignition system to trigger combustion. In order for combustion to take place, both propane and natural gas require a very precise ratio of oxygen to fuel. This ratio (5:1) is regulated by the size and shape of the grill's burners. Each burner mixes fuel and oxygen in the proper ratio and spreads it out over the burner's surface area, where it emerges as flame through small holes or ports. When the ratio is correct, gas flames look blue and clear. A yellow flame indicates insufficient oxygen for complete combustion of the fuel to take place. You can improve your grill's ability to achieve a clear blue flame by checking for leaks or cleaning the burners.

GAS OR CHARCOAL?

Grilling with gas is certainly more convenient than grilling with charcoal, and since it is possible to add smoky aroma with the addition of wood chunks or chips (see page 28), most grill recipes work equally well with gas or coals. The only exceptions are steaks and chops. To get a good sear on a steak, you need a raging-hot fire and a dry surface on the meat. Grill aficionados often sneer that you can't turn out a great steak with a gas grill. They're basically right, and here's why: charcoal burns drier than gas. When charcoal or wood burns, it produces primarily carbon dioxide, but when propane or natural gas (methane) burns, it produces carbon dioxide and vaporized water. That moisture prevents the temperature from rising as high as a charcoal grill, since steam can reach only 212°F (100°C). So unless a gas grill has a superheated infrared burner that will evaporate any moisture before it has time to settle, it can't produce the same sort of thick crust on a steak that you get when grilling with the high, dry heat of charcoal.

GRILL CLEANING, MAINTENANCE & REPAIR

The most important control you have over the performance of your grill is keeping it clean. That doesn't mean you need to scrub it until it gleams. A grill naturally develops a light patina on the grill grate and firebox that doesn't negatively affect performance. But allowing layers of soot and carbonized food to build up on the grill grate, firebox, or lid will affect its ability to produce and transfer heat uniformly. To keep a grill in good working order, you should complete a few brief cleaning steps every time you grill. More thorough cleaning needs to be done only about once a year. On a gas grill, turn off the gas supply before extended cleaning.

EVERY TIME YOU GRILL

- Check the grease catcher or ash catcher. If either one is full, empty it before beginning to grill.

- Go over the bars of the grill grate with a stiff wire grill brush once before adding food and then once after removing food. Do it while the grill grate is hot, as a hot grate cleans easier than a cold one.

- Wipe down the side tables with warm, soapy water just as you would wipe down a countertop.

- Dry any wet surfaces of the grill with a clean cloth to prevent rusting.

ONCE A YEAR

- Metal heat diffusers on a gas grill will develop a buildup of food debris. Scrape them clean with an old metal spatula or metal bristle brush.

- Clean the inside of the lid and firebox. Remove the grill grate and the fire grate of a charcoal grill and shovel any ashes from the firebox. On a gas grill, remove the heat diffuser and then scrape away any debris from the firebox. Wash the lid and firebox with warm, soapy water. For thick soot buildup on the interior, use a heavy-duty grill cleaner. If you see what looks like peeling paint hanging from the interior of the grill lid, don't grab a paint brush. The flakes are baked-on grease that has turned to carbon. Wipe them away with a damp paper towel.

- Check the burner tubes on a gas grill. If the flame is more yellow than blue, there may be cracks or obstructions in the burner tubes preventing the optimal mix of oxygen and fuel. When a grill is not in use for a while, spiders sometimes nest in the tubes. Check the tubes for visible cracks or holes (other than the ports). If you see any cracks, replace the tubes according to the manufacturer's directions. Scrape off any debris with a stiff brush and gently unclog any visibly clogged holes (ports) with a pin. Be careful not to enlarge the ports, as their original diameter provides an optimal fuel-oxygen mix. Remove the tubes from the firebox and shine a flashlight into the openings at the ends of the tubes. Clean the tube interiors with a long, narrow, flexible brush. You can also shoot a stream of water through the tubes with a garden hose. If you clean the burners at the beginning of your typical grilling season, thoroughly dry the tubes and reaffix them to the firebox. If you clean the burners at the end of your typical grilling season and will be storing the grill, coat the burners with vegetable oil and wrap them in foil to keep insects out during storage.

- Check the hoses on a gas grill. Make sure all of the connections are tight and the hoses have no holes, cracks, or excessively worn areas. Follow the manufacturer's directions to replace any cracked or worn hoses.

- Check the control panel on a gas grill and spray lubricant into any sticky knobs. Brush away any spider webs under the panel. Spot-check the exterior of the grill and remove any other spiderwebs.

- Check the igniter on gas grills or charcoal grills with a gas-assist function. If the igniter isn't working, scrub the tip of the electrode with rubbing alcohol. Some electric igniters also require small batteries (such as AA or AAA). Replace old batteries as necessary.

- Check for rust and corrosion. Scrub away any white spots or corrosion with a mixture of equal parts vinegar and water. Dry any wet surfaces to prevent rusting. Even though most grills are coated with enamel to prevent rusting, it is a good idea to keep your grill dry.

LEAK TESTING ON A GAS GRILL

If you smell gas coming from the grill, check to see if the gas valves are tightly closed and tighten if necessary. If they are tight and the odor persists, you need do a leak check to locate the source of the leak. Mix a 1:1 ratio of soap and water. Turn on the fuel supply at the fuel source only (the propane tank or the natural-gas line). Do not open the control knobs on the grill's control panel. Brush the soapy water over the hose(s) and connections between the fuel supply, fuel valve, and temperature control knobs. Anywhere that bubbles appear indicates a gas leak. Inspect the hose(s) and connections for cracks or worn spots. Next, brush the soapy water on the welds around the propane tank, its supply valve, and the bottom ring of the tank and check for bubbles. Tighten all connections and immediately replace the hoses, valves, or fuel tank as necessary.

GRILL TOOLS & ACCESSORIES

A lot of grill tools and grill toys are available for accessorizing your grilling activities. Some are essential and some are plain fun. Here's what we think you will need. They are listed roughly in order of necessity.

FOR ANY GRILL

- **Grill brushes, scrapers, and scrubbers.** These basic cleaning tools come in a variety of styles. Look for brushes with long handles and a large head of stiff bristles for easily cleaning grill grates. Because a steel brush can scratch a streel grill grate, stainless steel grates should only be cleaned with a brass-bristled brush. Iron grates can be scrubbed with any metal brush. Many brushes have metal scrapers at the tip of the head to remove stubborn debris. A V-shaped brush or scraper makes it easier to clean individual bars on a grill grate. Scrubbers resemble scouring pads and are designed to clean the interior of the firebox and lid.

- **Tongs.** Grill tongs should have long, sturdy handles, be spring-loaded so they close only with pressure, and have scalloped ends to ensure a good grip on foods. Avoid tongs with thin handles, which tend to bend when pressed, rendering them useless for grabbing food.

- **Spatula.** Another key grill tool, a spatula excels at flipping small, delicate foods like burgers and fish fillets that would be torn with tongs. Look for a stiff, long-handled spatula with a wide blade and beveled edge to reach easily beneath foods without mangling them.

- **Thermometer.** An instant-read thermometer, available in digital and analog models, gives you the precise internal temperature of foods as soon as the probe is inserted. It is unbeatable for judging the doneness of thick meats and roasts. A grill thermometer, the sensor of which you place right near the cooking surface, is helpful as well. The thermometers that are built into the lids of grills tend to be unreliable.

- **Long-stem lighter.** A form of contained butane, long-stem butane lighters make it easy to light both wood fires and chimney starters full of coals. Keep at least one on hand for effortless fire starting.

- **Basting brushes.** Essential for brushing on a glaze or brushing off debris. Natural bristle brushes won't melt on the grill like nylon and work well with all bastes, glazes, and sauces. Silicone brushes work best with thicker sauces; thinner sauces tend to slip right off the bristles.

- **Grill mop.** Resembling a diminutive kitchen mop, the grill mop is useful for dabbing or drizzling thin mop sauces onto large pieces of meat without brushing off any seasonings that may already be there.

- **Grill screens, trays, and grates.** Often made of enameled metal, these perforated grill toppers allow you to cook small or delicate foods, such as cut vegetables, meat chunks, and shrimp or scallops, without them falling through the grate and without the use of skewers. They often include handles on both sides and can also be used to cook dough on a grill.

- **Grill gloves.** Grilling means working with intense heat. Insulated heat-resistant gloves will protect your hands. Leather makes a good choice, but we also like to use silicone gloves, which are waterproof and heat-resistant to about 500°F (260°C). Wear them and you can grab a hot grill grate, grill screen, salt block, or roasted turkey right off the fire.

- **Skewers.** Keep at least three types on hand for kebabs and satays: metal, bamboo, and two pronged. Flat metal skewers help to keep the food from spinning around the skewer. Two-pronged skewers do a slightly better job but may not evenly pierce small foods. Bamboo skewers are inexpensive and compostable. Soak any wooden skewer in water for 30 minutes before grilling to keep it from burning.

- **Aluminum foil pans.** An aluminum foil pan has multiple uses on the grill: a drip pan to catch grease, a roasting pan to retain juices for making a pan sauce, a water pan for creating steam, a warming container for grilled food, and a soaking container for bamboo skewers. Keep several sizes on hand.

- **Grill lamp.** Handy for nighttime grilling, these lamps clamp to the side or lid handle of your grill and are often adjustable to position the light where you need it. Some lamps require an outlet and/or extension cord and others are battery powered. You could also use an inexpensive work lamp from a hardware store.

- **Vertical roasting rack.** Excellent for chicken and other poultry, this rack holds birds in an upright position so they cook and brown evenly and drain fat easily. Available in various sizes for small to large birds.

- **Rib rack.** Essential for grilling lots of ribs on a small grill, this simple metal accessory positions four racks of ribs parallel to one another on their long edges. With two of these racks, you can simultaneously grill eight racks of ribs on a standard charcoal kettle grill.

- **Grill frying pans and woks.** Similar to vegetable grill screens or grates, these perforated pans include a long handle on one side. Often the handle is foldable, making it possible to close the grill lid without the handle protruding. Good for quickly cooking small pieces of food, grill frying pans and woks allow you to replicate stove-top cooking on the grill but with the addition of live fire and a little smoke.

- **Grill baskets.** These long-handled cages enclose food between two hinged wire grids, creating a shallow basket. Lift the basket by the handle and you can easily flip the food over without it sticking or falling apart. Very useful for grilled sandwiches, fish, and other delicate foods that are prone to sticking or falling apart on the grill. For the best protection against sticking (and best searing), preheat and oil the basket the same way you would preheat and oil the grill grate. Always put food on a hot grill surface, never a cold one.

- **Spray bottle.** Handy for spraying flavored liquids onto slow-cooking foods to keep them moist, deepen their flavor, and allow them to take on more smoke.

- **Injector.** A marinade injector (aka kitchen syringe) looks like a large hypodermic needle. There's no easier way to inject flavor deep into the muscle tissue of meats. Any pulp-free liquid can be used. Metal injectors last longer than plastic models.

- **Pizza peel.** Not essential but nice to have if you like cooking pizza on the grill, a peel is a broad, flat spade-like tool that is perfect for shaping pizza dough and then effortlessly sliding it onto a hot grill grate. Peels can be made of wood or metal. We prefer wood because the dough is less likely to stick to it. You can also use a peel to help move or rotate a large roast, such as a whole turkey.

- **Grill fork.** We avoid using grill forks because they poke holes into food, especially the skins of poultry and sausage. An insignificant amount of fat and juice escapes, but it's often enough to cause flare-ups. Sturdy tongs are preferred, but you may want to have a grill fork on hand for the odd roast that is easily turned when stabbed. Some models feature a built-in instant-read thermometer—so silly!

ESPECIALLY FOR CHARCOAL &/OR WOOD

- **Chimney starter.** Resembling a big, perforated coffee can, a chimney starter eliminates the need to resort to lighter fluid. The starter ensures the coals will ignite quickly (15 to 20 minutes) due to the upward draft of oxygen.

- **Paraffin lighter cubes.** These fire starters resemble chunky white spotless dice and can be used instead of paper to light a wood fire, a pyramid of coals, or a chimney starter full of briquettes. They leave no aftertaste. Sawdust starters, which are made from compressed sawdust and look somewhat like small blocks of particle board, do the same thing.

- **Coal rake.** Use this simple tool to rake coals into beds of varying thicknesses and varying heat levels. A children's garden rake is just the right size.

- **Coal shovel.** A small shovel is ideal for removing hot or spent coals and ashes from the firebox. A child-size metal garden shovel or a long-handled gardening trowel works best for backyard grills.

- **Coal poker.** Although not strictly necessary, a coal poker is handy if you grill in a wood-burning grill, over a campfire, or in a fireplace. Look for a coal poker that's long, metal, and curved at the end to hook coals and logs easily for repositioning.

- **Temperature regulator.** Particularly useful if you do a lot of smoking and barbecuing on your charcoal grill, this device replaces the grill's intake vents with a small fan and temperature sensor. Set your desired temperature (say, 250°F/120°C) and the fan cycles on and off, adjusting the airflow to maintain a constant temperature.

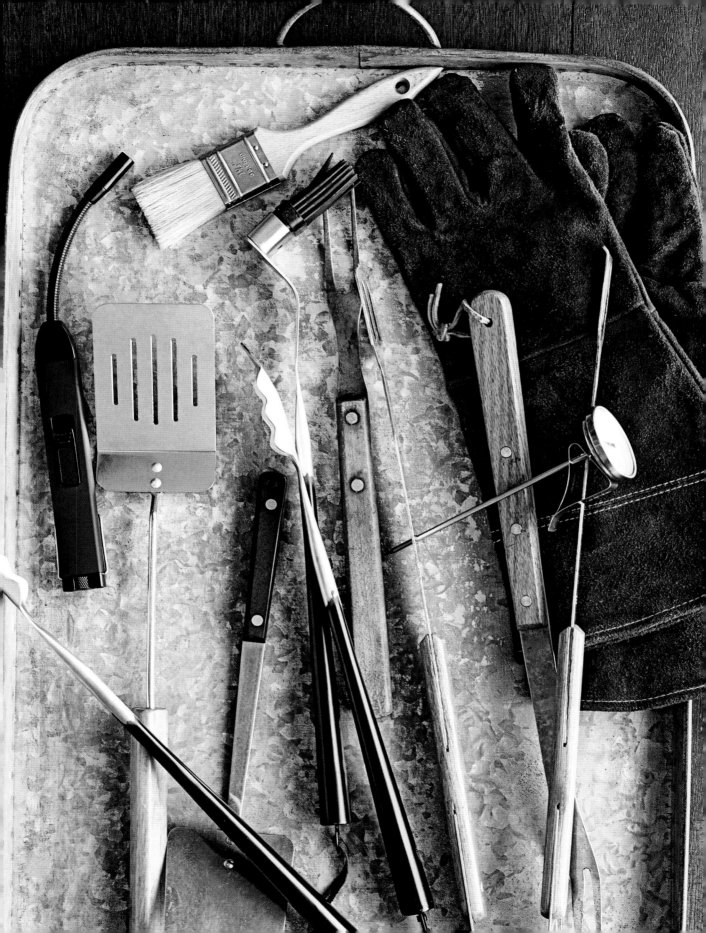

2
TECHNIQUES

THE POWER OF FIRE

Fire is incredibly powerful. It can create new, delicious flavor compounds on the surface of a grilled steak. It can also singe your hair and burn down your house, an element of danger that, we have to admit, is part of the fun of outdoor cooking. But don't worry. The grill itself already contains the fire, eliminating most of the danger. All that's left to do is to wield the power of fire by exploring ways to manipulate the heat and smoke for cooking.

DIRECT GRILLING

Put a marshmallow on a stick over a campfire and you are direct grilling. Put a rib-eye steak on a hot grate over a fire and you are still direct grilling. The most familiar form of outdoor cooking, this technique is marked by hot, fast cooking directly over the heat. The heat source could be the lit burners of a gas grill, the glowing coals of a charcoal grill, or the wood embers of a campfire. Whichever method you use, the food usually rests less than 6 inches (15 cm) from the heat source and cooks primarily by radiant heat, which is simply heat that radiates directly to the food, much like heat radiates from the sun to your skin.

Browned flavor and a crusty texture are what make grilled foods great. All forms of grilling develop that kind of flavor and texture, but they are especially pronounced with direct grilling. Protein-based foods like beef steak and tofu begin to brown when they reach a surface temperature of about 250°F (120°C), shortly after the moisture there evaporates. Amino acids, sugars, and fats all break down and react on the food's surface, creating new roasty, toasty flavor compounds. These chemical reactions are called Maillard reactions after Louis Camille Maillard, the French chemist who discovered them. Browning also occurs on the grill when sugar-rich foods caramelize. Slightly different from Maillard reactions, caramelization begins to occur around 350°F (180°C), when the sugar on the surface of, say, sliced pineapple melts and transforms from pale caramel to deep brown. As the sugar breaks down from heat, it creates new compounds that taste roasted, tart, bitter, fruity, floral, and buttery.

If the heating continues and the sugar burns, sweetness and other pleasant flavors eventually disappear, replaced by compounds that taste mostly sour, bitter, and burnt. Whether through Maillard reactions or caramelization, browning is what creates much of the flavor of grilled food. The brown color you see is a sign of flavor development—the delicious taste of grilled food. The goal here is to create a deeply browned crust on your food without burning it. This crust also adds to the textural appeal of grilled food. As moisture evaporates, the surface of the food gets dry and crisp, creating a crunchy crust. That texture contrast between a crunchy crust and a soft, juicy interior on a grilled steak or a toasted marshmallow is a huge part of the attraction of grilled food.

Best Foods for Direct Grilling

Hot and fast grilling is ideal for foods that are soft and porous, are less than 1 inch (2.5 cm) thick, and/or are likely to cook through in less than 30 minutes. That's actually most of what people tend to put on the grill, including hamburgers, hot dogs, sausages, thin chops and thin steaks (like skirt and flank steak), boneless chicken breasts and thighs, butterflied boneless turkey breast, a butterflied whole chicken, small whole birds like quail, most seafood like shrimp, scallops, clams, mussels, small whole fish, fish fillets and steaks, split lobsters, squid, and simmered octopuses. It also includes most tender vegetables and fruits like asparagus, onions, fennel, tomatoes, peppers, zucchini, eggplant slices, mushrooms, corn, peaches, bananas, and pineapple, as well as flatbreads like pizza and grill-toasted cakes like pound cake and doughnuts.

Setting Up a Grill for Direct Grilling

Create two heat levels. Most cooks spread hot coals all the way across the bottom of a charcoal grill or light all of the burners on a gas grill at the same heat level. But two heat levels give you better heat control, especially on charcoal and wood grills. You can sear and brown something like a thick pork chop on the hot side, creating a flavorful crust, and then

move it to the cooler side and cover the grill to finish cooking through without burning the surface. Two heat levels also help to control flare-ups. If the hot side is a blazing inferno of dripping fat from burgers, sausages, pork belly, chicken wings, or duck, just move the food to the cooler side until the flames subside. To create two heat levels on a gas grill, turn the burners on one side to high or medium-high and the burners on the other side to low or medium-low. On a charcoal grill, make a thicker bed of coals on one side and a thinner bed on the other. We like hardwood lump charcoal when direct grilling on a charcoal grill. It burns hotter (by weight) than charcoal briquettes, giving you a better crust and a bit more smoke. And if you're cooking over a blazing campfire, two heat levels (or even three) are absolutely essential. Think of high heat as a layer 4 inches (10-cm) thick of red-hot coals on one side of the fire and of low heat as a layer 1 inch (2.5-cm) thick of glowing orange coals on the other. See the chart on page 25 for more details on setting up charcoal and wood grills for different heat levels.

Heat the grill grate. Once your grill is set up for direct grilling, preheat the grill grate over the fire for 10 to 15 minutes. If there's a lid, close it to trap heat and speed the preheating. A hot grate helps to create a browned crust on the food and to keep it from sticking.

Brush and oil. Just before putting the food on the grill grate, brush the grate clean and then coat it with oil. We keep some paper towels and a widemouthed jar of vegetable oil (grapeseed or canola oil works well) near the grill. Dip a wad of paper towel in the oil, then grab it with tongs and rub it over the hot grate to lubricate it and remove any fine bits of soot. A hot, clean, well-oiled grill grate delivers more heat to your food and improves browning. For that reason, we usually give the grate a quick scrape right after food comes off, as well. A hot grill grate is easier to clean than a cold one.

Close the lid for most cooking. After you put the food on the grate, close the lid to trap heat and smoke and deliver both to your food. A lid is crucial for melting the cheese on grilled pizza. If you don't have one, improvise by inverting a large aluminum foil pan over the pie. Is a covered grill crucial for cooking shrimp and asparagus? Not so much. Any food that cooks through in 5 minutes or less does not need to be covered.

CONTROLLING TEMPERATURE

The temperature of a fire is controlled by the amount of fuel and oxygen. In a gas grill, the ratio of fuel to oxygen comes preset by a Venturi valve on the gas burner tube. Once the fire is lit, temperature control is simple: just turn the knob to raise or lower the temperature.

On charcoal and wood grills, the temperature is controlled by manually adding more or less fuel and oxygen. For high-heat direct grilling on charcoal and wood grills, build a bed of hot coals 3 to 4 inches (7.5 to 10 cm) thick. For lower heat, build a bed 1 to 2 inches (2.5 to 5 cm) thick. If the coals burn out and the temperature drops, add more hot coals.

Adjust the vents to maintain a steady temperature. The intake vents near the coals supply them with oxygen, which the fire needs to stay alive. Open the vents all the way for a fast-burning high fire. Close them to starve the coals and kill the fire. Anywhere in between gives you medium-high and medium-low heat. Think of these intake vents as your main temperature knob. The exhaust vents in the lid are your secondary temperature knob. The top vents help draw oxygen through the bottom vents and give smoke and combustion gases an escape hatch out of the grill. For superhot direct grilling on charcoal,

leave off the lid or close the lid and open the exhaust vents all the way. Partially close the exhaust vents for medium and low direct heat grilling. Try to position the exhaust vents over the food so heat and smoke are drawn from the coals over the food before exiting the grill.

Use a grill thermometer. If your grill has a thermometer in the lid, don't rely on it. The most accurate cooking temperature should be taken right next to the food on the cooking grate. Clip a grill thermometer to the grate within about 2 inches (5 cm) of the food so you can monitor the cooking temperature.

Factor in the weather. Wind, rain, and cold or hot weather will affect how much fuel you need to add and how you adjust your air vents to maintain a steady temperature.

Flip often for more flavor. Grill cooks are often seduced by pretty crosshatch marks. But a few burn marks on a steak are not as flavorful as even browning across its entire surface. For hot, fast grilling, flip the food often to help brown the entire surface and create more flavor. Frequent flipping also helps prevent overcooking.

DIRECT GRILLING

HEAT	TEMPERATURE	COAL APPEARANCE	COAL-BED THICKNESS	GRATE HEIGHT	VENTS	COUNTING BY THOUSANDS
High	450°–500°F/ 230°–260°C	Red-hot glow	4 inches/10 cm	2 inches/5 cm	100% open	2 times
Medium-high	400°–450°F/ 200°–230°C	Orange glow; light ash	3–4 inches/ 7.5–10 cm	3 inches/7.5 cm	80% open	4 times
Medium	350°–400°F/ 180°–200°C	Medium ash; visible glow	3 inches/7.5 cm	4 inches/10 cm	60% open	6 times
Medium-low	300°–350°F/ 150°–180°C	Medium-thick ash; faint glow	2 inches/5 cm	5 inches/13 cm	50% open	8 times
Low	250°–300°F/ 120°–150°C	Thick ash; spotty faint glow	1 inch/2.5 cm	6 inches/15 cm	40% open	10 times

INDIRECT GRILLING

HEAT	TEMPERATURE	COAL APPEARANCE	COAL-BED THICKNESS	GRATE HEIGHT	VENTS
High	400°–450°F/200°–230°C	Bright orange glow	4 inches/10 cm	2 inches/5 cm	100% open
Medium-high	350°–400°F/180°–200°C	Orange glow; light ash	3–4 inches/7.5–10 cm	3 inches/7.5 cm	80% open
Medium	300°–350°F/150°–180°C	Medium ash; visible glow	3 inches/7.5 cm	4 inches/10 cm	60% open
Medium-low	250°–300°F/120°–150°C	Medium-thick ash; faint glow	2 inches/5 cm	5 inches/13 cm	50% open
Low	225°–250°F/110°–120°C	Thick ash; spotty faint glow	1 inch/2.5 cm	6 inches/15 cm	40% open

COOKING IN THE COALS

Our mantra with direct grilling is "the fewer things between the fire and the food, the better." This technique takes that mantra to heart by dispensing with the grill grate altogether. Cooking steaks and chops right on hot coals gives you a fantastic crust due to the high, dry heat. It's perfect for campfires, especially when you can tuck a few vegetables like beets and sweet potatoes into the coals to round out the meal.

Stick with wood and lump charcoal. Charcoal briquettes produce too fine an ash for cooking steaks and chops in the coals. They'll just make your meat or fish taste like an ashtray. For this technique, you need wood embers or lump charcoal. (Of course, if you're burying foil-wrapped foods in the coals—or burying jacketed vegetables like potatoes—briquettes work fine because you won't be eating food that directly touches the coals.) The coals should be glowing orange and raked into a relatively flat bed with plenty of small air pockets between the coals. Those pockets will give you the best browning on the food. Blow off any excess ash with a portable fan, leaf blower, or a baking sheet and a strong arm, then lay the beef steak, pork chop, or fish steak right on the hot coals. Steaks less than 1 inch (2.5 cm) thick work best. To grill root vegetables in the coals, bury the unpeeled vegetables right in the hot embers and cook until they are tender, turning them as necessary for even cooking.

CHARCOAL & WOOD GRILL SETUP GUIDE

Use the chart (facing page) to set up charcoal and wood grills for various heat levels. For direct grilling with two heat levels (highly recommended), spread a layer of coals 4 inches (10 cm) thick on one side for high heat and a layer of coals 1 inch (2.5 cm) thick on the other for low heat. For indirect grilling, bank all of the coals to one side of the grill and leave the other side completely unheated. We recommend using a grill thermometer placed within 2 inches (5 cm) of the food to check the cooking temperature. Or you can check the approximate temperature with your hand: Hold your hand, palm down, about 4 inches (10 cm) above the grill grate and count by thousands, saying, "1 one thousand, 2 one thousand," and so on. The number of times you can count by thousands is the approximate temperature as listed in the chart.

INDIRECT GRILLING

Unlike direct grilling, for indirect grilling you place your food away from the fire. It's usually done at medium-high temperature of about 350°F (180°C) with the lid down. The food cooks primarily by convection currents of warm air traveling from the heat source and surrounding the food. It's essentially grill roasting. Indirect grilling is similar to oven roasting indoors except that you're doing it outdoors in a grill where you can add smoke. An even bigger advantage of setting up your grill for indirect grilling is that you can do a combination of direct and indirect grilling. Because you still have the hot side of the grill to work with, you can, say, get a crisp skin on Classic Barbecued Chicken (page 101) after it has cooked through to doneness on the unheated side of the grill. And you can grill different types of foods at once: sear a thick steak on the hot side, move it to the unheated side to finish cooking, and then grill asparagus on the hot side (see Steak, Potatoes & Asparagus on page 54). Plus, the unheated side is like an insurance policy against burning. If you get flare-ups or the food threatens to burn on the hot side, move it to the unheated side.

Best Foods for Indirect Grilling

Indirect grilling is the best choice for foods that are hard and dense, more than 1 inch (2.5 cm) thick, and/or likely to take more than 30 minutes to cook through. It is ideal for getting bronzed skin on your Thanksgiving turkey or serving a holiday meal of Grill-Roasted Rib Roast with Grilled Onion Toasts & Grilled Apple Horseradish (page 63). Use this technique for whole turkeys and chickens, whole turkey breasts, beef roasts, thick steaks, thick pork chops and pork shoulder, pork and beef ribs, pork loin roasts, beets, potatoes, and pears. Add wood chunks or chips for indirect grilling to allow you to replicate a barbecue pit to make succulent smoked brisket and pork shoulder.

Setting Up a Grill for Indirect Grilling

Separate the heat from the food. That's the key to keeping the cooking temperature from getting too high. On a gas grill, you'll need at least two burners so you can light only one side of the grill. For indirect grilling with medium heat, light the gas burner(s) on one side to medium and leave the other burner(s) off. On a charcoal grill, bank the coals to one side about 3 inches (7.5 cm) thick. See the chart (facing page) for specifics on other heat levels. We like charcoal briquettes for indirect grilling and

barbecuing because they burn more steadily and can maintain a lower temperature over a longer period of time than lump charcoal. We usually light one chimney of briquettes for shorter indirect grilling sessions of 1 to 2 hours. They last about 1 hour, and it's easy to add more hot coals as needed. For longer indirect grilling sessions, you can also add unlit briquettes, a handful or two at a time, to keep the fire burning steadily. Although you have two sides for indirect grilling in most charcoal and gas grills, egg-shaped ceramic grills call for a different arrangement. For these and other vertical setups, you'll need to raise the food 12 to 36 inches (30 to 90 cm) above the coals.

Put a drip pan under the food. Before you put the cooking grate on the grill, set an aluminum foil pan in the unheated side of the grill beneath where the food will sit. It will catch dripping fat and juices, which can then be used to make a sauce. If the food isn't particularly fatty or juicy, you may need to add water to the pan to keep the juices from incinerating. You can also set food directly in a pan on the grill grate, but you'll get less browning on the bottom that way.

Put a water pan over the heat. Even more important is an aluminum foil pan of water set directly over the heat. A water pan creates steam to help keep lean foods such as a skinless whole turkey breast, moist. Steam also gives smoke something to stick to on the food surface, helping to make food taste smokier. Add hot water as necessary to keep the water pan from going dry. Or, if the fire gets away from you and you need to cool down the grill temperature, add cold water to the water pan. On a gas grill, put the water pan under the grill grate and directly over the heat diffuser so the water will get hot enough to steam. On a charcoal grill, put it above the coals on the grill grate.

Maintain a steady temperature. Most grill roasting is done between 300° and 400°F (150° and 200°C). Stabilize the temperature in your gas grill and you're good to go. On a charcoal grill, use the intake vents at the bottom and exhaust vents at the top to adjust the airflow. Open the vents about 60 percent for medium heat (300° to 350°F/150° to 180°C). Be sure to position the lid with the exhaust vents over the food so heat and smoke are drawn over it. Clip a thermometer on the unheated side of the grill about 2 inches (5 cm) from the food to monitor the grill temperature. Put the food on the unheated side of the grill, cover the grill, and add more coals or adjust the vents as necessary to maintain a steady temperature.

Try vertical roasting. A form of grill roasting with indirect heat, this method is best for poultry. You stand the bird upright on the grill so the tender white meat is farther away from the heat and less likely to dry out. You can buy vertical roasting racks in various sizes for game hens, chickens, and turkeys. Alternatively, use the beer can method: perch the bird on a half-empty can of beer (or of beans or artichokes—get creative), stabilizing the bird's legs on the grill like a tripod. This type of vertical roaster also provides liquid that gently steams the interior of the bird and keeps the meat moist. It acts like a roasting pan, too, catching drippings that can become part of a sauce.

BLUE SMOKE

Gray and black smoke will make your food taste sooty. Blue smoke particles are less bitter and more agreeable. To get blue smoke, you want a hot burning fire rather than a low smoldering one. That's why food is placed so far away from the fire for barbecue. The temperature is actually pretty high near the fire but pretty low near the food. To keep a charcoal grill from emitting sooty-tasting gray or black smoke, replenish it with hot coals rather than unlit ones. It also helps to keep your grill clean to avoid buildup of sooty-tasting creosote.

ADDING SMOKE & BARBECUING ON A GRILL

Gas and charcoal add little smoke flavor to food. You get a bit from dripping fat in a gas grill, and charcoal produces some combustion by-products, but these are mere wisps of smoke. If you want to taste smoke on your food, you need to burn wood. Logs, chunks, and chips combust at about 575°F (300°C), releasing smoke and combustion gases that stick to the surface of food, adding flavor. We like the taste of smoke and often add wood to our gas and charcoal grills, especially for low and slow indirect grilling, also known as barbecuing. It takes time for food to pick up smoke flavor. A pounded chicken breast that cooks over direct heat in 10 to 15 minutes takes on much less smoke than a whole chicken grill roasted for an hour. Low-heat slow smoking is best done on a smoker designed to burn wood and to separate the food from the heat. But gas and charcoal grills can be adapted. You just need to get the food away from the fire, maintain a steady temperature, add some moisture, and keep the smoke going.

How to Add Wood to Gas & Charcoal Grills

Add the wood right away. Set up your grill for indirect grilling so the heat is separated from the food (see page 25). When the fire is hot, add the wood, and when you see smoke, add the food. The surface of food dries out as it cooks, creating a flavorful crust. But smoke sticks best to water, so the food will pick up the most smoke at the beginning of cooking when the surface of the food is moist.

Use wood chunks for long cooking. Chunks last longer than chips and work best when you're cooking for an hour or more. On a charcoal grill, to keep them burning slowly, place a chunk or two directly onto the hot coals but off to the side or near a thinner part of the coal bed. On a gas grill, place wood chunks over a lit burner beneath the grill grate while you preheat the grill. Add more wood chunks whenever the old ones stop smoking.

Make a smoke packet of wood chips. These burn up faster but work well in both charcoal and gas grills. Tear off a square of aluminum foil, add a single layer of wood chips, and then fold the foil around the chips into a relatively flat packet. Poke several large holes in the top to help release the smoke. Make a few perforated smoke packets when grilling for more than 1 hour. You can also buy perforated metal smoking tubes, boxes, or mesh pouches that do the same thing as the foil. On charcoal grills, place the smoke packet on top of the hot coals beneath the grill grate. On gas grills, place the smoke packet over the lit burner beneath the grill grate, directly on the V-shaped or flat heat diffuser if there is one. Add another packet to the grill whenever you stop seeing smoke. Or, if your gas grill has a built-in smoker box, place the wood in the box and replace it whenever it stops smoking.

Skip soaking wood. Don't bother soaking wood chips or chunks. It takes at least a day for the wood to absorb much water, and even then the water has to burn off for the wood to start smoking. For a slow burn and steady release of smoke, it's more effective to delay the wood's oxygen supply by wrapping wood chips in a foil smoke packet. Toss unsoaked wood chunks onto a cooler part of a charcoal fire, where they'll burn slowly.

Use any untreated hardwood. Unless you're using wood as the primary fuel, the type of wood chunks or chips hardly matters. As a general rule, if you want mild-tasting smoke on the food, go with woods like alder, cherry, maple, oak, or pecan. If you want stronger-tasting smoke, use apple, hickory, mesquite, or walnut. In addition to chips and chunks, you can burn pellets, blocks, and bisquettes. These are essentially different shapes of compressed hardwood sawdust. When using pellets, be sure to buy those meant for cooking not heating, as heating pellets may include soft pine wood and petroleum by-products. Compressed sawdust burns even faster than wood chips, so it's doubly important to wrap them in a foil smoke packet. Whatever wood you use, avoid resinous pine woods, which impart nasty flavors to grilled food.

Try other combustibles. For smoke, you can use pruned grapevines or even dried tea leaves. To make a classic blend for Chinese tea smoking (excellent on fish), mix together equal parts tea leaves, brown sugar, and raw rice along with some warming spices like star anise and cinnamon stick and maybe some citrus peels. Put the mix in a disposable aluminum pan or perforated foil and use it just as you would a smoke packet.

Add moisture. Smoke sticks to water pretty well. For the most smoke flavor, keep your cooking environment moist. Put an aluminum foil pan filled with water on the grill grate right next to the food and add hot water as necessary to keep the pan from going dry. A water pan can be used to cool down the grill if the fire gets away from you, too. Just add cold water instead of hot. You can also spritz, mop, or baste the surface of the food to keep it moist and to help it absorb more smoke. Use water, vinegar, apple cider, beer, or other flavored liquid that appeals to you. Subtle flavors will be left behind after the liquid evaporates. Apply the liquid after the food surface dries out and forms a crust. If you add it in the beginning of cooking, you could wash off whatever spice rub or flavoring you've placed there. Use warm liquid to avoid cooling down the meat surface and prolonging the cooking time. Moisture in the grill—applied or in a water pan—also helps to dissolve connective tissue in tough meat cuts like brisket, ribs, and pork shoulder, transforming the collagen into rich-tasting gelatin.

Use smoked ingredients. If you're having trouble getting enough smoke from your grill, get it from your ingredients instead. Use smoked salt and/or smoked paprika in the rub or smoked chiles, such as chipotles, in the sauce to bump up the smoky aromas. But don't go overboard. It is possible to oversmoke your food.

Cover the grill. A tightly closed grill traps the most smoke. If you have a leaky grill, you may need to add more wood to generate more smoke. On charcoal grills, be sure to position the lid with the exhaust vents over the food so the smoke is drawn over the food before it leaves the grill.

Maintain a steady temperature. The key to great barbecue is to maintain a low, slow, steady temperature (typically 225° to 250°F/110° to 120°C) with gentle moisture and blue wood smoke. This is how you get meltingly tender smoky brisket and pork. Use the grill's vents to adjust the airflow and stabilize the temperature. Put a thermometer near the food on the unheated side of the grill to monitor the cooking temperature. It can be tough to sustain a consistent low temperature in a charcoal grill, even when using steady-burning briquettes. There is a simple fix: a temperature regulator fan. This kit replaces the intake vents in the grill with a small fan and a temperature sensor. Set your desired temperature (say, 250°F/120°C) and the fan cycles on and off, adjusting the airflow to maintain that temperature. Highly recommended if you regularly use your grill to smoke meat.

Wrap in foil if necessary. Tough cuts of meats with a lot of connective tissue sometimes appear to cease cooking before they're fully tender. The internal temperature stops moving somewhere around 150° to 170°F (65° to 77°C). Here's what's happening: the moisture that's driven from the center of the meat evaporates on the surface, cooling down the surface and slowing down the cooking. The effect is much like the chill you feel on your skin when you sweat while running and the wind picks up. The wind in the grill comes in the form of convection currents of air. When barbecuing, this cooling effect can cause the internal temperature of meat to stall for hours. Avoid the temptation to raise the heat in your grill. Remember, a steady temperature is paramount. Patience and some extra moisture will help get you through the slow times. If hours have gone by and your brisket temperature still hasn't risen, wrap it in aluminum foil with some liquid like beer or apple juice. This sort of grill braising steams the meat and raises its temperature. Although this technique is often done with ribs and pork shoulder, we prefer these meats without the steamed, waterlogged taste. It is helpful for smoked brisket, however. Instead of wrapping, you can also just put the brisket in an aluminum foil pan to capture dripping juices and mop it frequently to add more moisture.

THE SMOKE RING

On heavily smoked meats such as brisket, you often see a thin layer of bright pink meat just beneath the surface crust. This thin pink line, the color of which is reminiscent of the color of corned beef, contrasts sharply with the interior gray meat. This so-called smoke ring is caused by carbon monoxide and nitrogen monoxide mixing with water in the meat, a chemical combination that prevents myoglobin, the red pigment in meat, from turning gray. But smoke usually penetrates only about 1/8 inch (3 mm) into the meat, so the pink color remains near the surface, creating a colorful ring. Water pans, mopping, spritzing, and basting help to deepen the smoke ring because they keep the meat surface moist, so more smoke and combustion gases can mix with water, stick there, and eventually penetrate the meat.

ROTISSERIE GRILLING

One of the most primitive forms of grilling, rotisserie grilling is simply rotating a piece of food slowly over the fire. When you rotate a hot dog on a stick over a campfire, you are rotisserie grilling. Enlarge the meat to a whole lamb or hog and spread out the fire and this form of grilling is called spit roasting. Constant rotation, which causes the dripping fat and juices to roll around the surface of the meat instead of falling into the fire, is what makes this grilling method effective. That constantly rolling moisture and melted fat makes spit-roasted meats self-basting. It's particularly useful for whole chickens, turkeys, and other lean birds because it creates an exceptionally crisp crust while keeping the tender meat moist. But don't stop there. You can put a rack of ribs, any large meat roast, or even a whole head of cauliflower on a spit to help grill it evenly and create a crisp, browned surface.

To set up the grill, slide the spit into the food (through the cavity of a whole bird, for example) and secure it with skewers, bolts, or kitchen string according to the directions that accompany your rotisserie (they're all a little different). Make sure there are no loose bits of food. It may help to truss birds to keep them tight (see page 111). Once secure, set the spitted food in the rotisserie assembly so it will rotate 6 to 12 inches (15 to 30 cm) away from the heat and turn freely. On gas and charcoal grills, you may need to remove the grill grate for the food to rotate unobstructed. If the food isn't very fatty, brush the surface with oil to help it brown evenly. Place a drip pan beneath the food to prevent flare-ups and capture drippings for making a pan sauce. We like to put a few vegetables like onions, carrots, and potatoes in the drip pan during cooking. If you intend to capture smoke, close the grill lid. If not using a lid, plan on slightly longer cook times.

WRAPPING

Loose, delicate, and wet foods like fish fillets and ground meats can be difficult to grill directly over the heat. Wrapping helps contain them and keep them moist. Almost any wrapper will do, from aluminum foil and thin wood sheets to grape leaves, banana leaves, and corn husks. Wood and leaf wrappers not only protect the food but also impart subtle flavors. To keep wood sheets and dried leaves from incinerating on the grill, soak them in water for at least 1 hour before using. Place the food on the wrapper, fold the wrapper around the food, and place the packet on the grill. Use this method to wrap ground beef in banana leaves, sausage links in grape leaves, fish in lotus leaves, or wheels of Brie cheese in grapevine leaves.

You can also wrap foods and liquid in aluminum foil to make a "hobo pack" for grill braising. For example, to make grilled shrimp scampi, bundle shrimp, butter, garlic, parsley, and lemon juice in foil and place directly over the fire on the grate. Or you can bundle together clams or mussels and tomato sauce, wine, or beer, or even chopped vegetables and pesto. A hobo pack is especially useful for making Grill-Roasted Garlic and Grill-Caramelized Onions (page 167).

LA PLANCHA

Solid planks make a handy surface for cooking food over a live fire. The traditional Spanish *plancha,* or metal plate, is like a flattop griddle. Made of cast-iron or steel, the metal plank gets screaming hot and conducts heat quickly to any food surface, creating an evenly browned exterior. Flatbreads like Indian chapati and Middle Eastern pita are traditionally cooked this way, as are such grilled sandwiches as the cubano, Cuba's famed ham, roast pork, cheese, and pickle combination. You can even heat up planks of salt, stone, and wood for cooking on a grill. It's not really grilling because the fire never touches the food, but it's a fun way to expand your outdoor repertoire.

Preheat and oil metal planks. As with a grill grate, it's important to get a metal plank hot and to lubricate it with oil to help prevent sticking. Thick metal griddles can get blisteringly hot over high heat.

They give beef steaks, octopuses, and other foods an incomparable sear. For more even searing, use a heavy pan on top of the food to make sure all surfaces touch the hot metal.

Gently heat stone and salt planks. These planks are like alternative sauté pans. You can cook any thin, quick-cooking food on them, but it's best to heat them up slowly to prevent cracking. Heated soapstone and ceramic planks give you a nice browned bottom crust on pizza, and salt planks both season and cook foods in a single step. The moisture from sliced flank steak, shrimp, and even eggs cooked on a hot salt plank dissolves some of the salt, depositing the salt onto the food. Stone and ceramic planks for grilling should be at least ¾ inch (2 cm) thick and salt blocks at least 1½ inches (4 cm) thick. Preheat them over low heat on the grill, gradually raising the temperature or moving the plank to a hotter part of the grill over a 30-minute period. Salt blocks can reach temperatures up to 650°F (345°C). Set the food on the hot plank and it will sear and cook in minutes. You can even use heatproof grill gloves to set the hot block on a table (over a trivet) and cook food on the hot block at the table. Clean metal, ceramic, and salt planks in the same way you handle most other pans. Let the plank cool down gradually, then clean it with warm water and a scouring pad. Allow to dry thoroughly before storing.

Char wood planks first. Unlike metal and stone, wood is not a good heat conductor, which makes grilling on a wood plank a gentle cooking method. It's perfect for soft food like a fillet of salmon or a wheel of Brie, and it makes a fantastic presentation because you can serve the cooked food on the wood plank. Use almost any untreated wood plank that's about ¼ inch (6 mm) thick. Cedar and alder are popular, but apple and cherry work just as well. For the most smoke flavor, char one side of the plank directly over the fire, then flip the plank over and set the food on the charred side. Cover the grill to trap the heat and send it to the top of the food to help cook it through. Wood planks can be washed clean and reused once or twice.

MEAT, GAME & FISH DONENESS

Cooking time is not a reliable indicator of doneness. Neither is color. Go by temperature to be sure. When the food reaches the internal doneness temperature listed in the chart below, it is done. Test foods by inserting the probe into the thickest part of the food without touching bone. Keep in mind that the internal temperature may rise 5° to 10°F (3° to 6°C) after the food comes off the grill (this applies mostly to foods more than 1 inch/2.5 cm thick).

The temperatures below are consistent with how most chefs serve food for the best texture and flavor. In some cases, the United States Department of Agriculture (USDA) temperatures are slightly higher to account for user error. For instance, the USDA defines most meats as rare at 135°F (57°C), medium-rare at 145°F (63°C), medium at 160°F (71°C), and well-done at 170°F (77°C) and above. At those temperatures, however, the meat will probably be cooked more than you wish.

MEAT	BLUE	RARE	MEDIUM-RARE	MEDIUM-DONE	MEDIUM-WELL	WELL-DONE
Beef, bison, & venison steaks & roasts	120°F/49°C	125°F/52°C	135°F/57°C	145°F/63°C	155°F/68°C	170°F/77°C
Beef, bison & venison tough cuts	---	---	---	---	155°F/68°C	170°F/77°C
Ground beef, bison & venison	---	---	---	150°F/65°C	155°F/68°C	160°F/71°C
Pork & boar chops & roasts	---	---	---	145°F/63°C	155°F/68°C	170°F/77°C
Pork & boar shoulders	---	---	---	145°F/63°C	165°F/74°C	170°F/77°C
Ground pork & boar	---	---	---	---	155°F/68°C	165°F/74°C
Lamb & goat chops & roasts	120°F/49°C	125°F/52°C	135°F/57°C	145°F/63°C	155°F/68°C	170°F/77°C
Lamb & goat shoulders	---	---	---	---	155°F/68°C	170°F/77°C
Ground lamb	---	---	---	---	150°F/65°C	160°F/71°C
Veal chops & roasts	---	---	135°F/57°C	145°F/63°C	155°F/68°C	170°F/77°C
Veal shanks	---	---	---	---	155°F/68°C	170°F/77°C
Ground veal	---	---	---	---	150°F/65°C	160°F/71°C
Whole chicken & turkey & all dark meat	---	---	---	---	165°F/74°C	175°F/80°C
Chicken & turkey breasts					155°F/68°C	
Duck, goose, & game birds	---	140°F/60°C	150°F/65°C	165°F/74°C	170°F/77°C	180°F/82°C
Fish	---	---	125°F/52°C	130°F/54°C	140°F/60°C	150°F/65°C

3
BURGERS

36 LESSON 1: BURGERS

37 UMAMI TURKEY BURGERS
WITH HARISSA KETCHUP

39 CLASSIC BEEF BURGERS
WITH LOTS OF TOPPINGS

43 LAMB KOFTA BURGERS
WITH ZA'ATAR TZATZIKI

44 SICHUAN TUNA BURGERS
WITH PICKLED-GINGER
RELISH

48 BLACK BEAN BURGERS
WITH SRIRACHA MAYO
& SESAME SLAW

LESSON
1

BURGERS

Grinding meat pulverizes its fibers, which affects the texture and juiciness in ground beef and how it is best handled and grilled. When a tough cut of meat is ground, you get the flavor of a well-exercised muscle with none of its toughness. Of the three most common cuts of beef that are ground, the most flavorful is chuck (from the well-exercised shoulder), followed by bottom round (from the leg) and sirloin (from the hip). If smooth texture is your goal, ground sirloin is the best choice. But if you want flavor, make your burgers from chuck. Round falls somewhere in the middle. If price is not a factor, opt for short rib or brisket, which can be even tastier than chuck.

WHAT MAKES BURGERS JUICY?

Grinding destroys the structure of meat. As the meat sits, most of the natural moisture once held by the muscle fibers runs out. To replace the missing juices, simply add liquid. Ice water is the most basic choice, but you can opt to use almost any liquid if you want to add both moisture and flavor.

Fat content contributes to juiciness, as well. That means that extra-lean ground beef that's 95 percent lean and 5 percent fat tastes unpalatably dry (in fact, any beef with a fat content of less than 10 percent tastes dry), lean beef that's 85 to 90 percent lean tastes lean and juicy, and beef that's 80 percent lean tastes a bit richer. You won't often see less than 80 percent lean sold in stores, and if you do, the beef may have full flavor but will also have a fatty mouthfeel verging on greasy.

DO SIZE & SHAPE MAKE A DIFFERENCE?

Some people like a thick, mounded burger to keep the center rare. Others prefer a flatter burger to provide a stable shelf for toppings. Either way, ground meat will swell up slightly in the center during grilling.

- If you like a puffy, mounded cooked burger, gently shape the raw meat into flat or disk-shaped patties that taper to the edge.

- If you like a flat cooked burger, make a slight depression in the center of the patty as you shape it. The center will swell and form a flat surface as the burger cooks.

WHEN IS A BURGER DONE?

We believe that ground meat should be thoroughly cooked but not overcooked. Here's why: During grinding, the surface and the interior of a piece of meat are mixed together, causing bacteria on the surface to become dispersed throughout the batch, which is why it is inadvisable to eat any ground meat that is not cooked to at least 145°F (63°C). The United States Department of Agriculture (USDA) recommends 160°F (71°C) to ensure that every area of the meat has reached a temperature of 140°F (60°C) or higher, but we have found that when the meat is cooked to that temperature, all of the moisture is gone, as well. We prefer stopping the cooking of beef burgers at an internal temperature of 145° to 150°F (63° to 65°F), at which point the meat will be slightly pink in the center and still relatively juicy.

Your mouth can pick up five tastes: sweet, salty, sour, bitter, and umami. Umami tastes savory like roasted meat, aged cheese, or sautéed mushrooms. In Japanese, umami translates roughly as "deliciousness," and it has been recognized in Japan as a unique taste since its discovery in 1908. Western science did not confirm the existence of specialized umami taste receptors on the tongue until 2001. These turkey burgers are loaded with rich umami flavors that send their roasty, toasty, meaty score over the top.

UMAMI TURKEY BURGERS WITH HARISSA KETCHUP

MAKES 6 SERVINGS

2 tablespoons finely chopped dried porcini mushrooms (3 to 4 medium pieces)

2 tablespoons soy sauce

1 tablespoon apple butter

3 tablespoons hot water

1 teaspoon anchovy paste

1 tablespoon tomato paste

Fine sea salt and freshly ground pepper

2 lb (1 kg) ground dark meat turkey

2 tablespoons canola oil or other mild vegetable oil

2 tablespoons honey

4 teaspoons Harissa (page 225 or store-bought)

1 large yellow onion, cut into rounds 3/8 inch thick

6 hamburger buns, split

1/4 cup tomato ketchup

1 Heat the grill for medium direct heat (350°–400°F/180°–200°C).

2 In a bowl, combine the mushrooms, soy sauce, apple butter, and water and mix well. Let stand for 1 minute to soften the mushrooms.

3 Stir in the anchovy paste, tomato paste, and ½ teaspoon each salt and pepper. Add the turkey and mix with your hands just until blended. Using a light touch, form the mixture into 6 patties, each about ¾ inch (2 cm) thick and 4 inches (10 cm) in diameter. Coat with 1 tablespoon of the oil. Refrigerate until ready to grill.

4 In a bowl, stir together the honey and harissa and set aside. Season the onion slices on both sides with salt and pepper and brush with the remaining oil.

5 Brush the grill grate and put a grill screen on the grate; oil the screen. Put the onions on the screen and grill, turning once, until soft and lightly browned, about 5 minutes per side. Transfer the onions to a plate and brush with half of the harissa-honey mixture; cover to keep warm.

6 Remove the grill screen and oil the grill grate. Put the patties on the grate, cover the grill, and cook for 9 minutes, turning the burgers after about 5 minutes for medium-well (160°F/71°C). Add 1 minute per side for well-done (170°F/77°C).

7 To toast the buns, place them, cut side down, on the grate over the fire 1 minute before the burgers are ready. If serving the burgers directly from the grill, serve on the buns. If the burgers will sit for even a few minutes, keep the buns and burgers separate until just before eating.

8 Mix the ketchup into the remaining harissa-honey mixture. Top each burger with a dollop of harissa ketchup and a pile of honeyed onions.

Every grill book claims to give you the best burger recipe ever. We don't. That's because we don't believe there is such a thing. Burgers are simple. Just a few techniques will increase your prospect for success. Once you have mastered a bare-bones burger, it is easy to expand your repertoire. We have included nine ideas for some delicious combos (see page 41), and once you try a few, we know you'll be inventing bigger and better extravaganzas all your own. Best burger ever? We're looking forward to chomping into the next great burger yet to come.

(see page 41)

MAKES 6 SERVINGS

2 lb (1 kg) ground beef chuck, 85 percent lean

5 tablespoons (3 fl oz/ 80 ml) ice-cold water

1 tablespoon tomato ketchup

1 teaspoon fine sea salt

½ teaspoon freshly ground pepper

Choice of toppings (page 41)

12 slices good-quality American, provolone, or Cheddar cheese (optional)

6 hamburger buns, split

CLASSIC BEEF BURGERS WITH LOTS OF TOPPINGS

1 Heat the grill for medium-high direct heat (400°–450°F/200°–230°C).

2 In a bowl, combine the beef, water, ketchup, salt, and pepper and mix with your hands until well blended; do not overmix. Gently form the meat into 6 patties no more than 1 inch (2.5 cm) thick. Refrigerate the patties until the grill is ready.

3 Choose your topping and prepare as needed.

4 Brush the grill grate and coat with oil. Put the patties on the grate, cover the grill, and cook for 7 minutes, turning the burgers after about 4 minutes for medium (150°F/65°C). They should be slightly pink at the center. Add 1 minute per side for well-done (160°F/71°C). If you are making cheeseburgers, put 2 slices of cheese on each burger 1 minute before the burgers are ready to be removed from the grill.

5 To toast the buns, place them, cut side down, on the grate over the fire 1 minute before the burgers are ready. If serving the burgers directly from the grill, serve on the buns with the chosen topping. If the burgers will sit for even a few minutes, keep the buns and burgers separate until just before eating.

Continued on page 40

Recipes for kofta (aka *kufta* and *kefta*) appear in the earliest Arabic cookbooks, and variations can be found from Croatia to Pakistan. The meat patties can be seasoned with anything from mint to chiles and are typically baked, fried, or simmered in curry. Ours are grilled, of course, made from lamb lightened with spinach and grilled onion and served on flatbread with *tzatziki* in the style of the eastern Mediterranean.

MAKES 4 SERVINGS

¼ cup (1 oz/30 g) fine dried bread crumbs

⅓ cup (3 fl oz/80 ml) vegetable juice such as V8

1½ lb (750 g) ground lamb, about 80 percent lean

¼ cup grated yellow onion

1 large egg, lightly beaten

1 teaspoon each fine sea salt and freshly ground black pepper

⅛ teaspoon cayenne pepper

1 teaspoon ground coriander

1 teaspoon cumin seeds, toasted in a dry pan until fragrant then ground

¼ teaspoon ground allspice

¼ teaspoon ground ginger

3 cloves garlic, minced

2 tablespoons chopped fresh flat-leaf parsley

2 tablespoon chopped fresh mint

3 tablespoons olive oil

¾ cup (6 oz/170 g) Za'atar Tzatziki (page 225)

1 teaspoon Za'atar (page 174 or store-bought)

4 whole-wheat pita breads

2 cups (2 oz/60 g) baby spinach leaves

4 lemon wedges

LAMB KOFTA BURGERS WITH ZA'ATAR TZATZIKI

1 Heat the grill for medium-high indirect heat (350°–400°F/180°–200°C).

2 In a large bowl, mix together the bread crumbs and vegetable juice until the crumbs are evenly moistened. Add the lamb, onion, egg, salt, black pepper, cayenne, coriander, cumin, allspice, ginger, garlic, parsley, and mint and mix everything together with your hands. Using a light touch, form the mixture into 4 oval-shaped patties about 5 by 3 by ¾ inches (13 by 7.5 by 2 cm). Coat the patties on both sides using 1 tablespoon of the oil and set aside on a plate or rimmed baking sheet.

3 In a small bowl, mix together the remaining 2 tablespoons oil and the za'atar. Brush the za'atar mixture on both sides of each pita.

4 Brush the grill grate and coat with oil. Put the patties on the grate directly over the fire and cook, turning once, until browned, about 3 minutes per side. Move the burgers away from the fire, cover the grill, and cook until an instant-read thermometer inserted horizontally into the burger registers 145F (63°C).

5 During the last minute of grilling, put the pitas on the grate over the fire for about 15 seconds per side to toast lightly. To assemble the burgers, cut one side off of each pita to expose the internal pocket. Coat the interior of each pocket with 2 tablespoons of the tzatziki. Put one-fourth of the spinach leaves in each pocket, followed by a burger, imbedding it deeply in the bed of spinach. Top with the remaining tzatziki and serve with the lemon wedges.

 EXTRA CREDIT

Instead of forming the lamb mixture into oval patties, you can shape it into long sausages on skewers and fold the pita around the grilled meat. To make a skewered kofta, form the meat mixture into 4 elongated meatballs. Thread each meatball onto a large skewer and mold it into an elongated oval (about 6 inches/15 cm long and 1½ inches/4 cm across) that comes to a point covering the tip of the skewer. Grill as you would burgers, but you will need to turn each skewer so that the kofta cooks on all four sides.

To up the flavor, add some chopped Preserved Lemons (page 226) to your tzatziki.

Any firm, fatty fish—salmon, mackerel, bluefish, swordfish—is sturdy enough for making burgers. But our favorite, without question, is tuna. Finely chopped raw tuna is surprisingly similar in appearance and texture to lean beef, and it holds its shape better when fashioned into a burger, without the aid of binders and starches, than extra-lean beef does.

MAKES 4 SERVINGS

1½ lb (750 g) tuna steak, cut into small chunks

1 tablespoon red miso paste

½ teaspoon prepared wasabi

1 teaspoon soy sauce

4 green onions, white and pale green parts, cut into ½-inch (12-mm) pieces

PICKLED GINGER RELISH

½ cup (3 oz/90 g) pickled ginger for sushi, finely chopped

Finely chopped zest and juice of ½ lemon

3 green onions, white and pale green parts, halved lengthwise and thinly sliced crosswise

1 tablespoon soy sauce

½ teaspoon fish sauce

1 tablespoon canola oil or other mild vegetable oil

4 hamburger buns, split

SICHUAN TUNA BURGERS WITH PICKLED-GINGER RELISH

1 Heat the grill for medium-high direct heat (400°–450°F/200°–230°C).

2 Chop the tuna finely enough so that when you press some between your fingers, it clings to itself. Do not chop so finely that it becomes mushy. You can use a sharp knife and a sturdy cutting board or a food processor. If using a food processor, use the pulse button and be careful to stop pulsing before the fish is reduced to a puree.

3 Transfer the fish to a bowl and mix in the miso, wasabi, soy sauce, and green onions just until well blended. Do not overmix. Using a light touch, form the mixture into 4 patties no more than 1 inch (2.5 cm) thick. Refrigerate until the grill is ready.

4 To make the pickled ginger relish, in a small bowl, combine all of the ingredients and mix well. Use immediately, or transfer to an airtight container and refrigerate for up to 1 week.

5 Brush the grill grate and coat with oil. Coat the patties on both sides with the oil. Put the patties on the grate, cover the grill, and cook for 3 minutes. Turn the burgers and cook uncovered for 3 minutes longer for medium-rare. Add 1 minute per side for medium-well.

6 To toast the buns, place them, cut side down, on the grate over the fire 1 minute before the burgers are ready. If serving the burgers directly from the grill, serve on the buns. If the burgers will sit for even a few minutes, keep the buns and burgers separate until just before eating. Top each burger with a heaping spoonful of the ginger relish.

Continued on page 47

Continued from page 44  **EXTRA CREDIT**

Switch your fish. Try bluefish for its creamy, rich consistency, or wild salmon for clean mouthfeel and a touch of gaminess.

Mix your fish. You can cut the fat in your fish burger by replacing up to one-third of the tuna or other fatty fish with something lean, like flounder, snapper, or bass.

Shrimp or Scallop Burgers: Replace one-half of the tuna or other fatty fish with ½ lb (250 g) peeled and deveined shrimp or sea scallops, finely chopped.

To take the flavor a step further, add one of the following:

- 1 teaspoon each minced garlic and peeled and minced fresh ginger

- 1 teaspoon fish sauce and/or Asian hot-pepper sauce (lately we've been adding Korean gochujang)

- 1 tablespoon pineapple or apple juice, for a mysterious sweetness

- 1 teaspoon smoked salt in place of the soy sauce or 1 drop of liquid smoke with the soy sauce, for a smoked fish burger

Keep the fish from sticking to your hands by dampening your hands with cold water before you mix and form the burgers.

Plank 'em! After browning the burgers directly over the heat for 1 minute on each side, transfer them to soaked cedar planks away from direct heat to finish cooking. Top with grilled green onions and Korean BBQ sauce.

Enhance the Japanese character of these burgers with some pickled daikon, wasabi mayonnaise, or a drizzle of teriyaki sauce, or coat them with Asian sesame oil rather than canola oil.

There are many tricks for making vegetable burgers taste meaty. Our favorites are adding mushrooms to up the umami ante; seasoning with cumin and smoked salt to lead the taste buds toward chili con carne and grilled meat; stirring in some beans for a creamy mouthfeel reminiscent of well marbled steak; and throwing in a shredded beet for some rare-meat redness. These burgers have it all.

MAKES 4 SERVINGS

2 teaspoons olive oil

¾ diced (3 oz/90 g) red onion

1 cup (3 oz/90 g) finely chopped mushrooms

1 teaspoon smoked salt

½ teaspoon freshly ground pepper

1 teaspoon ground cumin

1 teaspoon smoked paprika

1 can (15 oz/470 g) black beans, rinsed and drained

¾ cup (4½ oz/140 g) cooked quinoa

1 cup (3½ oz/105 g) finely shredded raw beet

1 tablespoon soy sauce, preferably shoyu

½ cup (2 oz/60 g) ground walnuts

1 tablespoon canola oil or other mild vegetable oil

Sriracha Mayo (page 223)

Sesame Slaw (page 230)

BLACK BEAN BURGERS WITH SRIRACHA MAYO & SESAME SLAW

1 Heat the grill for medium direct heat (350°–400°F/180°–200°C).

2 In a large frying pan, heat the olive oil over medium heat. Add the onion and mushrooms and sauté until tender, about 4 minutes. Remove from the heat and season with the smoked salt, black pepper, cumin, and paprika. Add the beans and mash with the back of a fork until a chunky puree forms. There should be no whole beans, but there should still be lots of visible chunks. Stir in the quinoa, beet, soy sauce, and walnuts. Form into 4 patties each about ¾ inch (2 cm) thick. Coat the patties on both sides with the canola oil and set aside on a plate or rimmed baking sheet.

3 Put a grill screen on the grill grate and oil the screen. Heat the screen for at least 5 minutes. Put the patties on the hot screen, cover the grill (vents completely open), and grill the burgers, turning once, until browned and heated through, about 5 minutes per side. To toast the buns, place them, cut side down, directly over the fire 1 minute before the burgers are ready.

4 To assemble the burgers, spread a thin layer of the mayo on the bottom half of each bun. Top with burgers, a little more mayo, and a generous dollop of slaw. Place the bun top askew to one side. You will probably have more slaw than can fit on the burgers. Serve the remainder on the side.

 **EXTRA CREDIT**

Try substituting bulgur and chickpeas, or brown rice and red beans for the quinoa and black beans.

Change up the spices. Trade out the Mexican palate for Italian, North African, Indian, or Chinese.

Replace a portion of the cabbage in your slaw with shredded carrot, fennel, apple, or sweet onion.

4

BEEF

52 LESSON 1: STEAKS

53 ESPRESSO-BUZZED
RIB-EYE STEAKS

54 STEAK, POTATOES
& ASPARAGUS

57 GARLIC-CRUSTED
T-BONE WITH
GORGONZOLA BUTTER

58 LESSON 2: ROASTS

59 GRILL-ROASTED
TRI-TIP WITH SPICY
KOREAN GLAZE

60 GRILL-ROASTED
TENDERLOIN WITH WILD
MUSHROOM MOSTARDA

63 GRILL-ROASTED RIB
ROAST WITH GRILLED
ONION TOASTS & GRILLED
APPLE HORSERADISH

64 LESSON 3: TOUGH CUTS

67 BBQ BRISKET WITH
ANCHO CHOCOLATE
BBQ SAUCE

STEAKS

Cattle carcasses are divided into eight primal cuts and then sold to retail butchers. The butchers in turn divide the primal cuts into steaks, roasts, and ground meats. Steaks are sections of roasts, usually made up of one or two muscles and crosscut ½ inch to 2 inches (12 mm to 5 cm) thick.

What distinguishes one type of steak from another depends on the primal cut from which the steak was sectioned.

- Rib steaks, including the popular rib eye, are cross sections of a rib roast. They have a great balance of flavor and tenderness and are the favorite of many grill masters.

- T-bone, porterhouse, and tenderloin (which includes fillet, tournedos, and chateaubriand) steaks all come from the short loin, a pair of tender muscles that run on either side of the spine. All loin steaks are tender and have a mild flavor and a minimum of bone and fat.

- Sirloin steaks and strip steaks come from the sirloin, the hip section of the steer or heifer. Sirloin steaks vary greatly in quality, depending from which end of the sirloin they are cut. At one end, a sirloin steak is very close to a high-priced porterhouse, and at the other end it is just a hairline away from rump or round. Because of this variety, sirloin is usually priced to sell, and for the most part, it is a good value with little waste. Since some pieces of sirloin can tend toward toughness, always look for visible marbling in the lean, and if you purchase a sirloin that is very lean, be careful not to overcook it.

- Of the tough cuts, the ones that are best for grilling are skirt steak, hanger steak, and flank steak. They have long, thick muscle fibers running parallel to one another that remain tough after grilling, but they can be tenderized by thinly slicing the steak against the grain of the fibers. Flat-iron steak is a similarly shaped cut taken from the interior of the shoulder (chuck).

Here are a handful of simple tips to help you turn out a great grilled steak.

- Buy the best grade of beef you can find, preferably choice or prime. Dry-aged beef will have more concentrated flavor.

- Cool-temperature meat sears better than ice-cold meat. That means you'll get a better crust on a steak if you remove the steak from the refrigerator 30 minutes before you plan to put it on the grill.

- To keep steaming to a minimum and crusting to a maximum, pat the steaks dry before seasoning them or putting them on the grill.

- For steaks thinner than ¾ inch (2 cm), use a raging hot fire to create a nice thick crust before the steak is cooked through.

- The more well-done you like your steak, the lower your fire should be. Low heat gives a steak the time it needs to cook through without scorching the surface.

- Grill steak thicker than ½ inch (12 mm) indirectly. Sear the steak over high heat, then move it away from the fire to finish cooking without burning.

- As beef cooks, the meat fibers get firmer: rare meat is soft, medium is resilient, and well-done is stiff. You can judge the doneness of a steak by either taking its temperature with an instant-read thermometer or by pressing on it. With practice, you will be able to judge a perfect medium-rare steak just by touch. For doneness temperatures, see page 32.

- Allowing a grilled steak to rest briefly before slicing into it gives its fibers time to set a bit, so they release less juice when the meat is cut.

A rib-eye steak, cut from the rib section of the steer, is the boneless center of prime rib. This steak includes a fair amount of intramuscular fat that keeps the meat moist, so we tend to flavor it with a dry rub and a sauce, rather than a brine or marinade. This cut also stands up to fairly bold seasonings. Here, we dust the meat with a dry espresso rub and then glaze it with classic steak sauce infused with coffee. The flavors are strong and dark, enhancing the rich beefiness of this stellar steak.

MAKES 4 SERVINGS

4 boneless rib-eye steaks, each 8 to 10 oz (250 to 315 oz) and about 1 inch (2.5 cm) thick

⅓ cup (1½ oz/45 g) Espresso Rub (page 215)

½ cup (4 fl oz/125 ml) Espresso Steak Sauce (page 220)

ESPRESSO-BUZZED RIB-EYE STEAKS

1 Heat the grill for medium-high direct heat (400°–450°F/200°–230°C).

2 Season both sides of the steaks with the rub. Set aside for 15 minutes.

3 Brush the grill grate and coat with oil. Put the steaks on the grate and cook, turning once, until grill marked on both sides, about 4 minutes per side. Cover the grill and cook for another 3 minutes per side for medium-rare or 4 minutes per side for medium-done.

4 Transfer the steaks to a platter and let rest for 5 minutes. Serve with the steak sauce.

 **EXTRA CREDIT**

Pairing a spice rub and a pungent sauce is a great way to dress up any steak. Look for couples with complementary flavors and be careful to avoid matches where both mates are predominantly spicy, salty, or sweet. Here are some of our favorites:

- Ancho Chile Rub (page 215) and Grilled Tomato Jam (page 223)

- Bedouin Spice Rub (page 215) and Za'atar Tzatziki (page 225)

- Berbere (page 217) and Gorgonzola Butter (page 227)

- Shichimi Togarashi (page 217) and Homemade Steak Sauce (page 220)

Most beef lovers agree that the rib section of beef has the perfect balance of tenderness and flavor.

Those two qualities are enhanced by marbling, the buildup of fine threads of fat within the lean parts of meat. Although numerous criteria go into grading beef (see facing page), marbling has the most influence on succulence, so it is no accident that meat producers will go to great lengths to get the rib sections of their cattle graded prime. Seek out prime rib eye whenever possible.

Very little beef sold commercially is aged, and for many cuts the effects of aging are not worth the exorbitant price. But rib eye is the exception. You should seek out aged rib eyes at least once in a lifetime. The concentration of flavor and the intense marbling make an aged prime rib eye one of the best pieces of meat you can find.

This dinner cooks entirely (well, almost) on the grill and takes less than half an hour. The tricks are choosing a flat steak that grills in minutes, precooking potatoes before putting them over the fire, and using a quick-cooking, tender vegetable like asparagus.

MAKES 4 SERVINGS

4 teaspoons flake sea salt such as Maldon

1 teaspoon coarsely ground black pepper

1 teaspoon red pepper flakes

1¼ lb (625 g) flat, boneless steak such as 2 flat-iron steaks, 1 flank steak, or 1 London broil if the first two are unavailable

4 large russet potatoes

3 tablespoons extra-virgin olive oil

¾ lb (375 g) thin asparagus, tough ends snapped off

Fine sea salt and freshly ground black pepper

STEAK, POTATOES & ASPARAGUS

1 In a bowl, stir together the flake salt, coarse black pepper, and red pepper flakes. Rub two-thirds of the mixture over the steak(s). Set aside. You should have about 2 teaspoons remaining. Heat the grill for high indirect heat (400°–450°F/200°–230°C).

2 Microwave the potatoes at full power until tender, 7–8 minutes. Let the potatoes cool until they can be handled, then cut in half lengthwise.

3 Drizzle the steak with 1 tablespoon of the oil. Divide the remaining 2 tablespoons oil evenly between the potatoes and asparagus, coating the cut sides of the potatoes and the length of the asparagus spears.

4 Brush the grill grate and coat with oil. Put the potatoes, cut side down, on the grate directly over the fire and cook until grill marked, about 2 minutes. Move the potatoes, cut side up, away from the fire and sprinkle evenly with the remaining seasoning mixture.

5 Put the steak on the grate directly over the fire, cover the grill, and cook, turning once, until blistered with char and resilient to the touch, about 4 minutes per side. If you like, you can insert an instant-read thermometer horizontally into the steak; it should read 130°F (54°C). Transfer the steak to a cutting board and let rest for 5 minutes. Leave the potatoes on the grill.

6 While the steak is resting, lay the asparagus on the grill grate directly over the fire, running them perpendicular to the bars. Cover the grill and cook the asparagus until dark green and charred in spots, about 5 minutes. Transfer the asparagus and potatoes to a serving plate; season the asparagus to taste with fine salt and ground pepper. Slice the steak against the grain and serve with the potatoes and asparagus.

 **EXTRA CREDIT**

Our current favorite is flat-iron steak, which comes from the center of the shoulder and looks a lot like a mini flank steak. It is similar to flank in flavor and tenderness. The big difference is flat-iron steak costs about 30 percent less than flank.

If asparagus are out of season or you don't like asparagus, substitute grilled romaine (page 166).

Use this recipe as a formula for scores of easy steak meals by changing up the spice rub (pages 214–217).

Great grilled steak is all about the palate-popping juxtaposition of a spicy, crunchy crust with the moist, relatively untouched meat beneath. This recipe takes that play to a higher level, adding a whiff of smoke and creamy, pungent blue cheese butter.

GARLIC-CRUSTED T-BONE WITH GORGONZOLA BUTTER

MAKES 4 SERVINGS

4 tablespoons (2 fl oz/ 60 ml) extra-virgin olive oil

4 cloves garlic, minced

1 tablespoon coarse sea salt, preferably sel gris

1 teaspoon coarsely ground pepper

1 T-bone or porterhouse steak, 2½–3 lb (1.25–1.5 kg) and at least 2 inches (5 cm) thick

2 large handfuls wood chips or chunks

½ cup (4 oz/125 g) Gorgonzola Butter (page 227)

1 In a small saucepan, heat 3 tablespoons of the oil over medium heat just until warm. Drop in the garlic; the oil should be hot enough to make the garlic bubble but not hot enough to brown it. Remove from the heat and let cool to room temperature. Rub the cooled garlic oil evenly over the steak. Let the steak rest for 1 hour while the grill heats.

2 Heat the grill for high indirect heat (400°–450°F/200°–230°C). If using charcoal, wrap the wood chips in a perforated aluminum foil packet and place on the hot coals, or place the wood chunks directly on the coals. If using a gas grill, wrap the chips in a perforated foil packet, and put the packet directly over one of the gas burners under the cooking grate. Or if your grill has a smoker box, use it.

3 Brush the grill grate and coat with oil. Put the steak on the grate directly over the fire, cover the grill, and cook, turning once, until darkly crusted on both sides, 4–6 minutes per side. Move the steak away from the fire, cover the grill, and cook for 6–12 minutes for medium-rare to medium–done. Transfer to a platter, cover loosely with foil, and let rest for 5–8 minutes.

4 While the steak is resting, make the butter.

5 Carve the steak and drizzle with the remaining 1 tablespoon oil. Top each portion with one-fourth of the butter.

 **EXTRA CREDIT**

Most supermarkets and some butcher shops don't regularly cut steaks this thick. Call the meat department or your butcher ahead of time to order it. On this steak, the T-shaped bone separates the smaller and more tender tenderloin (or fillet) from the larger and slightly tougher top loin (strip). To arrive at 4 servings, you have two options: you can cut the 2 pieces away from the bone, cut each piece into 4 pieces, and serve each guest a piece of tenderloin and a piece of top loin, or you can cut all of the meat into slices ½ inch (12 mm) thick and serve each guest a mix of tenderloin and top loin slices. The T-bone itself is up for grabs.

ROASTS

Any cut of meat that is larger than 2 inches (5 cm) thick must be grill roasted using indirect heat. For most boneless roasts, the meat is browned directly over the fire and is then moved away from direct flame and cooked, with the grill covered, until it reaches the desired internal temperature (see the doneness chart on page 32). Once the roast is moved away from direct heat, it will roast gently by convection without danger of scorching and with far less chance of overcooking.

Because bones are filled with air, they act as temperature insulators, greatly slowing down the rate that heat moves through meat. That's why bone-in roasts are typically grill roasted away from direct heat for their entire cooking time. Searing bone-in roasts over direct heat can cause the surface to brown too early in the grilling process so the roast ends up scorched before the meat is done inside.

HOW DO YOU KNOW WHEN A ROAST IS DONE GRILLING?

Roasts are too thick to judge doneness by touch. The only way to know if a roast is done is to take its internal temperature by inserting an instant-read thermometer into the center of the meat from any direction. Make sure the tip of the thermometer reaches the center of the thickest part of the roast and is not touching bone. The temperature of bone will always register cooler than the cooking meat around it, which could lead you to believe that a roast has not reached doneness, when in fact it has.

TO GET A GREAT CRUST

After their surface is seasoned and before they go on the grill, most meats are allowed to rest for an hour or more to encourage salt in the seasoning to draw some meat juices to the surface. Meat juices are a combination of protein, minerals, and water. Given a little time, the juices air-dry, gluing the flavorful seasonings to the surface of the meat. When the surface comes in contact with fire, the dried juices brown quickly, enhancing the color of the roast (or steak) and helping to form a thicker, more flavorful crust.

In the late 1950s, a butcher in Santa Maria, California, tried roasting the butt portion of a bottom sirloin, rather than grinding into hamburger, and created a regional barbecue specialty that practically defines California grilling. The tri-tip, a boomerang-shaped roast, is one of the tastiest beef cuts you can put on the grill. It is lean and has little waste. Here, we complement its rich, beefy flavor with an equally assertive rub and bold glaze that radiate with chiles, garlic, and ginger.

MAKES 4–6 SERVINGS

1 whole tri-tip, about 2 lb (1 kg), silver skin and excess fat trimmed to ¼ inch (6 mm)

3 tablespoons Basic Barbecue Rub (page 215)

1 tablespoon canola oil or other mild vegetable oil

1 cup (8 fl oz/250 ml) Spicy Korean Glaze (page 220)

GRILL-ROASTED TRI-TIP WITH SPICY KOREAN GLAZE

1 Coat the meat evenly with the rub. Set aside for 1 hour.

2 Heat the grill for direct medium-high heat (400°–450°F/200°–230°C) on one side and direct medium heat (350°–400°F/180°–200°C) on the other.

3 Brush the grill grate and coat with oil. Coat the meat with the oil. Put the tri-tip on the grate over the medium-high heat and cook, turning once, until browned on both sides, about 7 minutes per side. Move the meat to the lower heat, or if using a gas grill, turn the heat down to medium (350°–400°F/180°–200°C). Cover the grill and cook, turning once, for about 10 minutes per side for medum-rare. The meat is ready when an instant-read thermometer inserted into the center of the roast registers 130°F (54°F).

4 While the tri-tip is roasting, prepare the glaze.

5 Brush the roast with a thick layer of the glaze. You will use about half of it. Return the roast to high heat and cook, turning once, just long enough to brown the glaze, about 1 minute per side.

6 Transfer the roast to a cutting board and let rest for 10 minutes. Cut the roast in half at the center where it angles. Slice both halves against the grain. Serve the remaining glaze on the side for drizzling.

 **EXTRA CREDIT**

Because of the popularity of tri-tip in California, most meat packers in America ship all of their tri-tips west, making it difficult to find the cut anywhere but the West Coast. If you can't find it, you can substitute any sirloin roast.

Tri-tip steaks have a unique shape, hence their name, triangle steaks.

Replace the Spicy Korean Glaze with Ssam Jang (page 222) or Western Carolina Barbecue Sauce (page 219).

A steer has only two tenderloins. The short supply and high demand makes tenderloin the most expensive beef cut on the market. But if it's tenderness you're after, it doesn't get any better than this. Here we grill the whole tenderloin with a mushroom rub and an updated *mostarda* made from wild mushrooms, mustard, and spices.

2 dried porcini mushroom slices

1 teaspoon truffle salt

1 teaspoon coarsely ground pepper

1 tablespoon fresh rosemary leaves, finely chopped

2 cloves garlic, minced

1 beef tenderloin roast, about 3 lb (1.5 kg), trimmed and tied

2½ cups (30 oz/850 g) Wild Mushroom Mostarda (page 227)

1 tablespoon extra-virgin olive oil

GRILL-ROASTED TENDERLOIN WITH WILD MUSHROOM MOSTARDA

1 Grind the porcini mushroom slices into dust in a spice grinder or with a mortar and pestle. You should have about 1½ teaspoons. Transfer to a small bowl, add the truffle salt, ground black pepper, rosemary, and garlic, and mix well. Rub evenly over the tenderloin and set aside for 1 hour.

2 Heat the grill for indirect high heat (400°–450°F/200°–230°C). While the grill is heating, prepare the mostarda, if you haven't already, and keep warm.

3 Brush the grill grate and coat with oil. Coat the tenderloin with the oil. Put the tenderloin on the grate directly over the fire, cover the grill, and cook until browned on all sides, about 4 minutes per side. Move the tenderloin away from the fire, with the wider end closer to the fire. Cover the grill and cook for 15 minutes for medium-rare. If you like, you can insert an instant-read thermometer into the center of the tenderloin; it should read 135°F (57°C).

4 Transfer the tenderloin to a platter and let rest for 10 minutes before slicing. Serve with the warm mostarda on the side.

 **EXTRA CREDIT**

Prepare a fruit mostarda by substituting 2 lb (1 kg) fresh apricots or peaches for the dried and fresh mushrooms and 1 tablespoon marmalade for the tomato paste.

The loin and tenderloin run parallel to each other above and below the spine. Although the loin muscle helps the legs and hips in their movement, the sole anatomical function of the tenderloin is to allow the animal to straighten its back and stand upright, which is something that cattle never do. Thus, it's the least exercised and most meltingly tender cut of beef.

The tenderloin is shaped like a baseball bat, with the wider end sitting in the hips and the tapered end coming to a point just past the beginning of the rib cage. When the tenderloin is sliced into roasts and steaks, you get three cuts, distinguished by their dimension: the wide butt end yields chateaubriand, the center section yields fillet roast or fillet steaks. Small steaks, called tournedos, are cut where the center narrows to under 2 inches (5 cm), and the tapered end is sold as tips.

Roasting a standing rib roast over an open fire is spectacular all by itself, and it will graciously share its high status with you, even though it requires little effort on your part. In this boss-coming-for-dinner-worthy presentation, we're serving two accompaniments: savory-sweet bruschetta of caramelized onions and dollops of sweet-tart-pungent-fruity horseradish.

MAKES 6 SERVINGS

3-bone standing rib roast of beef

6 cloves garlic, minced

5 tablespoons (2½ fl oz/ 60 ml) extra-virgin olive oil

1 teaspoon coarse sea salt, preferably sel gris

1 teaspoon freshly ground pepper

2 large sweet onions, sliced ¼ inch (6 mm) thick

1 large tart apple such as Granny Smith, peeled, halved, cored, and cut into slices ¼ inch (6 mm) thick

1 teaspoon sugar

⅓ cup prepared white horseradish

2 teaspoons brown mustard

4 teaspoons honey

12 slices baguette

GRILL-ROASTED RIB ROAST WITH GRILLED ONION TOASTS & GRILLED APPLE HORSERADISH

1 Heat the grill for medium indirect heat (300°–350°F/150°–180°C), placing a drip pan under the grill grate away from the fire. Ask your butcher to cut the meat from the bone along the ribs but leave it attached at its widest end, or do this yourself. This will make the roast much easier to carve.

2 In a small bowl, combine the garlic, 2 tablespoons of the oil, and ½ teaspoon each of the salt and pepper and mix well. Rub the mixture evenly over the meat, including on the underside where it is sitting on the bones.

3 Brush the grill grate and coat with oil. Put the roast, bone side down, on the grate away from the heat (over the drip pan), cover the grill, and cook until an instant-read thermometer inserted into the thickest part registers about 130°F (54°C) for medium-rare, about 2 hours. If your grill has a temperature gauge, it should stay around 350°F (180°C). If you are using charcoal, you will need to replenish the coals after the first hour.

4 About 30 minutes before the roast is scheduled to be done, coat the onion and apple slices with 1 tablespoon of the oil. Put them on the grill grate directly over the fire keeping the onions and apple slices separated from one another, and cook, turning once, until all of the slices are deeply grill marked, about 3 minutes per side. Transfer the apple slices to a plate and the onion slices to a large piece of aluminum foil. Season the onions with the remaining ½ teaspoon each salt and pepper and the sugar and then separate the slices into rings. Fold the foil over the onions, crimp and seal the foil, and put the packet next to the beef away from the fire. Cook for 15–20 minutes.

5 Meanwhile, chop the apple finely and transfer to a small bowl. Add the horseradish, mustard, and honey and mix well. Set aside.

6 Transfer the beef to a large cutting board and let rest for 10–15 minutes. While the roast is resting, brush the baguette slices with the remaining 2 tablespoons oil. Put the baguette slices on the grill grate directly over the fire just long enough to toast, about 40 seconds per side. Put a small mound of grilled onions on each toast. Carve the roast and serve with the onion toasts and apple horseradish on the side.

TOUGH CUTS

Most meats are cross sections of muscles. Muscles are built of protein. The protein can be either in muscle fibers, which are the red bulky parts of meat, or in connective tissue, which is the transparent membrane that surrounds the fibers and the muscles themselves. As a muscle is exercised, its fibers take on protein, making the muscle bigger, redder, and more flavorful. At the same time, its connective tissue thickens and becomes more elastic, which makes the muscle harder and tougher. That means that when meat is taken from an older animal or an exercised muscle group, it will have lots of flavor, a dark red color, and a tendency to be tough.

Tender meats are usually preferred for grilling, but that leaves out a lot of the more flavorful cuts, simply because they're tough. Tough cuts, like brisket, chuck, shank, and round, can be cooked on a grill, but to do so, you need to turn your grill into a barbecue (read about barbecuing technique on page 27), which means reducing the heat, adding moisture, and moving the food away from the fire to slow down heat transference.

When meat cooks, two things happen: the protein in the fibers coagulates, becoming firmer and more opaque, and the connective tissue melts. Connective tissue is made mostly of collagen, a unique protein that liquefies in hot water (most proteins get harder when they are boiled). That's why tough, collagen-rich meat becomes tender only when it is cooked with liquid, that is, when it is stewed, braised, or barbecued. Tender meats with sheer fibers of collagen don't need moist cooking (in fact, it can ruin them). They are best cooked by a dry, direct heat method like grilling.

When collagen melts, it turns into gelatin, which is what gives great barbecue its succulence. To encourage the production of gelatin, a pan of water is placed on the grill, usually right above the fire, which has the advantage of billowing tons of steam into the closed grill and of keeping the barbecuing meat away from direct heat. The development of gelatin takes not only moisture but also time. So when grilling tough cuts of meat, the meat is kept as far away from the fire as possible, and the fire itself is monitored so it doesn't get too intense.

Because the flavor of traditional barbecue is largely dependent on smoke, adding steam boosts the ante. Smoke is encouraged to cling to meat by the presence of moisture, so if you want your barbecue to be both smoky and succulently tender, make sure steam is always present.

You will notice in the BBQ brisket recipe that follows that the meat is put on the grill directly out of the refrigerator (something that is never done for tender-cut grilling). That is to encourage extra condensation on the surface of the meat, which gives the smoke more moisture to cling to.

Brisket is a large, tough cut that takes hours of cooking over a low, slow fire to reach tenderness. The extended grilling time allows incredible flavor to permeate deep into the meat. We start by massaging the beef with a rub of hot chile and dark-roasted coffee. We enhance the rub with a savory beer-infused mop to help soften its tough fibers. The finished brisket is sliced and served with a bittersweet barbecue sauce.

MAKES 6 SERVINGS

1/3 cup (1 1/2 oz/45 g) Ancho Chile Rub (page 215)

2 2/3 cups (21 fl oz/660 ml) Beer Mop (page 212)

1 flat or center-cut beef brisket, 3–4 lb (1.5–2 kg), trimmed, with 1/4-inch (6-mm) fat layer on one side

1 cup (8 fl oz/250 ml) Ancho Chocolate BBQ Sauce (page 219)

BBQ BRISKET WITH ANCHO CHOCOLATE BBQ SAUCE

1 Combine 1 tablespoon of the rub with the mop. Set aside.

2 Rub the remaining rub evenly over the brisket. Wrap tightly in plastic wrap and refrigerate for at least 8 hours or up to a day.

3 Remove the meat from the refrigerator about 1 hour before grilling. Heat the grill for medium-low indirect heat (250°–300°F/120°–150°C), placing a drip pan under the grill grate away from the fire.

4 Brush the grill grate and coat with oil. Put the brisket, fatty side up, on the grate away from the fire (over the drip pan) and cover the grill. As the brisket cooks, mop or drizzle it with the mop on both sides whenever the surface looks dry, roughly every 45 minutes for the entire cooking time. After 2 hours of cooking, put the brisket in an aluminum foil pan, place the pan on the grate away from the fire, and then re-cover the grill and continue cooking. The pan helps to retain moisture in the brisket and keep it from drying out. Once the brisket is in the pan, you will need to mop only the top, fatty side. If your grill has a temperature gauge, it should stay around 250°F (120°C) during the entire cooking time. If you are using charcoal, you will need to replenish the coals about once an hour during the cooking. Cook until well browned and even blackened in spots (about 190°F/88°C on an instant-read thermometer), 4–6 hours total. The brisket should be very well-done and tender.

5 Make the barbecue sauce while the brisket is cooking.

6 Remove the brisket in the pan from the grill and let the brisket rest for 20 minutes.

7 Trim any excess fat from the brisket. Don't trim too much fat, however, as the crispy bits taste great. Slice the brisket against the grain. Serve with the barbecue sauce.

5

PORK

70 LESSON 1: PORK CHOPS

73 BRINED PORK CHOPS WITH CHIPOTLE RYE BARBECUE SAUCE

74 BUFFALO PORK STEAKS

76 LESSON 2: RIBS

77 FIVE-PEPPER RIBS WITH PEACH-BOURBON BARBECUE SAUCE

80 LESSON 3: PORK SHOULDER

81 NORTH CAROLINA–STYLE PULLED PORK BARBECUE

84 LESSON 4: PORK SAUSAGES & BELLY

85 GRILL-BRAISED CHORIZO WITH POBLANO CHILE, CILANTRO & LIME

87 GRILLED PORK BELLY WITH SPICY-SWEET KOREAN GLAZE

88 JALAPEÑO CHEDDAR BACON EXPLOSION

94 MUSTARD-SAGE PORK TENDERLOIN WRAPPED IN PANCETTA

LESSON 1

PORK CHOPS

Chops are to pork what steaks are to beef. Most pork chops are cut perpendicular to the backbone from the central loin section, which runs about 18 inches (45 cm) long from the hog's shoulders to its hips. The shoulders and hips support more weight than the central loin, so pork chops vary in tenderness, toughness, and fat content. How the hogs were raised matters, too. Pasture-raised pork tends to be richer and more flavorful but also a bit tougher and less consistent than commodity pork.

WHAT'S THE BEST CUT OF PORK CHOP?

For grilling, we prefer bone-in rib-eye chops that are at least 1½ inches (4 cm) thick. But try different cuts to see which you like best. Pork chops were renamed a few years ago so they would correspond more closely with the terms used for beef steaks.

- Blade Chops: Also called shoulder chops, these are cut from the shoulder blade of the hog. Blade chops include some bone and various intersecting muscles. When cut thick (at least 2 inches/5 cm), they're called pork blade steaks or shoulder steaks. Either way, the muscles here are well developed, interspersed with connective tissue and fat, and have a meaty flavor and chewy texture.

- Rib-Eye Chops: Just like beef rib-eye steaks, pork rib-eye chops are cut from the rib section of the loin, closer to the shoulder. They are somewhat tender and marbled with a moderate amount of fat, which keeps them from drying out on the grill. Formerly called rib chops, they fetch the highest price.

- Porterhouse Chops: While rib-eye chops have a single eye of loin meat on one side of the bone, porterhouse or T-bone chops also include a bit of pork tenderloin on the other side, like a T-bone steak. This cut used to be called a center-cut or bone-in loin chop.

- New York Chops: Once known as a top loin chop, this boneless cut is not the most flavorful, but it is the leanest and most tender. It is sometimes thinly cut (¼ to ½ inch/6 to 12 mm) and called a breakfast chop or pork minute steak.

- Sirloin Chops: The most economical cut, a sirloin chop comes from just above the hog's hind leg and often includes a bit of hip bone. Neither tender and lean nor tough and rich, sirloin chops represent the more variable middle ground.

HOW DO YOU KEEP PORK CHOPS JUICY?

The keys to juicy chops are brining and being careful not to overcook them. Most pork chops come from the leanest part of the hog, the loin, so they tend to dry out when grilled. Plus, modern hog breeds like Yorkshire and Poland China White that produce most of the retail pork have been bred to be leaner than heritage breeds like Duroc and Berkshire (also known as Kurobuta). Both wet and dry brines help pork chops stay juicy. For more on brining, see page 210.

WHAT'S THE BEST GRILLING METHOD FOR PORK CHOPS?

Most chops can go directly over the heat, but it helps to build a fire with two heat levels, especially if you're grilling thick chops. Use the higher heat area for searing and browning the surface, and use the lower heat area with the grill lid down to cook the chops through without burning the surface. Bone-in chops take a little longer to cook.

WHEN IS A PORK CHOP DONE?

A thermometer is indispensable. The color of meat is not a reliable doneness indicator, and it may be safe to eat pink pork. According to the USDA and the National Pork Board, pork chops are safe to eat when cooked to an internal temperature of 145°F (63°C).

NEW YORK CHOP

BONE-IN
RIB-EYE CHOP

BLADE CHOP

PORTERHOUSE CHOP

SIRLOIN CHOP

A simple dry brine keeps grilled pork nice and juicy. If you like, you could use a wet brine instead (see Extra Credit below). Either way, get a jump on prep by brining the chops the morning before or even the night before you plan to cook them. Then just grill the chops and brush them with sauce to add sweet, spicy, and savory flavors to the meaty pork. Serve with grilled pineapple and steamed rice.

MAKES 4 SERVINGS

4 bone-in center-cut pork chops, each about 14 oz (440 g) and 1½ inches (4 cm) thick

1½ tablespoons coarse sea salt, preferably sel gris

1½ teaspoons sugar

2 cups (16 gl oz/500 ml) Chipotle Rye Barbecue Sauce (page 219)

BRINED PORK CHOPS WITH CHIPOTLE RYE BARBECUE SAUCE

1 Set a large wire rack on a rimmed baking sheet. Pat the chops dry and sprinkle evenly on both sides with the salt and sugar. Place the chops on the rack on the pan and refrigerate uncovered for at least 8 hours or up to 24 hours.

2 Heat the grill for medium-high direct heat (400°–450°F/200°–230°C). Remove the chops from the refrigerator and let them rest at room temperature until the grill is ready.

3 Brush the grill grate and coat with oil. Put the chops on the grate and cook, frequently flipping and rotating their position on the grate for even browning, until nicely grill marked on both sides and an instant-read thermometer inserted into the center of a chop away from bone registers 140°F (60°C), 15–20 minutes total. During the last few minutes of cooking, brush the chops with some of the sauce and grill briefly on both sides to glaze the chops.

4 Transfer the chops to a platter and let rest for 5–10 minutes. Serve with the remaining sauce.

 **EXTRA CREDIT**

Brined Pork Chops with Fennel and Juniper Rub: Add 2 teaspoons each ground fennel seeds and ground juniper berries along with the salt and sugar. Omit the sauce. Serve with Anchovy Butter (page 226) and Grilled Fennel Basted with Rosemary Absinthe (page 164).

For an ultrasimple sauce, melt 1 teaspoon unsalted butter on each hot chop just before serving. Grill a halved lemon, cut side down, for a couple minutes and serve for squeezing on top of the chops.

Ask for porterhouse pork chops, which look like small versions of porterhouse beef steaks. This pork cut, which is not always labeled "porterhouse," has a small piece of tenderloin on one side and a larger piece of loin on the other.

To use a wet brine instead, dissolve the salt and sugar in 1½ cups hot water. Add 1 cup ice water to cool down the brine. Soak the meat in the brine in a zippered plastic bag for the same amount time. Remove, pat dry, and proceed as directed.

Pork steak is essentially a bisected portion of shoulder blade with the bones. This cut includes various muscle groups all held together with connective tissue and fat. As that "glue" softens and melts, it keeps the meat moist and juicy. It's a forgiving cut, too. You can cook a pork steak to medium doneness like a beef steak, or you can lower the heat and cook it until it is well-done and fall-apart tender like pork barbecue.

MAKES 6 SERVINGS

2 bone-in pork shoulder blade steaks, each about 2 lb (1 kg) and 2 inches (5 cm) thick

Coarse sea salt, such as sel gris, and freshly ground pepper

1¾ cups (14 fl oz/430 ml) Buffalo Sauce (page 227)

1¼ cups (10 fl oz/ 310 ml) Blue Cheese Dressing (page 222)

BUFFALO PORK STEAKS

1 Heat the grill for high direct heat (about 450°F/230°C) on one side and for low direct heat (about 275°F/135°C) on the other side. Season the steaks on both sides with salt and pepper.

2 Brush the grill grate and coat with oil. Place the steaks on the grate over the high-heat side and cook, frequently flipping and rotating their position on the grate for even browning, until nicely browned and the pork registers about 150°F (66°C) if serving like beef steaks, 30–35 minutes. Or, if serving like pork barbecue, brown the steaks for about 20 minutes on the hot side, then move the steaks to the low-heat area of the grate, cover the grill, and cook until the pork registers 190°F (88°C), 40–50 minutes total. Brush the steaks all over with the sauce during the last 10 minutes of cooking.

3 When the steaks come off the grill, brush them with more sauce. Serve with the remaining sauce and the dressing.

 **EXTRA CREDIT**

To help steam and soften the collagen in this cut of pork, put a pan of hot water directly over the hot side of the grill once the pork is moved to the unheated side.

Or, for extra tender pork steaks, skip the water pan. Instead, double the amount of sauce and pour it into a large foil pan. After searing the pork, put the steaks into the sauce and continue cooking on the unheated side of the grill as directed.

Maple Bourbon Pork Steaks: Replace the Buffalo Sauce with Maple Bourbon Barbecue Sauce (page 000).

Buffalo Pork Chops: Replace the pork steaks with bone-in pork rib chops.

Serve with celery ribs, cut in half lengthwise, lightly oiled, and grilled briefly over medium-high heat.

RIBS

Pork ribs are cut from the rib cage of the hog. Tough connective tissue, fat, and a mixture of fine-grained and coarse meat surround the rib bones. Coaxing a rack of ribs to tender, juicy succulence takes a little practice but is well worth the effort.

WHAT CUT OF RIBS WORKS BEST ON THE GRILL?

You can grill any cut of ribs. Here are your choices.

- Baby Back Ribs: Also known as loin back ribs, these are smaller than spareribs and come from the hog's back, hence the name. A slab of baby backs has eight to thirteen ribs and the meat is leaner, more tender, and less flavorful than spareribs.

- Spareribs: Cut from the side of the hog, spareribs come in a slab of at least eleven bones. The slab tapers at one end and has a flap of tough brisket meat attached to the wider end. Larger and richer tasting than baby backs and with a more satisfying chew, spareribs are our preferred cut of ribs for grilling.

- St. Louis–Style Ribs: A rack of spareribs includes a triangular section of rib tips with portions of breast meat, sternum, and diaphragm. When removed, the rack looks perfectly rectangular and is called a St. Louis cut. This cut of spareribs cooks more evenly than a full rack of spareribs and is easier to portion into individual servings, so we generally prefer it for grilling.

- Country-Style Ribs: These are not really ribs because they are not from the rib section. Often sold as individual "ribs," bone-in country-style ribs are cut from the shoulder blade, and boneless country-style ribs come from a rear portion of loin. The bone-in style can be grilled like pork blade chops, and the boneless style can be grilled like sirloin chops.

HOW DO YOU PREP RIBS FOR GRILLING?

Whichever ribs you prefer, be sure to remove the shiny white membrane from the underside (bone side) of the rack. This membrane tightens and toughens during cooking, keeping the finished ribs from tasting tender. Lift up a corner of the membrane with the tip of a knife, then grab it with a paper towel and slowly pull off the entire membrane in a single sheet. Removing the membrane also allows your seasoning to penetrate more deeply into the meat.

WHAT'S THE BEST WAY TO KEEP RIBS MOIST?

Ribs include a fair amount of tough connective tissue, and portions of the meat itself can be lean and prone to dryness, especially if you prefer baby back ribs. Slow cooking and adding moisture are the secrets to dissolving tough collagen into rich-tasting gelatin and keeping lean ribs from drying out. You can brine the ribs to help them hang onto moisture as they cook. You can keep a pan of steaming liquid in the closed grill to help introduce moisture. You can spritz, baste, or mop the ribs with liquid as they cook. And you can wrap cooked ribs in aluminum foil so they steam in their own juices while resting off the heat. All four methods work reasonably well, but our preferred methods are brining and using a water pan in the grill. These two methods result in juicy, tender ribs that still have a satisfying chew.

WHEN DO YOU APPLY BARBECUE SAUCE?

At the very end. Most barbecue sauces are high in sugar and burn easily on the grill. Brush on barbecue sauce only during the last 10 to 15 minutes of cooking and let your guests add extra sauce at the table.

Moisture is the key to great barbecued ribs. Some cooks wrap the ribs in aluminum foil, but we think that's overkill. It makes the ribs taste steamed. Instead, we put a pan of steaming water in the grill to keep the ribs both moist and meaty. With paprika and black, ancho, chipotle, and cayenne peppers in the rub, these ribs deliver tons of flavor. Peach nectar in the barbecue sauce brings sweet Southern aromas.

MAKES 4–6 SERVINGS

½ cup (1¾ oz/50 g) Basic Barbecue Rub (page 215)

1 teaspoon ancho chile powder

1 teaspoon chipotle chile powder

1 teaspoon garlic granules

2 slabs St. Louis–style pork spareribs, about 2 lb (1 kg) each

About 12 large handfuls wood chips or chunks

2 cups (16 fl oz/500 ml) Peach Bourbon Barbecue Sauce (page 219)

FIVE-PEPPER RIBS WITH PEACH-BOURBON BARBECUE SAUCE

1 In a small bowl, combine the rub, ancho chile powder, chipotle chile powder, and garlic granules and mix well.

2 Using a small knife, lift up a corner of the sheer white membrane that covers the underside of a slab of ribs. Grab the corner with a paper towel (the towel provides a good grip) and pull upward. The membrane should begin to lift away, at which point you should be able pull it off in a single, sharp motion. Generously coat the ribs all over with the seasoning mixture. Wrap the slabs in plastic wrap and refrigerate for at least 8 hours or up to 12 hours.

3 Heat a smoker to 250°F. Or heat a grill for medium-low indirect heat (250°–275°F/120°–135°C). If using charcoal, wrap the wood chips in several perforated aluminum foil packets and place one packet on the hot coals, or place a handful of wood chunks directly on the coals. If using a gas grill, wrap the chips in several perforated foil packets and put one packet directly over one of the gas burners under the cooking grate. Or if your grill has a smoker box, use it.

4 Brush the grill grate. Place an aluminum foil pan of hot water on the grate on the heated side of the grill. Put the ribs, meaty side down, on the grate away from the fire. If you have a rib rack, stand the ribs in the rack. Cover the grill and cook the ribs, rotating them 180 degrees once or twice for even cooking, until they are tender and the meat starts to pull back from the ends of the bones, 2–2½ hours. If you are using charcoal, you will need to replace the coals about once an hour during cooking. Whenever the wood stops smoking, add another foil packet of chips or handful of chunks. Refill the water pan with hot water as needed to keep the pan from going dry. If your grill has a temperature gauge, it should stay around 375°F (190°C).

Continued on page 79

Continued from page 77

5 During the last 15 minutes, brush the ribs with some of the sauce every 5 minutes or so. If cooking directly on the grill grate rather than with a rib rack, brush the bone side of the ribs with the sauce and then flip and cook that side until lightly browned. Brush the meat side and then flip and cook that side until lightly browned. Continue brushing and cooking until the ribs are nicely glazed with sauce and the meat side is face up.

6 Transfer the ribs to a platter and let rest for 10–20 minutes. Cut the ribs into 3- to 4-bone servings or cut into individual ribs. Serve with the remaining sauce on the side.

 **EXTRA CREDIT**

If you like your rib meat to fall apart and fall off the bone, wrap each slab in foil after it comes off the grill. Let rest for up to 1 hour.

When the ribs have rested, cut the slabs into individual ribs, toss with barbecue sauce, and grill directly over medium-high heat for a few minutes to firm up the glaze and create a nice, crisp texture.

You can replace the St. Louis–style spareribs with 2 slabs of baby back ribs. They will take a little less time to cook because they are smaller.

Espresso-Rubbed Ribs with Creamy Stout Barbecue Sauce: Replace the rub and spices with Espresso Rub (page 215) and the sauce with Creamy Stout Barbecue Sauce (page 219).

Brined Ribs with Cumin, Coriander, and Lime Butter: Skip the rub. Instead, brine the ribs in Cumin & Coriander Brine (page 212) for 5–6 hours. Grill as directed, then use melted Citrus Butter with lime (page 226) as the sauce, adding ¼ cup (⅓ oz/10 g) chopped fresh cilantro and the lower portion of 1 lemongrass stalk, peeled and finely chopped.

LESSON 3
PORK SHOULDER

The average hog weighs about 250 pounds (115 kg), and the shoulders bear much of that weight. As the animal moves, its shoulder muscles get quite a workout, becoming bigger, redder, and more flavorful. Connective tissue and fat also develops throughout various muscle groups, making the meat tougher and richer. Pork shoulder is among the toughest cuts on a hog. But low heat and moisture help to dissolve connective tissue, transforming tough meat into tender morsels. Pork shoulder is the most popular cut for pork barbecue, and smokers excel at the job, introducing the seductive taste of wood smoke. But you can smoke pork shoulder on a grill, too.

WHAT IS A BOSTON BUTT & A PICNIC HAM?

Butchers usually cut pork shoulder in half and sell the top half as "Boston butt" and the bottom half as "picnic ham." What's behind the names? Meat was once stored in wooden barrels called butts, and the upper half of pork shoulder was a specialty of Boston, so this cut became known as a Boston butt. The picnic ham is a small joint of cured meat made from the smaller front leg instead of the larger rear leg or "ham." Even when sold fresh, this shoulder portion goes by the name of picnic ham. Boston butts are usually sold without the skin, either bone in or boneless, while picnic hams are sold bone in and skin on. Both portions are relatively inexpensive and weigh 5 to 8 pounds (2.5 to 4 kg).

HOW DO YOU PREP PORK SHOULDER FOR GRILLING?

We prefer bone-in pork butts. Most are sold with the skin removed and the fat trimmed to about ¼ inch (6 mm). Season this cut with Basic Barbecue Rub (page 215) and smoke it on the grill (see North Carolina–Style Pulled Pork Barbecue, facing page). If you have time, refrigerate the seasoned meat so the flavors penetrate more deeply. If you're starting with a boneless butt, tie it with kitchen string to help it hold its shape. If you start with a bone-in, skin-on shoulder roast, cut off the skin, season the meat, and then retie the skin onto the meat so you get both seasoned meat and crisp skin. Either way, pork shoulder is fatty enough to keep the meat from drying out without using injections or brines.

HOW DO YOU MAKE PORK SHOULDER TASTE SMOKY?

Burning wood is best, as are low temperatures of 250° to 300°F (120° to 150°C). If you have a smoker, use it. Alternatively, separate the meat from the heat by setting up your grill for low indirect heat (see page 25). Introduce smoke by placing wood chunks or an aluminum foil pan of wood chips directly over the heat (see page 28). Keep in mind that water readily absorbs smoke. After a crust forms on the meat, keep the meat moist by periodically spritzing or mopping the surface with water or another flavored liquid. You can also keep a foil pan of steaming liquid on the heated side of the grill. If you're having trouble getting enough smoke from your grill, get it from your ingredients instead, adding smoked salt and/or smoked paprika to the rub and chipotles, moras, or other smoked chiles to the sauce.

WHEN IS A PORK SHOULDER DONE?

Arthur Bryant's and other Kansas City barbecue joints serve their barbecued pork shoulder sliced. If that's your preference, cook it to an internal temperature of 170°–180°F (77°–82°C). If you intend to pull the pork into shreds, cook it to 190°–200°F (88°–95°C) so the connective tissue will break down and be soft enough for the protein to fall apart. Use a thermometer to test the meat for doneness and, preferably, monitor the grill temperature with a thermometer as well. Maintaining a steady cooking temperature is the single most important factor when slowly smoking meat.

Pork barbecue takes many forms. Here is one of the most popular styles, a specialty of western North Carolina. The sauce is lean and vinegary, with a little tomato ketchup for sweetness and texture. The trick is keeping a steady, low temperature in the grill (see page 24). It also helps to add moisture, which dissolves the tough connective tissue in pork shoulder and makes the meat moist. We use a pan of steaming water, but you can instead mop the meat periodically with Beer Mop (page 212).

MAKES 6 SERVINGS

½ cup (1¾ oz/50 g) Basic Barbecue Rub (page 215)

1 bone-in pork shoulder roast (Boston butt), 6–7 lb (3–3.5 kg)

3¼ cups (26 fl oz/810 ml) Western Carolina Barbecue Sauce (page 219)

About 20 large handfuls wood chips or chunks

NORTH CAROLINA–STYLE PULLED PORK BARBECUE

1 Set a large wire rack on a rimmed baking sheet. Scatter the rub evenly over the pork, patting it in with your fingers. If you have any rub left over, mix it into the sauce. Place the pork on the rack on the pan and refrigerate uncovered overnight.

2 Heat a smoker to 225°F (110°C). Or heat the grill for low indirect heat (225°–250°F/110°–120°C). If using charcoal, wrap the wood chips in several perforated aluminum foil packets and place one packet on the hot coals, or place a handful of wood chunks directly on the coals. If using a gas grill, wrap the chips in several perforated foil packets, and put one packet directly over one of the gas burners under the cooking grate. Or if your grill has a smoker box, use it.

3 Brush the grill grate. Place an aluminum foil pan of hot water on the grate on the heated side of the grill. Put the pork, fatty side up, on the grate over the unheated side of the grill. Cover and cook until the pork is dark all over and fall-apart tender and an instant-read thermometer inserted into the thickest part away from bone registers about 190°F (88°C), 4–5 hours total. If you are using charcoal, you will need to replace the coals about once an hour during cooking. Refill the water pan with hot water as needed to keep the pan from going dry. If your grill has a temperature gauge, it should stay between 225° and 250°F (110°–120°C). Whenever the wood stops smoking, add another foil packet of chips or handful of chunks.

4 Transfer the meat to a cutting board and let rest for 20 minutes to allow the juices to redistribute. Using tongs and a knife, pull and/or chop the pork into shreds, breaking up crispy bits and discarding bones and excess fat. Put the shredded pork in a large disposable aluminum pan, add about 2 cups (16 fl oz/500 ml) of the sauce, and stir to mix evenly. Drizzle on more sauce to taste.

Continued on page 82

Continued from page 81  **EXTRA CREDIT**

Pulled Pork Sandwiches: In a large bowl, stir together ½ cup (4 fl oz/ 125 ml) of the barbecue sauce and ¼ cup (2 fl oz/60 ml) mayonnaise. Add 1 bag (16 oz/500 g) coleslaw mix (or 8oz/250 g each shredded cabbage and carrots) until thoroughly coated. Serve the pork and slaw on hamburger buns. The slaw is optional but traditional on North Carolina pulled pork sandwiches.

If your idea of pork barbecue includes a sweeter, smokier barbecue sauce, mix your favorite barbecue sauce into half of the sauce called for here. Or follow the recipe and then pour some of your barbecue sauce onto your sandwich.

Mexican Roast Pork with Sour Orange Marinade (Cochinita Pibil): Omit the rub and sauce. Cut the pork into 1½-inch (4-cm) cubes, discarding the bones and large pockets of fat.

Marinate the pork pieces in Mexican Sour Orange Marinade (page 212) in the refrigerator overnight. Line the bottom and sides of a large aluminum foil roasting pan with banana leaves (thawed if frozen), leaving about 12 inches (30 cm) hanging over the pan edges. Pour the pork and marinade into the pan and fold the banana leaves over the top, adding more leaves if necessary to cover the pork completely. Place the pan on the unheated side of the grill as directed and cook until the pork is tender, about 4 hours total. You can skip the hot water pan since the pork will be cooking in a liquid marinade. Serve with corn tortillas, pickled red onions, and habanero salsa.

PORK SAUSAGES & BELLY

Here we have the fat lover's section. Pork belly is essentially a big slab of uncured, uncut bacon that is about 40 percent fat. Pork sausages are also high in fat, ranging from 30 to 50 percent fat. All that fat makes pork belly and pork sausage incredibly delicious. But they're a challenge to grill because the fat constantly melts, drips, and causes flare-ups, the bane of a grillmaster's existence. Don't let the challenge scare you off. There are ways to tame the flames.

HOW DO YOU PREP SAUSAGES & BELLY FOR GRILLING?

SAUSAGES

Some cooks precook fresh sausages by microwaving or poaching them. But precooking can cause sausages to dry out on the grill. If you poach them, the extra liquid also prevents you from getting a cracklingly crisp skin. Some cooks prick the sausage casings, too. But the casing is there to hold everything in. Pricking can also cause the sausages to dry out—and it can create flare-ups from fat dripping into the fire. So what's the best prep? Nothing. Maybe let them sit at room temperature while the grill heats. That cuts down the cooking time a bit and helps prevent burning.

BELLY

You can take a raw pork belly, slice it thinly, and grill it directly over a medium-high fire. But you might as well grill thick-sliced bacon instead. We prefer our pork belly in thick slabs or "bricks." To avoid an inferno of dripping fat, we braise the belly first to render out some fat. That allows you to grill it directly over the heat and get it crisp. First remove the skin (rind) if intact and then either slowly braise the belly with some liquid (we like vinegar) in a pan in the oven or wrapped in aluminum foil over indirect heat on the grill. See Grilled Pork Belly with Spicy-Sweet Korean Glaze (page 87) for an example. You can even slow smoke pork belly using indirect heat, wood smoke, and a water pan in the grill.

HOW DO YOU AVOID FLARE-UPS?

Set up your grill for indirect heat or for two heat areas with a medium heat area and a low heat area.

Then, if you get flare-ups, you can move the sausages or pork belly around until the flames subside. At the very least, don't crowd the grill. Leave about one-third of the grill grate open so you can move the food around to avoid flare-ups. Be gentle with tongs, too. You don't want to prick the sausage casings and cause more fat to drip onto the fire.

HOW DO YOU GET CRISP SKIN ON SAUSAGES?

Avoid poaching sausages before grilling. That extra moisture dampens the skin and keeps it from getting nice and crisp. Use medium heat and turn the sausages often to avoid burning the surface before the center cooks through. For supercrisp skin, lightly oil the sausages before grilling.

WHEN ARE SAUSAGES & PORK BELLY DONE?

Sausage casings should be browned, crisp, and ready to explode at the seams. The internal temperature should register 155°F (68°C; 165°F/74°C if grilling poultry sausages). Insert the thermometer into the end of the sausage to avoid losing too many juices. For pork belly, use the same doneness temperature. Be sure to allow the cooked meat to rest before eating it, especially sausages. Whenever meat cooks, juices start flowing. The hotter the meat gets, the faster and more furious the juices flow. If you cut or bite into a hot sausage fresh off the grill, the juices will squirt everywhere. Let sausages rest for 5 minutes so the juices have time to redistribute inside the casings.

If you like classic grilled brats in beer, try this Mexican version. In place of bratwurst, we use fresh Mexican chorizo, and instead of beer and sauerkraut, the sausages are braised in a sauce of tomatoes, poblano chiles, olives, and capers, just like the sauces often used to poach fish in Veracruz, Mexico.

MAKES 8 SERVINGS

1 yellow onion, finely chopped

1 poblano chile, seeded and finely chopped

3 cloves garlic, minced

Juice of 2 limes

1 can (28 oz/875 g) petite-diced tomatoes, with juice

1½ teaspoons dried oregano

½ cup (2 oz/60 g) sliced pimiento-stuffed green olives

3 tablespoons capers

2 tablespoons drained canned chopped jalapeño chiles

2 lb (1 kg) fresh chorizo sausages (about 8 links)

2 tablespoons chopped fresh cilantro

GRILL-BRAISED CHORIZO WITH POBLANO CHILE, CILANTRO & LIME

1 Heat the grill for medium-high indirect heat (about 400°F/200°C).

2 Brush the grill grate. Place a 12-by-8-inch (30-by-20-cm) aluminum foil pan on the grate directly over the fire. Add the onion and poblano and cook, stirring occasionally, until soft, 4–6 minutes. Add the garlic, lime juice, tomatoes and juice, and oregano, stir well, and simmer until slightly reduced in volume, 8–10 minutes.

3 Stir in the olives, capers, and jalapeños. Bury the sausages in the pan, spooning some of the sauce over the top. Move the pan away from the fire, cover the grill, and cook until an instant-read thermometer inserted into the center of a sausage registers 145°F (63°C), about 20 minutes.

4 Transfer the sausages from the sauce to the grill grate directly over the fire. Cook, turning as needed, until browned all over, 3–4 minutes total. As the sausages are ready, return them to the sauce.

5 Scatter the cilantro over the sausages and sauce and serve.

 **EXTRA CREDIT**

Serve in Mexican bolillos (rolls) or in tortillas.

For a rich garnish, drizzle a little Mexican crema (or crème fraîche or sour cream) over each sausage. A little crumbled Cotija cheese never hurts, either.

Classic Grilled Sausage and Peppers: Replace the chorizo with Italian sausage and the Veracruz sauce with Marinara Sauce (page 220), sautéing 1 cup (4 oz/125 g)

each sliced green and red bell peppers along with the onion.

Classic Grilled Brats in Beer: Replace the chorizo with bratwurst and the Veracruz sauce with 1½ cups (12 fl oz/375 ml) beer; 1 green bell pepper, seeded and thinly sliced; 1 yellow onion, thinly sliced; and 4 tablespoons (2 oz/60 g) unsalted butter simmered together in the foil pan. Served on crusty steak rolls with coarse-grain German mustard.

The only way to grill pork belly is to render out some fat first. Otherwise, the fat drips into the grill and creates an inferno that incinerates the meat. A low, slow braise in the oven gets the job done. Then you can grill the belly and get a good, crisp exterior. At the very end of cooking, we like to glaze it with our version of *ssam jang,* a thick Korean spice paste. Wrap pieces of grilled belly in lettuce leaves with sticky rice, kimchi, and more spice paste and you have a knockout small plate or first course. You can buy *ssam jang* in Asian markets, but it's easy enough to stir it up yourself.

GRILLED PORK BELLY WITH SPICY-SWEET KOREAN GLAZE

MAKES 4 SERVINGS

1½ lb (750 g) center-cut pork belly

3 tablespoons coarse sea salt

1½ cups (12 fl oz/375 ml) unseasoned rice vinegar

¾ cup Ssam Jang (page 222)

2 cups cooked sweet glutinous (sticky) rice

2 tablespoons seasoned rice vinegar

1 head butter lettuce, separated into leaves

Kimchi for serving (optional)

1 Preheat the oven to 300°F (150°C). Rub the pork belly all over with the salt and set the pork, fat side up, in a baking dish just a little bigger than the pork itself. Add the unseasoned rice vinegar to the baking dish; it should come about halfway up the sides of the pork. Cover the baking dish tightly with aluminum foil and braise the pork in the oven for 3 hours.

2 Remove from the oven and let cool, still covered, to room temperature. When cooled, uncover the baking dish and then peel off and discard the skin and the top layer of fat that comes off with the skin. Cut the pork into bricks about 2 inches (5 cm) long and 1 inch (2.5 cm) wide.

3 Heat a grill for medium-high direct heat (400°–450°F/200°–230°C). Brush the grill grate and coat with oil. Place the belly bricks, meat side down, on the grate and sear on all sides, 2–3 minutes per side, including the ends. Grill the fatty side last. During the last few minutes, brush the bricks all over with the ssam jang. Transfer the pork to a plate.

4 Put the rice into a serving bowl, add the seasoned rice vinegar, and stir and toss to mix evenly. Invite your guests to wrap the pork belly in lettuce leaves with a little rice, more ssam jang, and some kimchi (if using).

 EXTRA CREDIT

Add pickled carrots or other pickled vegetables to the lettuce wrap.

You can refrigerate the braised pork belly for a few days before using it. Remove the skin first. You can also freeze the braised belly for up to 2 weeks. Thaw completely before grilling.

This dish was popularized by Jason Day and Aaron Chronister, barbecue competition veterans who posted it on their blog, BBQ Addicts. Here's our version made with pickled jalapeños and Cheddar cheese mixed into the sausage. The recipe starts with a lattice weave of bacon strips dusted with our Chef Salt Bacon BBQ spice rub. Next, you spread on a layer of seasoned sausage, followed by some barbecue sauce and crumbled cooked bacon, and then you roll the whole thing up. You smoke it on the grill and then glaze it with barbecue sauce. It's wickedly rich and never fails to elicit oohs and ahs from guests.

MAKES 10–12 SERVINGS

1½ lb (750 g) thick-cut bacon slices

2 tablespoons Chef Salt Bacon BBQ Salt or Basic Barbecue Rub (page 215)

1 lb (500 g) bulk Italian sausage

¼ lb (125 g) grated Cheddar cheese

½ cup (3 oz/85 g) pickled jalapeño chiles, finely chopped

1 cup Sweet, Rich & Smoky Barbecue Sauce (page 219)

About 12 large handfuls wood chips or chunks

JALAPEÑO CHEDDAR BACON EXPLOSION

1 Using 14 of the bacon slices, make a square lattice weave of the bacon slices like the lattice on top of a pie. First arrange 7 bacon slices side by side and parallel to one another on a large sheet of aluminum foil. Squish them together so the sides are touching and relatively straight. Lay a slice of bacon, perpendicular to the other slices, on one end of the weave. Fold back the first, third, fifth, and seventh bacon slices over this new slice. Then lay another bacon slice next to the new slice, placing it parallel to the slice. Unfold the first, third, fifth, and seventh slices; fold back the second, fourth, and sixth slices. Repeat with remaining bacon slices, squishing together all 14 slices until you have a weave that is tightly woven and straight.

2 In a frying pan, fry the remaining bacon slices over medium heat until crisp, 3–5 minutes. Transfer to paper towels to drain briefly. As the bacon cooks, scatter 1½ teaspoons of the rub over the bacon weave. In a bowl, combine the sausage, Cheddar, and jalapeños and mix well. Evenly press and spread the sausage mixture on top of the bacon lattice, pressing to the outer edges to create a square.

3 Spread about ½ cup (4 fl oz/125 ml) of the barbecue sauce evenly over the top of the sausage square. Chop the fried bacon into bite-size pieces and scatter evenly over the top. Sprinkle evenly with another 1½ teaspoons barbecue rub.

4 Carefully separate the edge of the sausage layer nearest you from the bacon weave and begin rolling the sausage away from you. The bacon weave should remain flat on the work surface. Tightly roll the sausage and pinch together the ends to enclose the filling. Press all around the sausage to remove any air pockets, creating a large, tight sausage link.

Continued on page 93

Continued from page 88

5 Now, roll the sausage toward you, but this time with the bacon weave, until it is completely wrapped and tight. The roll should be 2–3 inches (5–7.5 cm) in diameter. Carefully sprinkle the remaining 1 tablespoon barbecue rub all over the roll. Turn the roll seam side down.

6 Wrap the roll in aluminum foil and chill for at least 1 hour or up to 24 hours. (Great for taking to tailgates!)

7 Heat a smoker to 225°F (110°C). Or heat a grill for low indirect heat (225°–250°F/ 110°–120°C). If using charcoal, wrap the wood chips in several perforated aluminum foil packets and place one packet on the hot coals, or place a handful of wood chunks directly on the coals. If using a gas grill, wrap the chips in several perforated foil packets, and put one packet directly over one of the gas burners under the cooking grate. Or if your grill has a smoker box, use it.

8 Brush the grill grate. Unwrap the roll and put it on the grate away from the fire. Smoke or grill until an instant-read thermometer inserted into the center of the roll registers 165°F (74°C), about 1 hour for each 1 inch (2.5 cm) of the diameter or a total of 2–2½ hours. If using a grill, turn the roll once or twice to face opposite sides of the meat toward the heat. If your grill has a temperature gauge, it should stay between 225° and 250°F (120°–190°C). Whenever the wood stops smoking, add another packet of chips or handful of chunks.

9 When the roll is ready, immediately glaze the roll all over with barbecue sauce. Transfer to a cutting board and slice into rounds ¼–½ inch (6–12 mm) thick. Serve with the remaining barbecue sauce on the side.

 EXTRA CREDIT

To use sausage links, cut the links and squeeze the meat from the casings.

Season the sausage with chopped fresh sage or other seasonings if you like.

You can also cook the bacon on a rack set on a rimmed baking sheet in a 400°F (200°C) oven until crisp, about 15 minutes.

Serve on biscuits or soft rolls with more barbecue sauce for an instant sandwich.

Pork tenderloins are the new boneless, skinless chicken breasts. They're quick cooking and endlessly adaptable. You often see pork tenderloin brined, but this easier method wraps the pork in herbed mustard and pancetta to keep it moist and flavorful For more tips on cooking pork tenderloin, see the Roasts lesson (page 58).

MAKES 4–6 SERVINGS

¼ lb (125 g) thinly sliced pancetta

½ cup (4 oz/125 g) Dijon mustard

2 tablespoons chopped fresh sage

2 pork tenderloins, about 1 lb (500 g) each, silver skin removed

1 teaspoon fine sea salt

¼ teaspoon freshly ground pepper

MUSTARD-SAGE PORK TENDERLOIN WRAPPED IN PANCETTA

1 Heat the grill for medium-high indirect heat (about 400°F/200°C). Cut two 12-inch (30-cm) squares of waxed paper or parchment paper.

2 Place 1 paper square on a work surface. Lay half of the pancetta slices on the paper, overlapping them by about 1 inch (2.5 cm) to create a square large enough to accommodate the length of a tenderloin. Spread half of the mustard evenly over the pancetta and then scatter half of the sage evenly over the mustard. Season the tenderloins all over with the salt and pepper. Lay 1 tenderloin on the pancetta square about 1 inch (2.5 cm) in from the edge nearest you, placing it parallel to the edge. Fold the uncovered edge over the tenderloin and, using the paper as an aid, tightly roll up the tenderloin in the pancetta. Repeat with the second paper square and the remaining tenderloin and other ingredients. Let the meat rest in the paper for 15–20 minutes while the grill finishes heating.

3 Brush the grill grate and coat with oil. Remove the paper from each tenderloin, put the tenderloins on the grate away from the fire, and cover the grill. Cook until the pancetta is crisp and an instant-read thermometer inserted into the pork registers 145°F (63°C), 20–25 minutes. If the pancetta is not crisp, use a spatula and tongs to move the tenderloins directly over the fire for the last 3–4 minutes of cooking, leaving the grill uncovered and turning the tenderloins frequently. Transfer to a cutting board and let rest for 10 minutes. Cut into slices ½ inch (1.25 cm) thick.

 EXTRA CREDIT

Add a pinch of ground cloves along with the black pepper to give the pancetta a taste reminiscent of Italian lardo.

For a more complex taste, use a mix of herbs, such as rosemary, thyme, and flat-leaf parsley, along with the sage.

Bacon-Wrapped Pork Tenderloin with Chipotle Rye Barbecue Sauce: Use the same technique but replace the pancetta with thinly sliced bacon and the mustard mixture with Chipotle Rye Barbecue Sauce (page 219).

Cumin and Coriander Pork Tenderloin with Chimichurri: Brine the tenderloins for 3–4 hours in Cumin & Coriander Brine (page 212). Grill directly over the fire until browned all over, then move away from the fire to finish cooking through as directed. Slice and serve with Chimichurri (page 228).

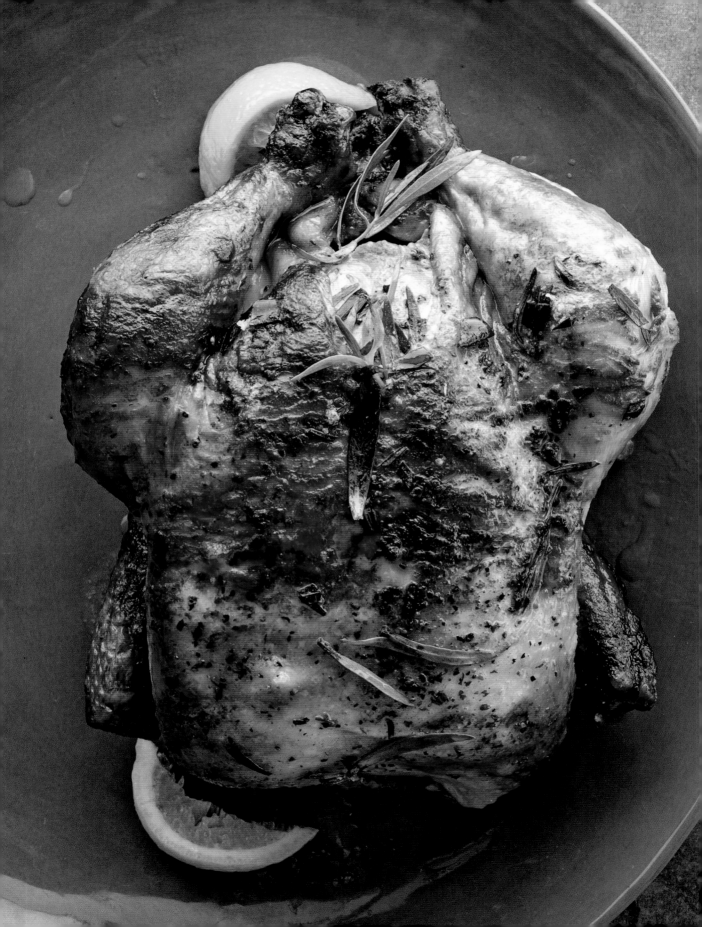

6
CHICKEN, TURKEY & OTHER BIRDS

98 LESSON 1: POULTRY PARTS

99 LESSON 2: WHOLE BIRDS & HALF BIRDS

101 CLASSIC BARBECUED CHICKEN

102 GRILLED QUAIL WITH APRICOT-SAGE SAUCE

103 GRILLED BUTTERFLIED CHICKEN WITH ARTICHOKE-PECORINO SLATHER

106 SPIT-ROASTED LEMON TARRAGON CHICKEN

108 GRILL-ROASTED TURKEY WITH LEMON-ROSEMARY DRY BRINE

112 LESSON 3: BONELESS BREASTS & THIGHS

113 GRILLED CHICKEN BREASTS IN BERBERE SAUCE

114 GRILLED CHICKEN TIKKA MASALA

117 GRILLED FIVE-SPICE DUCK BREASTS WITH HOISIN GLAZE

118 GRILLED CHICKEN THIGHS AGRODOLCE

119 BUTTERFLIED TURKEY BREAST WITH SPICY PEANUT GLAZE

POULTRY PARTS

In 2013, chicken consumption in the United States eclipsed that of beef for the first time in one hundred years. According to the National Chicken Council, most US shoppers buy chicken at grocery stores. Cooks often start with poultry parts, but it's much more economical to buy a whole bird and cut it up yourself (see page 100). Cutting poultry yourself also gives you a better sense of the bird's anatomy and how the different parts will respond to the grill's heat.

HOW DO YOU PREP POULTRY PARTS FOR GRILLING?

Skip marinating. It's common to marinate chicken in vinaigrette or barbecue sauce. But marinating fails on three counts. First, the flavor penetrates only ⅛ inch (3 mm) at most, so it doesn't deliver much seasoning to the food. Second, if you marinate in a high-sugar sauce (such as barbecue sauce), the chicken burns on the grill before the meat is fully cooked. Third, marinades moisten poultry skin, preventing you from getting crisp skin on the grill.

Start with a dry brine. Brining helps lean poultry hang onto more moisture as it cooks, so the cooked meat ends up tasting juicier. Both wet and dry brines work, but we prefer dry brines for skin-on poultry. Wet brines can saturate the skin and prevent you from getting a crisp skin. Dry brines do the opposite. They dry out the skin, making it easier to crisp it on the grill (see page 210 for more on brines).

Add flavor with a rub or sauce. Rubs, pastes, and sauces are more effective flavoring methods because you eat almost all of the seasoning rather than discarding it. Simply add seasonings to your dry brine, and if you're using a paste or sauce along with the brine, reduce the amount of salt in the sauce.

Keep the skin on. Poultry skin protects the meat from drying out. It provides a barrier to the hot fire and a source of slowly melting fat that drips over the meat, keeping it moist. Even if you plan to remove the skin later, keep it on for grilling. Just season the meat beneath the skin before you start.

WHAT'S THE BEST GRILLING METHOD FOR PARTS?

Go with indirect medium heat. To avoid serving burnt chicken, grill it slowly. Heat one side of the grill to medium and leave the other side unheated. Use the hot side for crisping the skin and the unheated side for cooking the meat through. We like to start the chicken on the unheated side then, when the chicken is cooked through, we move it to the heated side to crisp the skin and glaze it with barbecue sauce.

Give wings more direct heat. Chicken wings cook through faster than larger chicken parts, so give them more time over the hot side of the grill. To prep them, discard the wing tips (they'll just burn on the grill, leaving very little that's edible), then cut between the joint of the remaining two wing sections, bending and popping the joint to create two pieces.

WHEN ARE POULTRY PARTS DONE?

The primary advantage of grilling poultry parts instead of whole poultry is that parts cook more evenly. As each part is done, you can remove it from the grill. Go by temperature instead of color. Chicken and turkey breasts are done when they reach 155°F (68°C) in the thickest part. Thighs, drumsticks, and wings are done at 165°F (74°C). At this temperature, the meat may still appear pink near the bone and the juices may not run perfectly clear, particularly in young birds such as Cornish hens, broilers, and fryers. Because these young birds have built up limited calcium in their bones, the bones can leak red hemoglobin. But if the meat has reached the correct doneness temperature, it will be fully cooked and safe to eat, according to the USDA.

WHOLE BIRDS & HALF BIRDS

The challenge with grilling whole birds is cooking them evenly while keeping the meat moist and the skin crisp. One trick is to cut the bird in half, which also cuts the cooking time in half and allows you to grill both halves of a chicken directly over a medium fire. Here are some other tips.

HOW DO YOU PREP A WHOLE BIRD FOR GRILLING?

Avoid rinsing. According to the USDA, rinsing poultry actually increases the risk of bacterial contamination, as it can cause bacteria to migrate to your sink, countertops, and nearby food. Kill bacteria with heat instead. Use a thermometer to test for doneness. Harmful pathogens will be killed when you cook chicken to an internal temperature of 165°F (74°C) when tested in a thigh. See page 32 for other poultry doneness temperatures.

Halve the bird to speed cooking time. Cutting a chicken in half reduces the cooking time because the heat has to travel only half the distance to cook the bird through. Halving poultry also allows you to grill it directly over the fire. See page 103 for directions on cutting whole birds in half.

Dry brine. For whole and half birds, we prefer dry brining to wet brining. Brining keeps lean meat juicy by allowing the protein to hang on to more moisture as it cooks (see page 210 for details on the science). But unlike wet brining, dry brining also creates a crisp skin on grill-roasted poultry. The salt in dry brines draws moisture from the skin, drying it out so the skin browns and crisps more readily on the grill. Letting the salted bird sit in the refrigerator overnight enhances the effect, as the skin dehydrates from airflow in the refrigerator. Salt also denatures the protein in the skin, causing the skin to shrink and tighten around the meat, creating a cracklingly crisp surface.

Season under the skin. If you don't brine, it helps to season the meat beneath the skin to prevent the seasoning from scorching on the grill. Using your fingers and working gently, separate the skin from the meat over the breast, thighs, and drumsticks.

Distribute herbs, seasoning pastes, or rubs between the skin and flesh, replacing the skin so it covers the exposed meat completely. This is the most effective seasoning method if you plan to discard the skin after grilling.

WHAT'S THE BEST GRILLING METHOD FOR WHOLE BIRDS?

Chicken and turkey breast meat is done 10°F (6°C) before the dark meat on the thighs and drumsticks. That's why breast meat often tastes dry when birds are cooked whole. Here's how to achieve optimal doneness in all parts when grilling whole birds.

Vertical roasting. Stand the bird upright on the grill so the tougher dark meat is closer to the heat and cooks faster than the more tender white meat. Vertical roasting racks are available in a variety of sizes. See page 27 for more information on vertical roasting.

Indirect grill roasting. For large birds like turkeys, it's best to move the meat away from the heat and set it in an aluminum foil pan. This method replicates indoor oven roasting but with the added benefit of smoke (add wood chunks or chips for more smoke flavor). Position the legs closer to the heat and rotate the bird now and then for even cooking (see page 25 indirect grilling).

Spit roasting. Use this method for supercrisp skin. Constant rotation ensures more even cooking and a self-basting bird, as fat melts and rolls around the skin (see page 30).

Direct heat for small birds. Quail and other small birds can be cooked directly over medium heat. Or make a big bird thinner by butterflying it for direct grilling (see page 104).

CUTTING UP POULTRY

Position the bird breast side up on a cutting board and pull one of the legs away from the body. Using a knife or poultry shears, cut down to where the leg attaches to the body. Bend the leg away from the body to pop the ball of the thigh bone out of the socket. Cut between the ball and socket to remove the leg from the body. Repeat with the other leg. Separate the drumstick from the thigh on each leg by cutting down firmly between the joint. Pull a wing away from the body and cut near the joint at the base to remove it from the body. Repeat with the other wing. Pry the back away from the breast with your hands and cut the back from the breast. Cut the whole breast in half lengthwise down the middle of the breastbone. If you like, cut the breast crosswise in half to make smaller pieces.

We're big fans of dry brining poultry to create a crisp skin. The technique works especially well with barbecued chicken, which tends to develop rubbery skin from the moisture in the barbecue sauce. We also brown the chicken at the end of cooking (sometimes called a reverse sear) to make sure the exterior doesn't burn before the meat is cooked through to the center.

MAKES 4 SERVINGS

4 lb (2 kg) bone-in, skin-on chicken breasts, thighs, and drumsticks

1 tablespoon coarse sea salt

¼ teaspoon freshly ground pepper

2 tablespoons peanut or other vegetable oil

4 large handfuls wood chips or chunks

2 cups (16 fl oz/500 ml) Basic Barbecue Sauce (page 219)

CLASSIC BARBECUED CHICKEN

1 Place a large wire rack on a rimmed baking sheet. Trim any excess fat from the chicken parts, then coat them evenly all over with the salt and pepper. Place the chicken parts, skin side up, on the rack on the pan. Refrigerate uncovered for 2 days.

2 Heat the grill for medium indirect heat with (325°–350°F/160°–180°C). If using charcoal, wrap the wood chips in 2 perforated aluminum foil packets and place one packet on the hot coals, or place 2 handfuls of wood chunks directly on the coals. If using a gas grill, wrap the chips in 2 perforated foil packets, and put one packet directly over one of the gas burners under the cooking grate. Or if your grill has a smoker box, use it.

3 Coat the chicken all over with the oil and let stand at room temperature until the grill is ready and smoky. Brush the grill grate and coat with oil. Put the chicken parts on the grate away from the fire, cover the grill, and cook until an instant-read thermometer inserted into a thigh away from bone registers 165°F (74°C) or into a breast away from bone registers 155°F (68°C), 30–40 minutes. If your grill has a temperature gauge, it should stay between 325° and 350°F (160°–180°C). When the wood stops smoking, about halfway through the cooking, add the remaining foil packet of chips or handfuls of chunks. During the last 10 minutes, move the chicken directly over the fire to crisp and brown the skin (you can leave off the lid). During the last 2–3 minutes, brush the chicken parts all over with half of the barbecue sauce, briefly browning each side and taking care not to let the sauce burn. Transfer the chicken to a platter and serve with the remaining barbecue sauce.

 EXTRA CREDIT

Replace the Basic Barbecue Sauce with any of the sauce variations on page 218.

Barbecued Chicken with Alabama White Barbecue Sauce: Replace the Basic Barbecue Sauce with Alabama White Barbecue Sauce (page 219).

Grilled Ranch Chicken: Replace the Basic Barbecue Sauce with Ranch Dressing (page 222).

Grilled Chimichurri Chicken: Replace the Basic Barbecue Sauce with Chimichurri (page 228).

Grilled Citrus Chicken: Replace the salt and pepper with ⅓ cup (1 oz/ 30 g) Citrus Rub (page 215) mixed with 2 teaspoons fine sea salt such as fleur de sel. Proceed as directed, replacing the Basic Barbecue Sauce with Orange Vinaigrette (page 227).

The sauce here was inspired by a recipe in Darra Goldstein's *The Georgian Feast*. The classic sauce is a loose paste made with cilantro and dried apricots, but we use parsley and sage in place of the cilantro. Blanching the herbs before pureeing them keeps the sauce bright green. Serve the quail with *farro* or kasha.

MAKES 4 SERVINGS

⅓ cup (2 oz/60 g) dried apricots

4 cups (4 oz/125 g) packed fresh flat-leaf parsley leaves and small stems

1 cup (1 oz/30 g) packed fresh sage leaves

⅓ cup (1⅓ oz/40 g) walnut pieces

½ cup (4 fl oz/125 ml) walnut oil or olive oil

4 cloves garlic

Juice of 1 lemon

2 teaspoons fine sea salt

½ teaspoon freshly ground pepper

8 quail, about 5 oz (155 g) each

GRILLED QUAIL WITH APRICOT-SAGE SAUCE

1 Bring a large pot of water to a boil. Ready a large bowl of ice water. Place the apricots in a small heatproof bowl and ladle 1 cup (8 fl oz/250 ml) of the boiling water from the pot over the apricots. Let soak for 2 hours. Meanwhile, add the parsley and sage to the pot of boiling water and blanch until bright green, about 30 seconds. Using a slotted spoon, scoop the herbs out of the boiling water and transfer them to the ice water to stop the cooking. When the herbs have cooled, drain them and transfer them to a food processor. Let the herbs stand until the apricots are ready.

2 Pluck out the apricots and transfer them to the food processor. Reserve the soaking water. Add the walnuts, oil, garlic, lemon juice, salt, and pepper to the processor and pulse until the ingredients are finely chopped. Add about ½ cup (4 fl oz/125 ml) of the soaking water and process until a thick yet pourable sauce forms. Pour half of the sauce into a large zippered plastic bag and reserve the other half for serving.

3 Using poultry shears, cut off the wing tips from the quail (they burn easily on the grill). Remove the backbone from a quail by cutting along either side of it. Flip the bird over and flatten it by pressing down on the breast with your palm. Repeat with the remaining quail. Put the birds into the bag with the sauce and massage to coat the birds evenly with the sauce. Press out the air, seal the bag, and marinate the quail at room temperature while you light the grill. Or, for deeper flavor, refrigerate the quail for at least a few hours or up to overnight.

4 Heat the grill for medium direct heat (about 375°F/190°C). Brush the grill grate and coat with oil. Arrange the quail, breast side down, on the grate and brush the marinade evenly over the top. Cook, rotating the birds and turning them over a few times, until nicely browned all over and the meat is firm to the touch, about 15 minutes. It's difficult to test the internal temperature of birds this small with an instant-read thermometer, but if you can, the meat should register 155°–160°F (68°–71°C) in the thickest part of a thigh.

5 Serve the quail with the reserved sauce.

How do you get a whole chicken to cook faster? Cut out the backbone and open it up like a book. The chicken lays flat on the grill grate and because it's thinner it cooks quickly. We love the bright, citrusy Mediterranean flavors here, but experiment with other pastes such as basil pesto or Vadouvan (page 217) made into a paste with plain yogurt.

MAKES 4 SERVINGS

CHICKEN

1 whole chicken, about 4 lb (2 kg), butterflied

1½ teaspoons coarse sea salt, preferably sel gris

½ teaspoon freshly ground pepper

1 tablespoon olive oil

ARTICHOKE-PECORINO SLATHER

1 package (9 oz/270 g) frozen artichoke hearts, thawed

2 cups (8 oz/250 g) grated pecorino romano cheese

½ cup (2½ oz/75 g) pine nuts

2 large cloves garlic

½ teaspoon fine sea salt

¼ teaspoon freshly ground pepper

1 cup extra-virgin olive oil

Lemon wedges for serving

BUTTERFLIED CHICKEN WITH ARTICHOKE-PECORINO SLATHER

1 To prepare the chicken, set a large wire rack on a rimmed baking sheet. Season the chicken all over with the salt and pepper and place it, skin side up, on the rack in the pan. Refrigerate uncovered for at least 8 hours or up to 24 hours.

2 To make the slather, in a food processor, combine the artichokes, cheese, nuts, garlic, salt, and pepper and pulse until finely chopped, about 30 seconds. Scrape down the sides of the bowl, add the oil, and then process until well blended.

3 Heat the grill for medium direct heat (about 375°F/190°C). Meanwhile, using your fingers, gently separate the chicken skin from the top of the breasts, thighs, and drumsticks, being careful not to tear the skin. Spoon about half of the slather under the skin of the chicken breasts, thighs, and legs. Rub the oil all over the chicken, especially the skinless side. Let the chicken sit at room temperature for 15 minutes while the grill preheats.

4 Brush the grill grate and coat with oil. Put the chicken, skin side down, on the grate directly over the fire and cook until nicely browned, 15–20 minutes, using tongs and a spatula to rotate the bird 90 degrees after 8–10 minutes. Flip the bird over and grill the other side until nicely browned and an instant-read thermometer inserted into a thigh away from bone registers 165°F (74°C), 15–20 minutes longer. Transfer the chicken to a cutting board and let rest for 15 minutes.

5 Carve the chicken by removing the wings, cutting the legs into thighs and drumsticks, and removing each breast from the bone, then cutting each breast into 2–4 pieces (10–12 pieces to serve). Pour the juices from the cutting board over the chicken and serve with the remaining slather and the lemon wedges.

Continued on page 104

HALVING POULTRY

To cut a whole chicken or other bird in half for faster grilling, put the bird breast side down on a cutting board and, using poultry shears, cut along both sides of the backbone. Remove the backbone (save it for stock if you like). Flip the bird over and cut down along the middle of the breastbone to separate the bird into halves. Trim away any excess fat or skin.

Continued from page 103

EXTRA CREDIT

How to butterfly: The butcher can butterfly the chicken for you, or you can do it yourself. First, remove the giblets from the chicken cavity, if included, and reserve them for another use. Using poultry shears and starting at the neck end, remove the chicken backbone by cutting along both sides of the bone from top to bottom. Cut the bone into several pieces and refrigerate for making stock. Remove and discard any excess fat and skin. Flip the chicken over and, using your palms, press down firmly on the breastbone to crack it. The chicken should lie flat. Tuck the wings behind the chicken "shoulders" to hold the wings flat, and position the legs so the "knees" look knock-kneed and point inward.

After rubbing the slather beneath the chicken skin, you can help the chicken holds its shape and keep the skin in place by making two 1-inch (2.5-cm) slits through the apron of skin at the rear of the chicken. Tuck the drumsticks into the slits.

Pair this dish with a Mediterranean tomato salad if you like. Finely chop 1 heirloom tomato and transfer to a bowl. Add 1 tablespoon minced red onion, ¼ cup (1¼ oz/37 g) chopped Kalamata olives, 2 tablespoons extra-virgin olive oil, 1 teaspoon red wine vinegar, 1 tablespoon chopped fresh oregano, ½ teaspoon fine sea salt, ⅛ teaspoon freshly ground pepper, and ½ cup (2½ oz/75 g) crumbled feta cheese.

POULTRY PRODUCTION METHODS

Since the 1950s, industrial production methods (and marketing) have more than tripled the per capita consumption of chicken in the United States. In more recent years, less industrialized production methods have gained ground, leading to more choices in the marketplace.

FREE-RANGE. Unlike mass-produced chickens, these birds have access to the outdoors. Unfortunately, the birds may not avail themselves of the opportunity to exit the access door and may spend very little time outside. Credible producers of free-range chickens raise their flocks outdoors for a specified time each day. The meat of this type of free-range chicken may be slightly firmer and more flavorful than that of a cage-raised chicken, depending on how much exercise the bird gets.

PASTURED. A more precise form of free-range production, pastured chickens live in outdoor pens that are moved from field to field, providing them with a diet containing a high percentage of natural forage. The meat is firmer and much more flavorful than the meat of mass-produced chickens.

ORGANIC. In the United States, organic chickens and their feed must be produced without the use of antibiotics, genetic engineering, chemical fertilizers, sewage sludge, and synthetic pesticides. An organic label can be given to mass-produced chickens that meet these criteria. Organic chickens are not necessarily raised free-range or pastured, but they must be given access to pasture.

KOSHER. In accordance with Jewish religious law, kosher chickens are raised and harvested humanely with strict bacterial controls. They must be slaughtered by hand by a certified kosher butcher and are salted for up to an hour to draw out their blood. The birds are then rinsed, but because they are still slightly saltier than other chickens, you should not brine them.

The late Judy Rodgers served a spectacular dry-brined roast chicken at her popular Zuni Café in San Francisco. She chilled the bird uncovered until the skin dried itself to the meat. That makes for supercrisp skin when the chicken is roasted. We use the same brining technique but grill the chicken on a spit so the melting fat rolls around the meat, keeping it moist and juicy.

MAKES 6 SERVINGS

1 roaster chicken, about 5 lb (2.5 kg)

7 fresh tarragon sprigs, plus 2 tablespoons chopped leaves

3½ teaspoons coarse sea salt, preferably sel gris

½ teaspoon freshly ground pepper

2 lemons, quartered

2 tablespoons olive oil

½ cup (4 oz/125 g) unsalted butter

SPIT-ROASTED LEMON TARRAGON CHICKEN

1 Set a large wire rack on a rimmed baking sheet. Remove the neck and giblets from the cavity of the chicken, if included, and reserve for another use. Remove any large lumps of fat, as well. Using your fingers, gently separate the chicken skin from the top of the breasts, thighs, and drumsticks, being careful not to tear the skin. Slip 1 tarragon sprig into each of the 6 pockets you have created. Season the chicken all over with the salt and pepper, sprinkling a little inside the cavity, too. Slip 4 of the lemon quarters and the remaining 1 tarragon sprig into the cavity. Truss the chicken so that it holds its shape (see page 111). Place the chicken, breast side up, on the rack on the pan. Refrigerate uncovered for 2 days. The skin will dry and tighten over the meat.

2 Remove the grate from the grill and set up a rotisserie in the grill. Heat the grill for medium-high indirect heat (350°–375°F/180°–190°C).

3 Secure the chicken onto the spit, then rub the oil all over the chicken. Insert the spit into the rotisserie motor, making sure the chicken can rotate without touching the grill. Cover the grill and cook until the skin is golden and an instant-read thermometer inserted into the inside of a thigh away from bone registers 165°F (74°C), 1–1¼ hours.

4 Remove the spit from the rotisserie and place the chicken, still on the spit, on a cutting board. Let rest for 15 minutes.

5 Meanwhile, in a small saucepan, melt the butter over low heat and stir in the chopped tarragon.

6 Remove the chicken from the spit and tilt the bird to pour the juices from the cavity into the tarragon butter. Carve the chicken by removing the wings, cutting the legs into thighs and drumsticks, and removing each breast from the bone, then cutting each breast into 2–4 pieces (10–12 pieces to serve). Pour the juices from the cutting board into the tarragon butter, transfer the tarragon butter to a serving bowl, and serve the tarragon butter and the remaining lemon wedges for squeezing alongside the chicken.

EXTRA CREDIT

Grill-Roasted Chicken with Shichimi Togarashi: Skip everything but the chicken. Season the skin of the bird all over with 2 tablespoons Shichimi Togarashi (page 217) mixed with 1 tablespoon coarse sea salt, preferably sel gris. Refrigerate as directed. Heat the grill for medium indirect heat (about 350°F/180°C). Brush the grill grate. Oil the bird with a mixture of equal parts peanut oil and Asian sesame oil and then put it on the grill grate away from the fire. Cover the grill and cook, pivoting the bird a few times for even cooking, until the skin is golden and an instant-read thermometer inserted into the inside of the thigh away from bone registers 165°F (74°C), 1–1¼ hours. Transfer to a cutting board, let rest for 15 minutes, and carve as directed. Serve with orange wedges for squeezing.

Beer Can Chicken with Barbecue Rub: Skip everything but the chicken. Season the skin of the bird all over with 2 tablespoons Basic Barbecue Rub (page 215) mixed with 2 teaspoons fine sea salt. Refrigerate as directed. Heat the grill for medium indirect heat (300°–350°F/150°–180°C). Brush the grill grate. Drink about ¼ cup (2 fl oz/60 ml) of beer from a can of beer, then oil the outside of the can with canola oil or another mild vegetable oil. Oil the chicken all over with more of the same oil, then lower the bird onto the can, inserting the can into the cavity. Position the chicken so the legs form a tripod that holds the chicken upright. Put the beer can chicken on the grate away from the fire, cover the grill, and cook, pivoting the bird a few times for even cooking, until the skin is golden and an instant-read thermometer inserted into the inside of the thigh away from bone registers 165°F (74°C), 1–1¼ hours. Using tongs, lift the chicken off the can, let rest for 15 minutes, and carve as directed.

Here's our new favorite way to cook a juicy Thanksgiving turkey. Using the grill frees up space in the oven for cooking casseroles and other dishes. Look for a good-quality turkey that is not "self-basting," since those birds have already been pumped full of brine. Start this recipe at least 4 days before you plan to cook the turkey, as it will need to brine for 3 days in a bag and then 1 day out of the bag.

MAKES 12 SERVINGS

1 high-quality turkey, about 12 lb (6 kg)

2½ tablespoons coarse sea salt or 1½ tablespoons fine sea salt, or as needed depending on size of bird

3 large fresh rosemary sprigs

1 lemon

½ teaspoon freshly ground pepper

GRILL-ROASTED TURKEY WITH LEMON-ROSEMARY DRY BRINE

1 Note the total weight of the turkey. Remove the neck and giblets and set aside for making gravy, if desired (see Extra Credit, page 111). Use 1 tablespoon coarse sea salt for every 5 lb (2.5 kg) of turkey. For a 12-lb (6-kg) turkey, use 2½ tablespoons coarse sea salt; for a 15-lb (7.5-kg) turkey, use 3 tablespoons coarse sea salt. Place the salt in a small bowl. Chop enough of the rosemary to equal 2 tablespoons, add it to the salt, and stir well. Grate the zest from the lemon into the salt mixture and then stir to mix. Rub 1 tablespoon of the mixture lightly inside the turkey cavity. Sprinkle the rest of the mixture evenly all over the outside of the turkey, moving the legs and wings to reach every area. Cut the lemon into quarters and place in the turkey cavity along with the remaining rosemary.

2 Truss the turkey (see page 111) if you want it to hold a compact shape. Slip the bird into an extra-large zippered plastic bag, seal closed, and refrigerate for 3 days, turning the turkey over once a day.

3 Set a large wire rack in a roasting pan. Remove the turkey from the bag and place it, breast side up, on the rack in the pan. Refrigerate uncovered overnight or up to 24 hours to dry the skin so it will crisp as it cooks.

4 Remove the turkey from the refrigerator 1 hour before cooking. Heat a grill for high indirect heat (about 450°F/230°C). Brush the grill grate.

5 Turn the turkey breast side down on the rack in the roasting pan. Place the pan on the grill grate away from the fire, close the lid, and cook for 30 minutes. Remove the pan from the grill and use silicone grill gloves to turn the turkey breast side up. Lower the grill temperature to 325°F (165°C), return the pan to the grate away from the fire, cover the grill, and grill roast the turkey until an instant-read thermometer inserted into the inside of a thigh away from bone registers 165°F (74°C), 2–3 hours longer; the timing depends on the weight of the bird. If you are using charcoal, you will need to replace the coals about once an hour during cooking.

6 Remove the pan from the grill and let the turkey rest on the rack in the pan for at least 30 minutes or up to 1 hour. Tilt the bird to pour the juices from the cavity into the roasting pan. Transfer the turkey to a platter. Reserve the juices in the pan for making gravy, if you like. Carve the bird and serve.

Continued on page 111

Continued from page 108  **EXTRA CREDIT**

Turkey Gravy: To make gravy while the turkey cooks, put the turkey neck and all of the giblets except the liver (reserve the liver for another use) into a saucepan and add ½ cup (2 oz/60 g) chopped yellow onion, ½ cup (2½ oz/75 g) chopped celery, 1 bay leaf, and 1 tablespoon chopped fresh or 1 teaspoon dried thyme or flat-leaf parsley. Add water to cover by 1 inch (2.5 cm) and bring to a boil over high heat. Reduce the heat to low and cook for 2 hours. Strain through a fine-mesh sieve into a bowl and discard the solids. When the turkey is removed from the roasting pan, add the liquid to the pan. Place the pan on the stove top over high heat, bring to a boil, and scrape up any browned bits from the pan bottom with a wooden spoon or spatula. In a small bowl or cup, dissolve 3 tablespoons cornstarch in ¼ cup (2 fl oz/60 ml) cold water and then add the mixture to the roasting pan. Boil over medium-high heat, stirring constantly, until the gravy thickens. Season with pepper.

For a deep bronze color, baste the bird with a mixture of ¼ cup (2 fl oz/60 ml) melted unsalted butter and 3 tablespoons dark corn syrup during the last hour of roasting.

For smoke flavor and color, if using charcoal, wrap a couple handfuls of wood chips (apple and/or cherry are nice) in a perforated foil packet and place the packet on the hot coals right before you put the bird on the grill. Or put a wood chunk or two directly on the hot coals. If using a gas grill, place the perforated foil packet of wood chips directly over one of the burners under the cooking grate. Or use your grill's smoker box. Replace the wood whenever it burns out (or when you are adding more coals), about once an hour.

HOW TO TRUSS A BIRD

Put the bird, breast up and with the legs pointing toward you, on a work surface. Cut a 24-inch (60-cm) length of kitchen string and put the center of the string around the neck of the bird to anchor the string. Slip two lengths of string under the bird, pulling them tight. Bring the strings up around the middle of the body, then run them down the bird between the breasts and legs. Bring the strings around the outsides of the ends of the drumsticks, cross the strings, and pull tightly to bring the drumsticks together. Push the ends of the drumsticks under the bottom of the breast and pull tightly again to push up the entire breast. Now flip the bird over lengthwise so the neck is facing you and bring the strings up around the back of the bird. Cross the strings into an X and then draw them toward the neck. Cross them again around the neck and pull tightly. Tie a knot onto the back of the bird and cut off the excess string. Find the string between the thigh and breast on each side and tuck the wing "elbows" deep under the string on the backside to hold the wings in place. Flip the bird over so it is breast up and tuck the wing tips deep in between the thighs and breasts on the front side.

BONELESS BREASTS & THIGHS

Boneless, skinless chicken breasts are the most ubiquitous meat cooked at home. But boneless poultry is so lean that it can easily dry out on the grill. Here's how to grill juicy, flavorful boneless breasts and thighs every time.

HOW DO YOU PREP BONELESS POULTRY FOR GRILLING?

Pound breasts for even cooking. Poultry breasts tend to be thick on one end and thin on the other. For more even cooking, gently pound chicken breasts with a meat pounder or heavy skillet between sheets of plastic wrap or parchment paper (with a few drops of water to help ease the way). Pound to an even thickness of ½ to ¾ inch (12 mm to 2 cm). Or you can keep pounding to make chicken paillards, superthin disks of chicken breast that grill up in seconds. Poultry thighs generally have a more uniform thickness and don't require pounding.

Remove the tendon. To prevent shrinking and curling, remove the white tendon from the underside of poultry breasts (see step 1 facing page).

Use a wet brine for juiciness. Brining makes lean meats juicier. We use a dry brine on skin-on poultry to create a crisp skin, but a wet brine works well for skinless, boneless poultry breasts and thighs. These cuts can brine for as little as 30 minutes or as long as 2 hours.

Apply some fat. Boneless, skinless poultry breasts have almost no fat (3 grams in a cooked 3-ounce/ 90 g portion of chicken breast). To keep them from drying out and sticking to the grill grate, oil the surface or coat them with an oil-rich paste like pesto. Skinless poultry thighs contain a bit more fat, but we usually oil them as well to prevent sticking.

Season generously. Boneless chicken and turkey taste fairly bland. Use a spice rub, wet paste, or sauce to amp up the flavor. Just reduce the amount of salt in the seasoning if the meat has been brined. Watch the sugar, too. When boneless poultry is grilled over direct heat, sugary pastes or sauces can burn.

Cut boneless turkey breasts for direct grilling. To grill a large boneless roast like a whole turkey breast directly over the fire, cut it into medallions (cutlets). Or you can butterfly the breast and open it up flat like a book; the thinner halves will cook more quickly than the whole breast. See the recipe for Butterflied Turkey Breast with Spicy Peanut Glaze on page 119.

Trim duck breasts to prevent burning. A duck has a thick layer of fat under its skin. If the fat isn't fully rendered during cooking, the skin gets flabby. But a duck breast cooks through on the grill long before all of its fat has rendered. For this reason, before grilling a boneless duck breast, we trim off all of the skin except for a strip of skin and fat 2 inches (5 cm) wide over the center of the breast. You'll still get some flare-ups, so leave a little room on the grill to move the duck around.

WHAT'S THE BEST WAY TO GRILL BONELESS POULTRY?

Use direct heat for thinner pieces. Any boneless poultry less than 2 inches (5 cm) thick is tender enough to be grilled directly over the heat. Use higher heat for thinner pieces and lower heat for thicker pieces. A chicken breast pounded to an ultrathin paillard (⅛ inch/3 mm or less) can be grilled over direct high heat in less than 30 seconds per side. A thicker pounded chicken breast, a boneless chicken thigh, or a turkey tenderloin (¾ inch/2 cm thick or less) grills better over medium-high heat and takes about 5 minutes per side. A slightly thicker butterflied turkey breast cooks best over medium heat and takes 30 to 40 minutes. Even when using direct heat, it's helpful to create two heat areas on the grill so you can move the meat around in case of flare-ups.

Use indirect heat for very thick pieces. For thick boneless roasts like a whole boneless turkey breast, set up the grill for medium indirect heat so the meat cooks through without burning on the surface.

Here's a superflavorful take on Ethiopian *niter kibbeh* (spiced clarified butter) and *tibs* (seared meat in spicy butter sauce). Instead of clarifying the butter, we make a simple butter sauce with caramelized onions, ginger, and garlic spiked with a berbere spice mix. Serve with *injera* or other flatbread to soak up the sauce.

MAKES 4 SERVINGS

CHICKEN & BRINE

4 boneless, skinless chicken breast halves, 1½–2 lb (750 g–1 kg) total weight

3 cups (24 fl oz/750 ml) warm water

¼ cup (2¼ oz/70 g) coarse sea salt

2 tablespoons sugar

8 ice cubes

2 tablespoons peanut oil

BERBERE SAUCE

½ cup (4 oz/125 g) unsalted butter

1 large yellow onion, finely chopped

1 tablespoon peeled and grated fresh ginger

4 cloves garlic, pressed or crushed

2 tablespoons Berbere (page 217)

½ teaspoon ground turmeric

¾ cup (6 fl oz/180 ml) chicken broth

Juice of ½ lemon

½ teaspoon fine sea salt

GRILLED CHICKEN BREASTS IN BERBERE SAUCE

1 To prepare the chicken, remove the tough white tendon that runs along the length of each breast, which will prevent the chicken from shrinking as it cooks. You'll find the tendon on the underside in the center of the little muscle (the chicken tender). Grasp the exposed wide end of the tendon with a paper towel, lift it gently, and scrape the sharp edge of a knife down the tendon as if shaving it from the meat with a straight razor. Discard the tendon.

2 One at a time, place each chicken breast between 2 sheets of plastic wrap and, using a heavy frying pan or meat pounder, flatten the meat to an even thickness of ½–¾ inch (12 mm–2 cm).

3 To make the brine, in a bowl, whisk together the warm water, salt, and sugar until the salt and sugar have dissolved. Add the ice to cool down the mixture. When the ice melts, pour the mixture into a large zippered plastic bag and add the chicken. Press out the air, seal, and refrigerate for at least 30 minutes or up to 1½ hours.

4 To make the berbere sauce, in a large, heavy frying pan, melt the butter over medium heat. Add the onion, ginger, garlic, Berbere, and turmeric and cook slowly, stirring occasionally, until the onion is a deep golden brown, 30–40 minutes. Stir in the broth, lemon juice, and salt. Set aside.

5 Heat the grill for medium-high indirect heat (about 375°F/190°C).

6 Remove the chicken from the brine and pat dry with paper towels. Evenly coat the chicken all over with the oil.

7 Brush the grill grate and coat with oil. Put the chicken, smooth side down, on the grate directly over the fire and cook until nicely browned on the underside, 4–6 minutes. Flip the chicken over and cook until the second side is browned and an instant-read thermometer inserted into the center of a breast registers 155°F (68°C), 4–6 minutes longer. If the chicken threatens to burn, move it away from the fire to finish cooking.

8 When the chicken is almost ready, reheat the sauce over low heat. Transfer the chicken to the sauce and turn each breast to coat evenly. Let rest for a few minutes in the sauce, then serve with the sauce spooned over the top.

Yogurt makes a great marinade for lean meats like boneless chicken breasts and thighs. It adds both fat and acidity to bump up the flavors. This classic tandoori chicken then gets doused in tomato-based curry sauce. Serve with basmati rice and naan to soak up the juices.

MAKES 4 SERVINGS

CHICKEN TIKKA

½ cup (4 oz/125 g) yogurt

Juice of 1 lemon

4 cloves garlic, minced

1 tablespoon peeled and grated fresh ginger

1½ teaspoons paprika

1 teaspoon garam masala

1 teaspoon ground cumin

¼ teaspoon cayenne pepper

¼ teaspoon fine sea salt

1½ lb (750 g) boneless, skinless chicken breasts and/or thighs, cut into 1-inch (2.5-cm) pieces

MASALA SAUCE

2 tablespoons canola oil

½ cup (2½ oz/75 g) finely chopped red onion

4 cloves garlic, minced

1 tablespoon peeled and grated fresh ginger

2 teaspoons each paprika and ground coriander

½ teaspoon ground turmeric

⅛ teaspoon cayenne pepper

2 cups (16 fl oz/500 ml) tomato puree

1 teaspoon fine sea salt

½ teaspoon garam masala

¼ cup (2 oz/60 g) yogurt

2 tablespoons chopped fresh cilantro

GRILLED CHICKEN TIKKA MASALA

1 To make the chicken tikka, in a small bowl, combine the yogurt, lemon juice, garlic, ginger, paprika, garam masala, cumin, cayenne, and salt and stir to mix well. Put the chicken pieces in a zippered plastic bag, add the yogurt mixture, and massage to coat the chicken pieces evenly with the yogurt mixture. Press out the air, seal, and refrigerate for at least 8 hours or up to 24 hours.

2 To make the masala sauce, in a large, deep frying pan, heat the oil over medium heat. Add the onion and cook, stirring occasionally, until soft, about 5 minutes. Stir in the garlic, ginger, paprika, coriander, turmeric, and cayenne and cook for 1 minute. Stir in the tomato puree and bring to a boil. Cover, reduce the heat to low, and simmer until slightly thickened, about 20 minutes. Keep warm.

3 Heat the grill for medium-high direct heat (about 400°F/200°C).

4 Remove the chicken from the marinade and discard the marinade. Brush the grill grate and coat with oil. If there is any chance the chicken might fall through the bars of the grate, thread the pieces onto metal skewers. Put the chicken on the grate and cook, turning as needed, until nicely browned all over, about 3 minutes per side. The chicken will finish cooking in the sauce.

5 Stir the salt and garam masala into the sauce, then transfer the chicken to the sauce and simmer until the chicken is cooked through, 4–5 minutes. Stir in the yogurt and cilantro, heat through, and serve.

 **EXTRA CREDIT** ━━━━

To make fresh tomato puree, core 4 large tomatoes (about 1¼ lb/625 g), then puree in a food processor.

Duck burns easily on the grill. Chalk it up to that thick layer of fat under the skin. To avoid massive flare-ups, it's essential to trim away some of the fat from the duck. Once that's done, you can flavor and grill a duck breast much like you would a chicken breast. Serve this Chinese version with steamed rice, grilled plums, and bok choy.

MAKES 4 SERVINGS

4 boneless duck breast halves

½ cup (2 oz/60 g) Chinese Five-Spice Rub (page 215)

⅓ cup (3 oz/90 g) hoisin sauce

¼ cup (3 oz/90 g) honey

2 cloves garlic, pressed or crushed

2 teaspoons chile garlic paste

2 teaspoons soy sauce

2 teaspoons Asian sesame oil

1 navel orange, cut into wedges, for serving

GRILLED FIVE-SPICE DUCK BREASTS WITH HOISIN GLAZE

1 Cut away enough skin and fat from the meat on each duck breast to leave a strip of skin and fat only 2 inches (5 cm) wide over the center of the breast. Score the strip of skin and fat with a few diagonal slashes being careful not to cut into the flesh. Coat the duck all over with the rub. Cover and refrigerate overnight for the most flavor. Alternatively, let the duck stand at room temperature as the grill heats.

2 Heat the grill for medium indirect heat (about 325°F/160°C). While the grill heats, in a small bowl, combine the hoisin sauce, honey, garlic, chile garlic paste, soy sauce, and sesame oil and mix well.

3 Brush the grill grate and coat with oil. Put the duck breasts, skin side down, directly over the fire and cook until nicely browned, 5–6 minutes. As the fat drips and flares up, move the duck around the grill to avoid burning. Flip the duck breasts over and cook directly over the fire until lightly browned on the meat side, 2–4 minutes. Move the duck away from the fire and brush on both sides with the hoisin mixture. Cover the grill and cook until the glaze sets and an instant-read thermometer inserted into a duck breast registers 150°F (65°C) for medium-rare, 2–3 minutes more. Glaze the breasts again, then transfer them to a cutting board.

4 Cut the duck across the grain in slices ½ inch (12 mm) wide. Serve with the orange wedges for squeezing.

 **EXTRA CREDIT**

Grilled Ras El Hanout Duck Breast with Orange Glaze: Replace the Chinese Five-Spice Rub with Ras El Hanout (page 217) and the hoisin glaze with Orange Vinaigrette (page 227), using fresh flat-leaf parsley or cilantro in the vinaigrette.

Agrodolce is Italian for "sweet and sour." When applied to a sauce, it can take many forms, with various ingredients providing the right balance. This Sicilian-inspired version features the aromas of oranges, rosemary, olives, and capers. Serve it with a simple pasta and grilled fennel. Add freshly grated pecorino for a nice final touch.

GRILLED CHICKEN THIGHS AGRODOLCE

MAKES 6 SERVINGS

CHICKEN & BRINE

3 cups (24 fl oz/750 ml) warm water

¼ cup (2¼ oz/70 g) coarse sea salt, preferably sel gris

2 tablespoons sugar

8 ice cubes

1½ lb (750 g) boneless, skinless chicken thighs

1 tablespoon olive oil

½ teaspoon freshly ground pepper

AGRODOLCE SAUCE

2 tablespoons extra-virgin olive oil

1 small yellow onion, chopped

2 cloves garlic, minced

¾ cup (6 fl oz/180 ml) red wine vinegar

½ cup (4 fl oz/125 ml) fresh orange juice

1½ cups (12 fl oz/375 ml) chicken broth

1 teaspoon sugar

¼ cup (1 oz/30 g) halved and pitted green olives

1 tablespoon small capers

¼ teaspoon red pepper flakes

1 tablespoon chopped fresh rosemary

½ teaspoon fine sea salt

2 tablespoons unsalted butter

1 To make the brine, in a bowl, whisk together the warm water, salt, and sugar until the salt and sugar have dissolved. Add the ice to cool down the mixture. When the ice melts, pour the mixture into a large zippered plastic bag and add the chicken. Press out the air, seal, and refrigerate for at least 30 minutes or up to 1½ hours.

2 To make the sauce, in a large, deep frying pan, heat the oil over medium heat. Add the onion and cook, stirring occasionally, until soft, 4–5 minutes. Add the garlic, vinegar, orange juice, broth, and sugar and stir well. Raise the heat to high, bring to a boil, and cook, stirring, until slightly thickened and reduced to about 1 cup (8 fl oz/ 250 ml), about 15 minutes. Reduce the heat to medium and stir in the olives, capers, pepper flakes, and rosemary. Simmer gently for 5 minutes. Stir in the salt and butter and set aside.

3 Heat the grill for medium-high indirect heat (about 375°F/190°C).

4 Remove the chicken from the brine and pat dry with paper towels. Coat the chicken all over with the oil. Season all over with the pepper.

5 Brush the grill grate and coat with oil. Put the chicken, smooth side down, on the grate directly over the fire and cook until nicely browned on the underside, 4–6 minutes. Flip the chicken over and cook until the second side is browned and an instant-read thermometer inserted into the center of a thigh registers 165°F (74°C), 4–6 minutes longer. If the chicken threatens to burn, move it away from the fire to finish cooking.

6 When the chicken is almost ready, reheat the sauce over low heat. Transfer the chicken to the sauce and turn each thigh to coat evenly. Let rest for a few minutes in the sauce, then serve with the sauce spooned over the top.

 **EXTRA CREDIT**

Grilled Chicken Thighs with Romesco: Replace the agrodolce sauce with Romesco (page 228). Garnish with sliced almonds and chopped fresh parsley and pass the lemon wedges for squeezing.

You see this flavor combo on grilled kebabs all over West Africa. Before grilling, the raw meat gets dipped in oil and then in the spice mixture used here. We like to brine the meat first to keep it juicy on the grill. We also mix the oil right into the spices with some lime juice to create a glaze on the meat. Some extra spice mix gets scattered over the top at the table. To save time, replace the spices with 4 teaspoons pumpkin pie spice. For a description of the turkey London broil, see below.

MAKES 8 SERVINGS

1½ cups (12 fl oz/375 ml) Cumin & Coriander Brine (page 212)

1 turkey London broil, about 2 lb (1 kg)

1 cup (5 oz/155g) roasted salted peanuts

1 teaspoon ground ginger

1 teaspoon freshly grated nutmeg

1 teaspoon ground cloves

1 teaspoon ground cinnamon

1 teaspoon cayenne pepper

1 teaspoon salt

6 tablespoons (3 fl oz/ 90 ml) peanut oil

2 limes, halved

BUTTERFLIED TURKEY BREAST WITH SPICY PEANUT GLAZE

1 Combine the brine and turkey in a gallon-sized (4-l) zippered plastic bag. Press out the air, seal, and refrigerate for 3–4 hours.

2 To make the glaze, grind the peanuts to a coarse powder in a mortar or a food processor. Add the ginger, nutmeg, cloves, cinnamon, cayenne, and salt and stir or process until mixed. Set aside ¼ cup (1 oz/30) of the mixture. Add 5 tablespoons (2½ fl oz/75 ml) of the oil and the juice of ½ lime to the remaining peanut mixture and stir or process until well mixed. This mixture will glaze the turkey.

3 Heat the grill for medium direct heat (about 350°F/180°C). Remove the turkey from the brine, discard the brine, and pat the turkey dry with paper towels. Coat the turkey all over with the remaining 1 tablespoon oil.

4 Brush the grill grate and coat with oil. Put the turkey on the grate and cook until slightly pink in the center and an instant-read thermometer inserted into the thickest part registers 155°F (68°C), 30–40 minutes. Turn the turkey often to brown it evenly on all sides. During the last 15–20 minutes of grilling and turning, repeatedly brush the turkey all over with the glaze to coat it evenly. The glaze should be crusty and browned in spots.

5 Transfer the turkey to a cutting board and let rest 5 minutes. Cut into slices about ½ inch (12 mm) thick and arrange on a platter or plates, then sprinkle all over with the reserved spice mix. Cut the remaining lime halves into wedges and serve with the turkey for squeezing.

WHAT IS TURKEY LONDON BROIL?

Turkey London broil is a boneless, skinless butterflied turkey breast. It's perfect for grilling because butterflying makes the breast thin enough to cook through in about a half hour over direct heat. If you can't find this cut at the market, buy a boneless, skinless turkey breast half and cut it open like a book to make the roast thinner.

7

FISH & SHELLFISH

122 LESSON 1: WHOLE FISH

125 SALMON STUFFED WITH CILANTRO PESTO

128 BEDOUIN-SPICED SNAPPER WITH LIME BUTTER

130 LESSON 2: FISH FILLETS

131 PLANKED SALMON WITH CITRUS RUB & ARTICHOKE RELISH

133 GRILLED TILAPIA TACOS

134 GRILLED HALIBUT ESCABECHE

136 LESSON 3: FISH STEAKS

137 VIETNAMESE COCONUT SWORDFISH

140 LESSON 4: SHRIMP & SCALLOPS

141 SCALLOPS WITH RAS EL HANOUT & PRESERVED LEMON YOGURT

143 VADOUVAN GRILLED SHRIMP

144 LESSON 5: SQUID & OCTOPUS

145 VIETNAMESE-STYLE OCTOPUS LETTUCE WRAPS

147 GRILLED SQUID WITH CHORIZO & ROMESCO

148 LESSON 6: CLAMS & OYSTERS

149 GRILLED OYSTERS WITH FINES HERBES BUTTER

151 CHIMICHURRI CLAMS ON THE GRILL

152 LESSON 7: LOBSTERS

153 LOBSTER WITH CHERMOULA

WHOLE FISH

When buying fish, take a look to see if it's fresh. If the fish has already been filleted, there's not much to look at. Aside from checking on how it smells, which tells you only whether it is good or bad, not how fresh it is, there are few signs. Starting with a whole fish is the only way to tell the freshness of the fish you are about to purchase.

FIVE SIGNS OF A FRESH FISH

1 Fresh fish have firm flesh. Poke the side of a fish in its thickest portion. The imprint of your finger should spring right back. If an impression remains, it indicates that the flesh has already begun to decompose.

2 A fresh fish will have clear, clean eyes that bulge outward slightly. Reject specimens with sunken or cloudy eyes.

3 Looking more closely at the head of the fish, lift the gill flaps at the back of the head and inspect the spongy gills inside. They should be bright red or pink without hints of brown or gray.

4 The skin of the fish should have a full covering of firmly attached scales. The color should be bright and the skin should have no blemishes or reddish patches visible beneath its surface.

5 Perfectly fresh fish has no odor except possibly the faint briny aroma of seawater. Any fishy odor is an indication of decay. A smell test is a fairly accurate way of choosing a purveyor: when a fish store smells fishy, something's not right behind the counter.

HOW TO CLEAN & GRILL A WHOLE FISH

Once you have determined the fish is fresh, have your fish seller gut it, remove its scales and gills, and clip its fins. To gut a fish yourself, slit it down the center line of its belly from its pelvic fin to its anal fin. Open up the belly. Near the back opening, find the end of the intestine and separate it from the body by snipping it with kitchen scissors. You will now be able to lift all of the organs from the body cavity in one piece. They will be attached by the esophagus to the interior of the head. Snip the esophagus as close to the back of the mouth as possible. Remove all of the guts and discard. Hook a finger around the gills, which lie just under the gill flaps on either side of the head, and pull away from the head with some force. The gills will disconnect and you can discard them. Rinse the interior of the fish thoroughly with cold running water.

To remove the scales, put the fish in a deep sink or move outdoors. This is a messy job. Moving from the tail to the head, scrape the fish skin with the back of a knife blade, working against the grain of the scales as if shaving the skin. The scales will pop off. You will need to do this several times to remove all of the scales. Rinse the fish under cold running water.

Whether a whole fish is grilled by direct or indirect heat is a question of size. Most whole fish weigh less than 2 pounds (1 kg) and serve one or two people. Fish of this size can be grilled directly over the fire. It's a good idea to make several diagonal slashes through the flesh on each side of the fish down to the bone to help the fish cook through evenly. Use indirect heat for grilling fish that are thicker than 2 inches (5 cm) and/or weigh more than 2 pounds (1 kg). They can be slashed or not.

COMMON FISH FOR GRILLING

FISH	SHAPE	DESCRIPTION	HOW TO GRILL
Bluefish	Round	Soft, dark meat, fatty, strong flavor, vary in size	Large fillets: indirect, medium-high Small fillets: direct, medium-high
Catfish	Round	Freshwater, firm, pale flesh, meaty, sweet	Fillets: direct, medium-high
Cod	Round	Large, lean, firm flesh, white meat, large flakes, mild	Steak: indirect, medium-high
Dolphin (mahimahi)	Round	Lean, firm, white meat, large flakes, meaty, sweet	Steaks: direct, medium-high
Eel	Round	Fatty, rich, fine flakes	Skinned whole: direct, medium
Flounder	Flat	Lean, white meat, delicate flakes, mild	Whole or fillets: direct, medium-high
Halibut	Flat	Large flounder (see above)	Fillets: direct, medium-high
Herring	Round	Rich, dark meat, assertive flavor, delicate flakes	Fillets: direct, high
Mackerel	Round	Rich, dark meat, assertive flavor, delicate flakes	Fillets: direct, medium-high
Monkfish	Round	Eat only tail, white meat, meaty, sweet	Tail: indirect, medium-high
Pompano	Round	Mostly white meat, mild, sweet, flaky	Whole: direct, medium
Red Snapper	Round	White meat, sweet, large flakes, mild	Whole: indirect, medium-high
Salmon	Round	Red to pink flesh, rich, assertive flavor, wild has less fat than farmed	Whole: indirect, medium Fillets or steaks: direct, medium-high
Shad	Round	Rich, dark meat, assertive flavor, delicate flakes	Fillets: direct, medium-high
Shark	Round	Firm, grey-beige, meaty, strong flavored	Steaks: direct, medium
Striped Bass (Rockfish)	Round	White meat, large flakes, mild, sweet	Whole: Indirect, medium-high
Sturgeon	Round	Very large, firm flesh, dark, rich, meaty	Medallions: direct, medium
Swordfish	Round	Dark meat, firm, meaty, assertive flavor	Steaks: direct, medium
Trout	Round	Freshwater whole fish, meaty, tender	Whole: direct, medium-high
Tuna	Round	Dark red meat, firm, meaty, assertive flavor	Steaks: direct, medium-high; cook only to rare
Turbot	Flat	Large flounder (see above)	Fillets: direct, medium-high

A whole, farm-raised salmon is a bit tricky to grill. The fish tends to be large and thick, making it difficult to cook it through before it dries out on the surface. Wild salmon are much leaner and cook through more quickly. This wild one is slashed and embedded with cilantro pesto and then doused with fresh lemon juice.

MAKES 6 SERVINGS

1 oz (30 g) whole almonds (about 20)

3 cups (3 oz/90 g) packed fresh cilantro leaves (from about 2 bunches)

2 cloves garlic

5 tablespoons (2½ fl oz/ 75 ml) extra-virgin olive oil

½ teaspoon fine sea salt

¼ teaspoon freshly ground pepper

1 whole wild salmon, about 5 lb (2.5 kg), cleaned and head, scales, and fins removed

2 lemons, halved

SALMON STUFFED WITH CILANTRO PESTO

1 Heat the grill for medium indirect heat (300°–350°F/150°–180°F). Set a grill screen on the grate over the fire.

2 To make the pesto, in a food processor, pulse the almonds until chopped. Add the cilantro and garlic and process until all of the ingredients are finely chopped (or chop everything with a knife). Scrape into a bowl and mix in 4 tablespoons (2 fl oz/60 ml) of the oil, the salt, and the pepper.

3 Moving from the tail to the head, scrape the dull side of a knife against the skin of the salmon to remove excess moisture and any fine scales. Cut 6 evenly spaced diagonal slashes through the flesh on each side of the fish down to the bone. Fill the slashes with the pesto and rub more pesto into the interior cavity. It's fine if you have pesto left over, as it can be served with the salmon. Squeeze the juice from 1 lemon over the fish.

4 Coat the salmon on all sides with the remaining 1 tablespoon oil. Oil the grill screen and put the salmon on the screen. Put the screen on the grill away from the fire, cover, and cook the salmon, turning it over after about 10 minutes, until an instant-read thermometer inserted into the thickest part of the fish registers 130°F (54°C) or the fish barely flakes when gently pressed, about 20 minutes. If your grill has a temperature gauge, it should stay around 350°F (180°C).

5 Transfer the fish to a platter. If the skin tore when you flipped the fish, don't worry about it. Simply peel the skin off before serving. Squeeze the juice from the remaining lemon over the fish. Use the slashes in the flesh to help portion the fish. Serve with any extra pesto.

 **EXTRA CREDIT**

If using farmed salmon, choose a whole fillet instead of the whole fish. The finished trimmed weight will be about the same, 2–3 lb (1–1.5 kg), and because the meat is thicker and fattier, it will cook in about the same time as a larger whole wild fish.

Nearly any combination of chopped fresh herbs, garlic, and olive oil can be substituted for the pesto.

One of our favorite pesto flavors is marjoram and walnuts. A mix of dill and pine nuts is also delicious with salmon.

Red snapper is one of the world's great eating fish. Its sturdy bone structure makes it easy to fillet, and its fine texture and sweet flavor take to a wide range of seasonings and accompaniments. Plus, it is spectacular grilled whole, with its elegant symmetry and dappled red color. A spice rub tinted with turmeric adds yet another color dimension, and the delicate flesh readily absorbs the aromatics from the spice blend.

MAKES 2 SERVINGS

1 whole snapper, about 1½ lb (750 g), cleaned and scaled

1 tablespoon Bedouin Spice Rub (page 215)

1 tablespoon olive oil

2 tablespoons unsalted butter

1 clove garlic, minced

1 teaspoon ground coriander

Grated zest and juice of 1 lime

2 tablespoons finely chopped fresh cilantro

Fine sea salt and freshly ground pepper

BEDOUIN-SPICED SNAPPER WITH LIME BUTTER

1 Heat the grill for direct medium heat (about 375°F/190°C). Set a grill screen on the grate over the fire.

2 Moving from the tail to the head, scrape the dull side of a knife against the skin of the snapper to remove excess moisture and fine scales. Cut 3 or 4 evenly spaced diagonal slashes through the flesh on each side of the fish down to the bone (see photo). Season the fish inside and out with the spice rub and rub the olive oil all over the outside.

3 Oil the grill screen liberally and put the fish on the screen. Cover the grill and cook the fish, turning it over after about 4 minutes, until browned all over and an instant-read thermometer inserted into the thickest part of the fish registers 130°F (54°C), 7–8 minutes per side. Transfer the fish to a platter and keep warm.

4 To make the butter, in a small frying pan, heat the butter, garlic, and coriander over medium heat until the garlic sizzles, about 1 minute. Stir in the lime zest and juice and bring to a boil. Remove from the heat, stir in the cilantro, and season with salt and pepper. Pour the butter over the fish and serve.

 EXTRA CREDIT

The technique of grilling a whole fish rubbed with a spice or herb blend and served with seasoned butter or oil lends itself to near endless variation. Here are some good combinations:

• Italian herb rub with garlic butter

• Herbes de Provence with lemon butter

• Sichuan pepper salt (mix of 1 part Sichuan peppercorns, 2 parts fine sea salt, and ½ part toasted sesame seeds) with ginger, green onion, and Asian sesame oil

• Greek herb rub with lemon juice and olive oil

• Ginger, green onion, and lemon rub with Vietnamese Dipping Sauce (page 222)

Substitute any small, lean whole fish for the snapper. Good substitutes include black bass, striped bass, opa, porgy, ocean perch, or a small grouper.

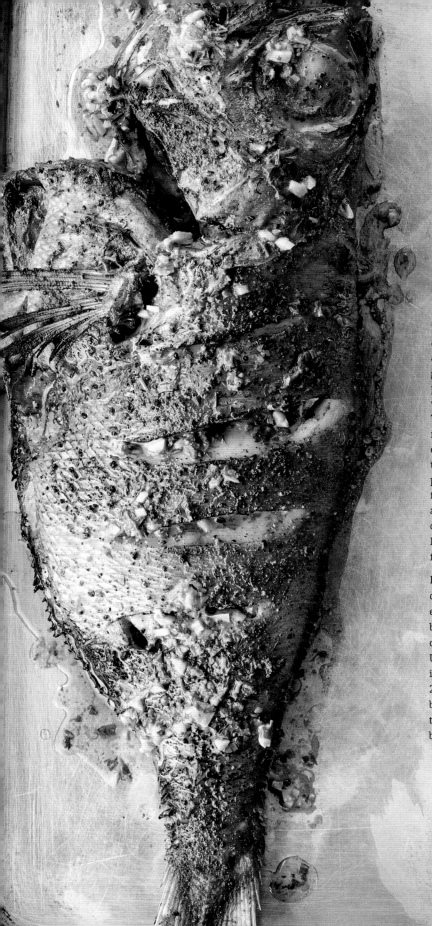

FARMED VS WILD

What Is the Difference Between Wild Caught and Farmed Fish?

Fish are the largest source of edible wildlife in the world. Wild fish can be delicious, but their quality and availability are subject to environmental variables like seasonality, weather conditions, pollution, and predators. The fishing industry has tried to control some of the vagaries of the wild by farming the most popular fish varieties, such as salmon, trout, sea bass, turbot, tilapia, and catfish.

Farmed fish, like other meats, grow faster than their counterparts in the wild. They are also often more tender, richer in fat, and blander tasting because they tend to get less exercise. Raising fish in ocean pens has contaminated nearby waters with waste products, food, and antibiotics. There have been cases of genetically modified farmed fish escaping into the environment, where they infiltrate the diversity of the surrounding wild population, and studies show that fish meal, the primary component of aquaculture feed, has elevated levels of environmental toxins, particularly PCBs, that accumulate in the flesh of farmed salmon.

How a fish lived determines most of its culinary attributes. Wild and farmed examples of the same fish species can be more radically different than two fish of different species. According to the USDA, the fat content of farmed salmon is twice that of wild salmon and contains 20 percent more saturated fat. That is a bigger difference than the difference in the amount of fat between snapper and bass or bluefish and mackerel.

FISH FILLETS

The term fillet refers to the sides of a fish cut lengthwise and freed from its backbone. Fillets from large fish, like salmon, are often sold cut into servable portion sizes. The rib cage can be removed or not. Fillets are popular because they cook quickly and the eater doesn't have to deal with separating meat from bone. The only problem with calling a piece of fish a fillet is that not all fillets are necessarily boneless. Industry standards say that only the central spine and its attached ribs need be removed. Fish fillets can still contain belly ribs and pin bones buried in the flesh. Consumer beware.

HOW DO YOU REMOVE PIN BONES?

Pin bones are small floating bones that parallel the ribs but are not attached to the spine. When the central skeleton is removed, pin bones remain in the flesh. They must be removed separately, usually by being pulled out individually with needle-nose pliers. If your fish seller doesn't do this, it is easy to do yourself. Run your finger down the crest of the widest part of the fillet and you will feel the ends of small bones protruding from the flesh. It is helpful to press the flesh around the pin bone with two fingers, which will better expose the tip of the bone. Grip the end of each bone with the pliers and pull at an angle toward the wider end of the fillet. The bone will slip out easily, though large pin bones closer to the wider end of the fillet might require a forceful tug. Do not pull toward the tail end of the fillet or you risk ripping the flesh.

Some fish, like shad, have an elaborate pin bone setup with two series of pin bones, some of which curve like fish hooks halfway through the fillet. They are complicated to remove, and the task is best done by a professional. When shad fillets are boned completely, they are sold as "boneless" fillets. Always purchase shad fillets boneless or you will be picking out suture-thin fish bones from between your teeth with every bite.

Several kitchenware companies sell sturdy fish bone tweezers for removing pin bones.

HOW DO I KEEP FISH FILLETS FROM STICKING TO THE GRILL?

Fillets pose some challenges for grilling. The grain of the flesh is exposed to the cooking surface, so if the meat should stick to the grill grate, a fillet is prone to tearing when it is turned. Here's what you can do to prevent sticking:

- Make sure your grill grate is free of all debris, so the cooking surface is completely smooth.

- Oil the grill grate and the flesh side of the fish liberally.

- Keep the skin on during cooking. Even if the flesh tears a bit, the skin will help hold it together.

- Grill the flesh side first just long enough to brown it. Flip the fillet and finish cooking it on its skin side. That way, if the skin sticks to the grill grate, you can slide your spatula between the flesh and the skin and skin your fillet as you lift it from the grill.

- Some fish fillets, such as catfish, red snapper, and flounder (and other flatfish like sole), are too thin to grill directly on the grill grate. For thin, delicate fillets, use a grill screen, which has a wide surface area to support the fillet as it cooks.

- For further protection, grill fish fillets on wood planks (see page 31). Fragrant woods like cedar and alder add some aroma, as well.

For centuries, Native Americans in the Pacific Northwest have tied whole sides of salmon to long planks, driving the planks vertically into the ground around a huge fire pit, where the salmon cooks through and smokes slowly. The modern planking method is not as elaborate and much faster. Charring the plank before laying the fish on it delivers smoky flavor, and the plank keeps the direct flame away from the fish.

MAKES 4–6 SERVINGS

1 cedar or alder plank, about 6 by 12 by ¼ inches (15 cm by 30 cm by 6 mm)

1 wild salmon fillet with skin intact, about 1½ lb (750 g), pin bones removed

¼ cup (¾ oz/20 g) Citrus Rub (page 215)

¼ cup (2 fl oz/60 ml) buttermilk

2 tablespoons extra-virgin olive oil

1 can (14 oz/440 g) artichoke hearts, drained and finely chopped

2 cloves garlic, minced

1 lemon, cut into wedges

PLANKED SALMON WITH CITRUS RUB & ARTICHOKE RELISH

1 Soak the wood plank in cold water for 20–60 minutes.

2 Heat the grill for medium-high direct heat (400°–450°F/200°–230°C). Remove the wood plank from the water, put it over the fire, and grill until the surface is charred, about 5 minutes. Remove from the heat and let cool.

3 Lay the fillet, skin side down, on the burnt side of the plank.

4 In a small bowl, combine 3 tablespoons of the rub, the buttermilk, and 1 tablespoon of the oil and stir to mix well. Brush the mixture over the top side of the salmon.

5 Put the planked fish on the grill, cover the grill, and cook until the fish is just a bit filmy and moist in the center, 10–15 minutes; the timing will depend on the thickness. Avoid overcooking the fish as it will continue to cook slightly after it is removed from the grill.

6 While the fish is cooking, in a bowl, combine the artichoke hearts, garlic, the remaining 1 tablespoon oil, and the remaining rub and mix well.

7 Transfer the fish to a platter and cut crosswise into 4 to 6 equal pieces. Serve with the artichoke relish and with the lemon wedges for squeezing.

 EXTRA CREDIT

If using farmed salmon, extend the cooking time by 5–7 minutes, depending on the thickness of the fillet.

Look for cedar planks in well-stocked supermarkets and gourmet kitchen shops. You can also use untreated cedar shingles from a home improvement center or lumberyard. Just be sure the wood is untreated.

We like to use skin-on fillets for flavor, but skinless fillets work just fine.

Oil the bottom of skinless fillets before laying them on the plank.

Be sure all of the bones are removed from the fillet before grilling. Run your fingers along the flesh in both directions, feeling for tiny bones and pulling them out with needle-nose pliers or tweezers.

Make a more traditional planked salmon by using a chile rub on the fish and accompany it with a simple vinaigrette.

Along with catfish, tilapia is among the most extensively farmed fish in North America. It's also one of the leanest white fish fillets with a honey-like sweetness and fine texture that make it ideal for tacos. Grilling has to be the easiest way to make fish tacos. Everything can be cooked over the open fire, there's minimal clean up, and there's no oil for frying or sautéing.

¼ cup (2 fl oz/60 ml) canola oil or other mild vegetable oil

1 tablespoon ancho chile powder

1 teaspoon ground cumin

1 jalapeño chile, finely chopped

1 teaspoon fine sea salt

1 lb (500 g) tilapia fillet

8 corn or flour tortillas

Cooking spray for tortillas

1 cup (8 fl oz/250 ml) Ranch Dressing (page 222)

2 cups (8 oz/250 g) Grilled Radicchio Slaw (page 165) or other coleslaw

1 avocado, pitted, peeled, and diced

GRILLED TILAPIA TACOS

1 Heat the grill for medium-high direct heat (425°–450°F/220°–230°C).

2 In a wide, flat bowl, combine the oil, chile powder, cumin, jalapeño chile, and salt and mix well. Cut each fillet down its center line, dividing it into thicker and thinner sections. Turn the fish pieces in the chile oil mixture, coating them evenly, and set aside in the mixture for 15 minutes.

3 Set a grill screen on the grill and coat with oil. Place the thicker fish pieces on the screen and cook, turning once, until opaque all around the edges, about 3 minutes per side. Cook the thinner pieces the same way but for only about 2 minutes per side. Transfer the fish to a platter and keep warm. Remove the grill screen.

4 Lightly spray the tortillas on both sides with cooking spray and brown directly over the fire, turning once, until grill marked and flexible, about 20 seconds per side. Wrap the tortillas in a clean kitchen towel to keep warm.

5 To serve, invite the diners to assemble their own tacos, piling a fish fillet, a splash of ranch dressing, a pile of slaw, and some avocado on each tortilla.

 EXTRA CREDIT

Substitute any white-fleshed skinless fish fillet or grilled shrimp for the tilapia.

To save time, use a good-quality bottled ranch dressing from the refrigerator section or your favorite deli coleslaw.

Although ranch dressing is classic (and spectacular) on fish tacos feel free to change things up with any vinaigrette or seasoned mayonnaise. Some suggestions: Roasted Tomato French Dressing (page 222), Real Russian Dressing (page 222), Sriracha Mayo (page 223), Pickled Salsa (page 223), Green Chile Queso (page 223), Za'atar Tzatziki (page 225).

Escabeche originated in Spain as a way of preserving fish. The marinade serves as a sort of pickling solution. Also popular in Provence, Mexico, and Jamaica, *escabeche* can be served cold, warm, or at room temperature. We give this *escabeche* a Mexican slant by grilling a mild white halibut fillet and marinating it in a searing blend of chiles and citrus juice. Halibut has snow-white flesh with extra-large satiny smooth flakes that maintain their meatiness even after days of soaking in the marinade.

MAKES 4 SERVINGS

4 pieces halibut fillet, about 6 oz (185 g) each

¼ teaspoon salt

¼ teaspoon freshly ground pepper

1 tablespoon olive oil

1⅓ cups (11 fl oz/340 ml) Spicy Citrus Marinade (page 212)

2 tablespoons sherry vinegar or white wine vinegar

2 tablespoons olive oil

GRILLED HALIBUT ESCABECHE

1 Heat the grill for medium-high direct heat (425°–450°F/220°–230°C).

2 Pat the fish dry and sprinkle with the salt and pepper. Let rest at room temperature for 10–15 minutes.

3 Brush the grill grate and coat with oil. Coat the fish on both sides with the oil. Put the fish on the grate, cover the grill, and cook, turning once, until the fish is just slightly filmy and moist in the center, about 2 minutes per side. If your grill has a temperature gauge, it should stay around 450°F (230°C).

4 Transfer the fillets to a wide, shallow baking dish. In a saucepan, heat the marinade over high heat until boiling. Stir in the vinegar and pour over the fish. Let cool to room temperature.

5 Serve the fish at room temperature, or cover and refrigerate for at least 2 hours or up to 24 hours. Serve chilled or bring to room temperature before serving.

 EXTRA CREDIT

The largest flatfish in the sea, some halibuts have been known to live for more than four decades and weigh upward of 700 pounds (350 kg). Fishermen call the biggest specimens "barn doors," which halibut resemble as their huge flat bodies rest on the ocean floor waiting to close in on small fish, squid, and octopuses.

This fish is so big it can be cut into not only steaks and fillets but also roasts and loins.

To lend this *escabeche* a Spanish accent, add 1 tablespoon tomato paste and ¼ cup (1 oz/30 g) sliced green olives to the marinade.

FISH STEAKS

While fillets are cut down the length of fish, steaks are cut across the whole body of round fish. A portion of backbone is usually left on the steak to help hold it together. The exception is superlarge fish like tuna, where the steak is a cross section of one of the fillets, because a cross section of the whole fish would be too big to handle. When a fish steak has a horseshoe shape, it is referred to as center cut and has come from the section nearest the head. If the steak has an oval shape, it has come from the loin, the section closer to the tail.

Fish steaks tend to be easier to grill than fillets. Because a steak is cut against the grain of the muscle (rather than with the grain, the way a fillet is cut), if the meat sticks to the grill grate, it will not tear the steak during turning. Steaks tend to sell for less money than fillets from the same fish, mostly because they require less labor in processing and also because you are buying a small portion of the total weight as bone.

WHAT ARE THE BEST FISH STEAKS FOR GRILLING?

Fish steaks can be made only from round-bodied fish, so there is no such thing as a flounder or halibut steak. The fish also needs to be fairly large. A steak cut from a 1- or 2-pound (500-g or 1-kg) fish would yield barely a mouthful. Most fish steaks are cut about 1 inch (2.5 cm) thick, though tuna steaks are frequently thicker to ensure the center remains raw during grilling. The best fish for steaks are fatty and/ or dark fleshed, including salmon, tuna, swordfish, and shark. Cod, which are large, are the only white-fleshed fish that are commonly cut into steaks. But cod steaks tend to fall apart on the grill.

ARE FISH STEAKS GRILLED THE SAME WAY AS FISH FILLETS?

In general, fish steaks require fewer precautions than fillets.

- Because steaks are less likely to break apart during handling, you don't need to as concerned about lubricating the grilling surface and the fish itself.

- Like all steaks, fish steaks lend themselves to aggressive crusting, so crank up the heat.

- Fish steaks are frequently paired with rubs. Here are some of our favorite crusty combos:

  - Ancho Chile Rub (page 215) on salmon or tuna
  - Bedouin Spice Rub (page 215) on salmon or swordfish
  - Espresso Rub (page 215) on shark
  - Citrus Rub (page 215) on any fish
  - Shichimi Togarashi (page 217) on tuna

Coconut inspires this fanciful grilled fish in three ways: first as a spicy marinade, then as an exotic "breading" on the surface, and finally as the base for a tangy satay sauce. Overfishing of swordfish during the 1990s sparked the first widespread public ban of fish and raised consumer awareness about the sustainability of wild fishing. Since then, swordfish populations have increased, and the Monterey Bay Aquarium Seafood Watch program now lists most varieties of swordfish as a best or good choice. It is one of the easiest fish to grill because it doesn't stick and it is difficult to overcook.

MAKES 4 SERVINGS

1 cup (8 fl oz/250 ml) Vietnamese Dipping Sauce (page 222)

1 cup (8 fl oz/250 ml) canned coconut milk, can well shaken before opening

2 lb (1 kg) swordfish, cut into 4 equal steaks

1 cup (4 oz/125 g) unsweetened shredded dried coconut (see Note)

Cooking spray for swordfish steaks

¼ cup (2½ oz/75 g) creamy or chunky peanut butter

1 lime, cut into 4 wedges

VIETNAMESE COCONUT SWORDFISH

1 Pour the dipping sauce and the coconut milk into a 2-cup (16 fl oz/500 ml) measuring cup and mix well. Put the swordfish into a large zippered plastic bag. Add half of the coconut milk mixture, press out any air, and seal. Refrigerate for at least 1 hour or up to 6 hours.

2 Heat the grill for medium-high direct heat (425°–450°F/220°–230°C).

3 Spread the shredded coconut out on a plate or on a sheet of aluminum foil or waxed paper. Remove the swordfish from its marinade and wipe off the excess marinade. Do not pat dry. Coat the swordfish steaks on both sides with the coconut and then spray liberally with cooking spray. Discard the marinade.

4 Brush the grill grate and coat with oil. Put the swordfish on the grate, cover the grill, and cook, turning once, just until a bit filmy and moist in the center, 3–5 minutes per side, depending on thickness.

5 While the swordfish is cooking, in a small saucepan, bring the reserved coconut milk mixture to a boil over medium-high heat. Remove from the heat and mix in peanut butter to make a lightly thickened sauce.

6 Serve the swordfish steaks with the sauce and lime wedges.

NOTE: Do not use sweetened shredded dried coconut. It will burn within seconds on the grill.

 **EXTRA CREDIT**

The swordfish in this recipe can be replaced by other large, sturdy-fleshed fish, such as halibut, mahimahi, shark, monkfish, salmon, or tuna.

SHRIMP & SCALLOPS

Shrimp are crustaceans (cousins to lobster and crayfish), and scallops are double-shelled mollusks (related to clams and oysters). They come from different families, yet shrimp and scallops are often grilled in similar ways: shells removed and cooked directly over the fire.

WHAT TYPES ARE BEST FOR GRILLING?

Frozen shrimp can be high quality. Shrimp freeze particularly well, and most shrimp are beheaded, quick frozen at sea, and then thawed just before sale, making the meat high quality. Shrimp with the heads on spoil more quickly due to protein-digesting enzymes in the head. If you're buying head-on shrimp, make sure they are very fresh (few to no black spots on the heads and no ammonia odor), keep them on ice, and grill them as soon as possible.

Buy bigger shrimp. To avoid sacrificing shrimp to the fire, buy extra-large shrimp or larger (see Shrimp Counts on page 142). If using extra colossal, butterfly the shrimp so they grill more evenly: slit each shrimp lengthwise along the back and open it up like a book.

Look for unsoaked sea scallops. Calico and bay scallops are too small to grill. Go with sea scallops at least 1½ inches (4 cm) in diameter. They should be ivory white or pale pink. If they look bright white, shiny, and clumped together, the scallops have probably been soaked in sodium tripolyphosphate to preserve them, a process that dilutes the flavor and increases the weight. Soaking also makes scallops too wet to brown properly on the grill. Unsoaked scallops (aka dry scallops) have the best flavor, caramelize beautifully, and shrink less when grilled.

HOW DO YOU PREP SHRIMP & SCALLOPS FOR GRILLING?

Devein shrimp if you like. The vein on the outer curve is part of the digestive tract. If it is large and dark, it may contain sand or grit, so we remove it. Otherwise, we leave it in for convenience.

Save the shrimp shells. Shrimp shells are full of briny flavor and help keep the meat from drying out on the grill. To grill shell-on shrimp, slit the shells through the back with kitchen scissors before putting the shrimp over the fire. If you remove the shells before grilling, simmer the shells in liquid to extract their flavor (see Vadouvan Grilled Shrimp, page 143).

Remove scallop tendons. To keep a scallop from toughening, peel off the small, rough, half-moon-shaped muscle from the larger white muscle.

Marinate or rub. Liquid marinades of oil, citrus juice, and garlic, ginger, ground spices, and/or chopped herbs work well with shrimp and scallops, particularly if you plan to discard the shells after grilling. The shellfish will pick up these flavors in as little as an hour. You can also use a simple spice rub for a more direct flavor impact, but rubs work best with peeled shrimp.

Skip the skewers. If you don't plan to serve them on skewers, and they're large enough not to fall through the grate, grill shrimp and scallops directly on the grate, turning them with tongs.

Oil them to prevent sticking. Use oil with a high smoke point, like canola or grapeseed, to prevent sticking and improve browning.

WHAT'S THE BEST WAY TO GRILL SHRIMP & SCALLOPS?

Use medium-high direct heat. Both shrimp and scallops are small enough to cook through in just 5 to 10 minutes over a medium-high fire (400° to 450°F/200° to 230°C). Both shellfish are done when they are grill marked and firm on the outside yet slightly soft on the inside, with an internal temperature of 120°F (49°C) for shrimp and 130°F (54°C) for scallops.

Here's a Middle Eastern take on basic grilled scallops rubbed with spices and served with sauce. *Ras el hanout* means "top of the shop" and often includes a mix of top-shelf spices like saffron, mace, and Aleppo pepper. The preserved lemon yogurt wakes up all of the aromas and adds richness and creaminess to the scallops.

MAKES 4 SERVINGS

1½ lb (750 g) large sea scallops (about 16), side muscle removed

3 tablespoons olive oil

¼ cup (¾ oz/20 g) Ras El Hanout (page 217)

2 cups (16 fl oz/500 ml) Preserved Lemon Yogurt (page 226)

1 teaspoon sweet paprika, preferably smoked

SCALLOPS WITH RAS EL HANOUT & PRESERVED LEMON YOGURT

1 Heat the grill for high direct heat (about 450°F/230°C).

2 Coat the scallops evenly with the oil and then dust them all over with the ras el hanout. Let stand while the grill heats.

3 Brush the grill grate and coat with oil. Put the scallops on the grate and cook, turning once, until nicely browned and springy to the touch but still soft in the center, or until an instant-read thermometer inserted into the center of a scallop registers about 130°F (54°C), 3–4 minutes per side.

4 Spread the yogurt on individual plates and top with the scallops. Dust with the paprika.

 **EXTRA CREDIT**

To keep a scallop from toughening as it cooks, peel off and discard the gristly, half-moon–shaped muscle on its side.

If you're starting with whole scallops (lucky you!), shuck them and remove them from the shell. Or grill them on the half shell just like oysters. Follow the directions for shucking oysters on page 149 and discard the black stomach sac, leaving only the white scallop flesh and pink coral (roe).

For a beautiful presentation, cook the scallops on a salt block (see page 31 for directions) and bring the hot salt block to the table for serving.

Grilled Scallops with Citrus Rub and Fines Herbes Butter: Replace the Ras El Hanout with ⅓ cup (1 oz/30 g) Citrus Rub (page 215) and the Preserved Lemon Yogurt with ½ cup (4 oz/125 g) Fines Herbes Butter, melted (page 226), drizzling the butter over the grilled scallops.

SHRIMP COUNTS

Shrimp are sold by the number of them in 1 pound (500 g). The lower the count, the larger the shrimp. Consumers like to buy food by size, so shrimp are also sold by retail names such as jumbo and small. Here's the cheat sheet for both labels.

COUNT PER POUND	RETAIL NAME
Under 10 (U10)	Extra Colossal
10/15 (U15)	Colossal
16/20 (U20)	Extra Jumbo
21/25 (U25)	Jumbo
26/30 (U30)	Extra Large
36/40 (U40)	Medium Large
41/50 (U50)	Medium
51/60 (U60)	Small
61/70 (U70)	Extra Small (Titi)

It sounds Indian, but *vadouvan* is actually a French take on curry with a base of caramelized onions and shallots. Mixed with butter and a simple shrimp stock, it makes a fantastic sauce for grilled shrimp. Cucumber *raita* brightens the deep flavors.

MAKES 6 SERVINGS

CUCUMBER RAITA

¾ cup (6 oz/185 g) plain yogurt

½ English cucumber, peeled, seeded, and shredded

3 tablespoons chopped fresh mint

½ teaspoon sea salt

¼ teaspoon ground cumin

SHRIMP & VADOUVAN

2 lb (1 kg) extra-large shrimp (26–30 count)

2 lemons

½ cup (4 fl oz/125 ml) canola oil or other mild vegetable oil

4 cloves garlic, crushed or pressed

1 tablespoon peeled and grated fresh ginger

¼ cup (⅓ oz/10 g) chopped fresh cilantro

2 teaspoons fine sea salt

½ teaspoon freshly ground pepper

4 tablespoons (2 oz/60 g) unsalted butter

¾ cup (5 oz/155 g) Vadouvan (page 217)

2 cups (14 oz/440 g) hot cooked basmati rice

Chopped fresh cilantro for garnish

VADOUVAN GRILLED SHRIMP

1 To make the raita, in a serving bowl, combine the yogurt, cucumber, mint, salt, and cumin and stir well. Cover and refrigerate until ready to serve.

2 To prepare the shrimp, peel and devein the shrimp and set aside. Place the shells in a saucepan, add water to barely cover the shells (about 3 cups/24 fl oz/750 ml), place over low heat, and simmer gently to make a stock, about 1 hour.

3 Grate the zest and squeeze the juice from the lemons into a large zippered plastic bag. Add the oil, garlic, ginger, cilantro, 1 teaspoon of the salt, and the pepper and stir well. Add the shrimp, press out the air, seal, and let marinate at room temperature while the shrimp stock simmers.

4 Heat the grill for medium-high direct heat (about 400°F/200°C).

5 While the grill heats, strain the stock through a fine-mesh sieve, discard the solids, and return the liquid to the pan. You should have about 1 cup (8 fl oz/250 ml). Stir in the butter, vadouvan, and the remaining 1 teaspoon salt and heat over low heat just until heated through to make a sauce.

6 Remove the shrimp from the marinade and, if necessary to prevent the shrimp from falling through the bars of the grill grate, thread the shrimp onto metal skewers. Brush the grill grate and coat with oil. Put the shrimp on the grate and cook, turning once, until firm and lightly browned, 2–3 minutes per side.

7 Serve the grilled shrimp with the rice, sauce, and raita. Garnish with the cilantro.

 **EXTRA CREDIT**

Save the lemon rinds from the shrimp marinade and add them to the simmering shrimp stock for more flavor.

You can make the vadouvan weeks or even months ahead of time. But if you make it the same day as everything else, use the pan in which you made it to simmer the shrimp stock for even more flavor.

SQUID & OCTOPUS

Squid and octopuses are mollusks in the same family as scallops, clams, and oysters. But these cephalopods have internalized their shells in the form of long, thin translucent "quills" or "pens." They also consist of tougher meat and more connective tissue than their shelled cousins. To grill squid and octopus without making them rubbery, it helps to buy them small and use high heat.

HOW DO YOU PREP SQUID & OCTOPUS FOR GRILLING?

Start with small squid. The largest invertebrates on earth, squid can grow to weigh nearly a ton (900 kg). But they are tough, and your grill isn't that big. Look for small squid that weigh 2 to 3 ounces (60 to 90 g) and are 4 to 5 inches (10 to 13 cm) long. If you buy frozen squid (or a frozeon octopus), you'll get a jump on tenderness because the freeze-thaw process stretches the cell walls, making the shellfish easier to chew. Both frozen and fresh squid are sold cleaned, but you can also clean fresh squid yourself (see facing page). Once cleaned, you can cook the squid whole (bodies and tentacles), or you can separate the tentacles from the bodies. Squid bodies can be stuffed or simply marinated, grilled, and cut into rings. You can also cut the bodies lengthwise to create a large, flat rectangle of squid that will cook in about a minute on each side. As for the tentacles, they can be marinated or rubbed with seasoning and then grilled whole. It helps to skewer small tentacles to keep them from falling into the fire as they curl up during cooking.

Simmer an octopus first. Octopus flesh is so tough that it's best to tenderize it before grilling. A frozen octopus, like frozen squid, will be slightly more tender than fresh. Regardless, we like to simmer the octopus gently until it is tender enough for a knife to enter the thickest part of the flesh easily, about 1 hour. You can simmer it up to 2 days ahead and keep it refrigerated until it is time to grill. Separate the head and tentacles and then grill and serve both portions if you like. Most octopuses are sold cleaned and frozen, but if you are starting with a fresh octopus, see facing page for cleaning directions.

Oil it. Whether you are cooking an octopus or squid, pat the surface and then oil it all over. A dry, oily surface ensures quick browning, helping to prevent these shellfish from becoming rubbery on the grill.

WHAT'S THE BEST WAY TO GRILL SQUID & OCTOPUS?

Use high direct heat. On the grill, it's best to cook raw squid and simmered octopus over the highest possible heat for the shortest possible time. Otherwise, the muscle fibers and connective tissue will toughen. You're really just searing the surface to create a layer of browned grill flavor. As soon as they are seared and firm, they will be done. The internal temperature should be about 130°F (54°C). If it reaches 140°F (60°C), the connective tissue will start to shrink and contract, making the squid or octopus tough and chewy. On the grill, this toughness can be transformed only by long, slow grill braising in a pan of liquid to dissolve the tough connective tissue into creamy-tasting gelatin.

Weight them down. To help squid and octopus grill quickly and evenly, put a heavy weight, such as a cast-iron pan, on the shellfish as it cooks. This technique also creates exceptional grill marks.

"Cook it fast or slow but nowhere in between." That's the mantra for preparing octopus that's tender and not rubbery. This recipe takes both approaches. First, we slowly braise it in olive oil and sparkling mineral water to infuse the octopus with briny minerals, then we quickly sear it on the grill for a kiss of char.

MAKES 4 SERVINGS

1 lb (500 g) cleaned baby octopus

1 cup (8 fl oz/250 ml) plus 2 tablespoons peanut oil or mild vegetable oil

½ cup (4 fl oz/125 ml) sparkling mineral water

1 small clove garlic, smashed

1 thick slice bacon, cooked and crumbled

1 Thai chile or small jalapeño chile, seeded and minced

1 teaspoon minced lemongrass

1 small green onion, finely chopped

1 teaspoon grated fresh ginger

2 tablespoons chopped fresh cilantro and/or mint

Juice of 1 lime

2 teaspoons fish sauce

1 teaspoon Asian sesame oil

4 large leaves romaine lettuce

Sriracha sauce, for garnish

VIETNAMESE-STYLE OCTOPUS LETTUCE WRAPS

1 Place the octopus head and tentacles in a pot just big enough to fit them. Add 1 cup of the oil, the sparkling water, and garlic. Bring the liquid to 180°F (82°C) over medium-high heat, and then reduce the heat to maintain a steady 180°F (82°C) temperature. Braise the octopus uncovered at 180°F (82°C) until it is tender, 1–1½ hours. Remove the pan from the heat and let the octopus cool in the liquid (once cooled it can be refrigerated for up to 1 day).

2 Heat the grill for medium-high direct heat (about 400°F/200°C). Brush the grill grate and coat with oil. Put the octopus on the grate and cook, turning once, until nicely grill marked, about 3 minutes per side. For more even cooking and great grill marks, put a heavy cast-iron pan on the octopus as it grills.

3 Transfer the octopus to a cutting board and chop it into bite-size pieces. Toss it in a bowl with the bacon, chile, lemongrass, green onion, ginger, herbs, lime juice, fish sauce, sesame oil, and the remaining 2 tablespoons peanut oil. Divide among the lettuce leaves, garnish with the Sriracha, and roll up.

HOW TO CLEAN AN OCTOPUS

Insert your fingers into the body (head) and turn it inside out. Scrape away the ink sac and reserve it for making dark "squid ink" sauces. Discard all of the innards and rinse the body well. Turn the body right side out and remove the eyes and black mouth (beak) where the tentacles meet the body. Scrub the tentacles well with coarse salt, rinse, and repeat until the tentacles are clean.

HOW TO CLEAN SQUID

Pull away the head and tentacles from the hood (tube-like body). Reach into the body and pull out the innards and plastic-like quill, taking care not to puncture the pearly ink sac. Cut off the tentacles just above the eyes and discard the head. Squeeze the base of the tentacles to force out the hard "beak," and rinse the tentacles and body thoroughly. Using the back of a paring knife, pull and scrape off the gray membrane from the body. Cut off and discard the two small wings from the body. Chill the squid in ice water until ready to use.

If the only shellfish you've ever grilled is shrimp, give squid a try. It's supereasy. Just marinate the squid in olive oil and lemon juice and give them a quick sear on a hot grill. Topping the squid with a cast-iron pan helps to keep them in place and creates great grill marks. We like to pair grilled squid with the Spanish flavors of chorizo sausage and thick roasted red pepper sauce over plenty of fresh, peppery arugula.

MAKES 4 SERVINGS

1½ lb (750 g) cleaned small whole squid bodies with tentacles attached

5 tablespoons (2½ fl oz/ 75 ml) extra-virgin olive oil

½ teaspoon fine sea salt

¼ teaspoon freshly ground pepper

½ small clove garlic, pressed or finely minced

1 tablespoon fresh lemon juice

3 cups (3 oz/90 g) small arugula leaves

4–6 oz (125–185 g) cured Spanish chorizo sausages, halved lengthwise

¾ cup (6 fl oz/180 ml) Romesco (page 228)

GRILLED SQUID WITH CHORIZO & ROMESCO

1 Cut the tips off of the squid bodies to allow steam to escape. In a bowl, toss the squid with 2 tablespoons of the oil, ¼ teaspoon of the salt, and ⅛ teaspoon of the pepper. Let stand at room temperature.

2 For the salad, in a small bowl, whisk together the garlic, lemon juice, and the remaining 3 tablespoons oil, ¼ teaspoon salt, and ⅛ teaspoon pepper. Save the arugula until just before serving.

3 Heat the grill for medium-high direct heat (about 425°F/220°C). Brush the grill grate and coat with oil. Put the squid and chorizo on the grate and cook, turning once, until nicely grill marked, about 2 minutes per side. For more even cooking and great grill marks, put a heavy cast-iron pan on the squid as they grill.

4 Cut the grilled squid bodies into rings and leave the tentacles whole. Cut the sausages into half-moons about ¼ inch (6 mm) thick.

5 Toss the arugula with the dressing and divide the arugula salad among individual plates. Top each salad portion with the grilled squid, chorizo, and a large dollop of Romesco.

 **EXTRA CREDIT**

Grilled Squid with Soppressata and Spicy Marinara Sauce: Replace the chorizo with soppressata and the Romesco with 2 cups (16 fl oz/500 ml) Spicy Marinara Sauce (page 220). Skip the arugula salad and spoon the sauce onto the plates and then top with the squid and soppressata.

CLAMS & OYSTERS

Bivalve mollusks are among the easiest shellfish to grill. Just cook them in the shell over a hot fire and they will steam in their own juices until the shells open. This method works best for clams and mussels. For oysters, it's best to shuck them first and grill them on the half shell to prevent overcooking.

WHAT TYPE OF CLAMS WORK BEST ON THE GRILL?

Look for hard-shell clams. Soft-shell clams like steamers and razor clams are nearly impossible to rid of sand. Hard-shell varieties like cherrystones and littlenecks keep out the sand much better. For the same reason, it pays to buy farmed (cultured) mussels, which are grown on ropes and will be free of grit. Clams, mussels, and oysters should all be tightly closed when you buy them and can be refrigerated on ice for a day or two before grilling.

HOW DO YOU PREP BIVALVES FOR GRILLING?

Scrub the shells clean. Clams, mussels, and oysters need firm scrubbing to clean the shells of grit. For the freshest taste, remove the beards from mussels just before cooking by snipping the black hairs from the shell with kitchen scissors.

Shuck oysters. You can cook oysters in the shell on the grill just as you do clams and mussels, but they tend to overcook before the shells open. We prefer to shuck oysters and grill them in the half shell.

WHAT'S THE BEST WAY TO GRILL BIVALVES?

Toss them right over the fire. Put whole clams and mussels in the shell directly over medium-high heat. When the shells open, they are done. Remove each clam or mussel from the grill as it opens (larger, older ones may take a bit longer) and handle them carefully with tongs to retain the briny juices. Add them to a pan of sauce or top each with a spoonful of sauce. Discard any that fail to open.

Grill them in a pan. In general, we eschew grill pans and trays. The fewer things between the fire and the food, the better. But the shells of bivalves already shield them from the fire, so we use pans occasionally for grilling this type of shellfish. Put whole clams and mussels in cast-iron pans or large aluminum foil pans directly over medium-high heat. Add a splash of wine and some butter if you like. You'll retain a bit more of the briny shellfish liquor if the bivalves open up in a pan.

Use medium heat for oysters. To prevent overcooking, grill oysters on the half shell over medium heat, drizzling them with butter, lemon juice, or other liquid as they cook. They are done when the shells char and the oysters are hot (about 130°F/54°C internal temperature), 8 to 10 minutes. Incidentally, you can grill scallops on the half shell using the same method.

BIVALVE	SHELL CHARACTERISTICS
Butter Clams	3–5 inches (7.5–13 cm)
Cherrystone Clams	2–3 inches (5–7.5 cm)
Littleneck Clams	1–2 inches (2.5–5 cm)
Manila Clams	3–4 inches (7.5–10 cm)
Ocean Quahog Clams	2–3 inches (5–7.5 cm)
Pismo Clams	5–7 inches (13–18 cm)
Surf or Bar Clams	4–8 inches (10–20 cm)
Blue Mussels	2–3 inches (5–7.5 cm), blue-black
New Zealand Mussels	3–4 inches (7.5–10 cm), green
Prince Edward Island Mussels	2 inches (5 cm), beardless
Atlantic or Bluepoint Mussels	2–4 inches (5–10 cm), gray-brown
European or Belon Mussels	1½–3 inches (4–7.5 cm); round and flat
Olympia Mussels	1–1½ inches (2.5–4 cm)
Pacific Japanese (farmed) Mussels	6 inches (15 cm), gray-brown

GRILLED OYSTERS WITH FINES HERBES BUTTER

MAKES 6 FIRST-COURSE SERVINGS

24 large oysters, shucked (see below)
1 cup (8 oz/250 g) Fines Herbes Butter
(page 226), melted
6 lemon wedges

Heat the grill for medium direct heat
(about 375°F/190°C). Brush the grill
grate and coat with oil.

Place the oysters directly on the grate and
top each oyster with about 1 teaspoon
of the butter. Grill until the oyster shells
char on the edges, 8–10 minutes.

Transfer the oysters to a platter and
drizzle another 1 teaspoon butter over
each oyster. Serve hot with the lemon
wedges for squeezing.

SHUCKING OYSTERS

Freeze the oysters for 20 minutes to numb
them and make them easier to shuck.
Working with 1 oyster at a time, press
a sturdy, dull knife between the hinged
end of the shell to pop the top and bottom
shells apart. Run the knife along the
inside of the top (flatter) shell to cut the
meat from the shell and then lift off the
top shell, holding the bottom oyster shell
level to retain its liquor (juices). Run the
knife under the oyster to detach it from the
bottom (rounded) shell, but leave the oyster
nestled in the liquor in the shell. Pick out
any bits of shell. The liquor should be clear.
If it's cloudy, the oyster is older, has begun
to break down, and should be discarded.

This method couldn't be easier for cooks new to grilling shellfish. Just toss the whole clams right on the grill. You could put them in an aluminum foil pan if you want to retain every last drop of clam juice, but right on the grill is simpler. Serve with crusty bread to soak up the sauce and juices.

MAKES 4 FIRST-COURSE SERVINGS

1 cup (8 fl oz/250 ml) Chimichurri (page 228)

24 clams (about 2 lb/1 kg), scrubbed clean

CHIMICHURRI CLAMS ON THE GRILL

1 Have the chimichurri and a platter or plates ready. If you have made the chimichurri in advance, bring it back to room temperature.

2 Heat the grill for medium-high direct heat (about 450°F/230°C). Brush the grill grate. Toss the clams onto the grate and grill until the shells pop open, 8–10 minutes. As they open, use tongs to carefully transfer the clams to the platter or plates, retaining as much clam juice as possible.

3 Drizzle or spoon some chimichurri into each clam, drizzle the rest around the platter or plates, and serve.

 EXTRA CREDIT

Grill a few spicy sausage links alongside the clams. Slice and serve with the saucy clams.

To capture more of the clam juices, grill the clams in a couple of large aluminum foil pans.

Grilled Mussels Marinara: Substitute 2 lb (1 kg) mussels, scrubbed clean and beards removed, for the clams.

They should open a bit more quickly, after 4–6 minutes on the grill. Transfer to a large bowl and toss gently with 2 cups (16 fl oz/500 ml) Marinara Sauce with Red Wine (page 220). Serve with crusty bread or spaghetti.

LOBSTERS

Just a brief time on the grill helps to caramelize sweet lobster meat, adding deep, roasty flavors. You can grill whole lobster, lobster tail, or lobster's smaller freshwater cousins, crayfish. Either way, it's best to leave these crustaceans in the shell.

WHAT TYPE OF LOBSTER IS BEST FOR GRILLING?

Whole Maine lobsters. They have a large amount of sweet, tender meat in their claws and knuckles.

Spiny lobster tails. Most lobster tails sold in the United States come from spiny lobsters (aka rock lobsters), which have large tails and a distinctive spotted pattern on the shell. This clawless lobster grows in warmer waters, and the meat tastes slightly less tender and sweet than a Maine lobster.

Buy them live. Look for feisty lobsters with a clean scent and no ammonia odor. Cook live lobsters the same day you buy them. Or, refrigerate them for up to 1 day in a box with some damp newspaper.

Buy them under 2 pounds (1 kg). Each year, lobsters molt, or shed their shells, in order to grow new, larger shells. These crustaceans can grow to 40 pounds (18 kg), but large lobsters are less tender, cook unevenly, and can be difficult to handle. For the grill, stick with 1- to 2-pound (500-g to 1-kg) lobsters. In the summer months, lobster shells tend to be somewhat soft because molting occurs in the spring and the new shells have not fully hardened. Soft-shell lobsters yield about one-third less meat by weight than hard-shell lobsters because they retain more water. But the meat of soft-shell lobsters is a bit sweeter. These summertime lobsters are also easier to crack and pick than hard-shell lobsters. Both types work well on the grill.

HOW DO YOU PREP LOBSTERS FOR GRILLING?

Split whole lobsters in half. Lobsters must be split for the meat to pick up any flavor from the grill. You can kill a lobster by boiling it first, but we prefer to cook whole lobsters completely on the grill for maximum grill flavor. It's best to split a live lobster in half lengthwise right through the head for a quick and efficient kill (see facing page for details) and then put the lobster on the grill immediately. As soon as a lobster (or any crustacean) is killed, protein-digesting enzymes near the head begin to break down the meat. The enzymes can cause the meat to become unpleasantly mushy in as little as an hour.

Butterfly lobster tails. For the best presentation, cut down to the bottom of the shell but not through it so the tail can be splayed open, exposing the meat to the grill but retaining the shell for its flavor, moisture, and good looks.

Oil the meat. To keep lean lobster meat from sticking to the grill, coat the meat with oil or an oil-based paste before grilling. Better yet, go with butter, preferably clarified butter to prevent burning.

WHAT'S THE BEST WAY TO GRILL LOBSTERS?

Quickly. Whenever the internal temperature of lobster (and other crustaceans like shrimp, crab, and crayfish) stays between 130° and 140°F (54° and 60°C) for an extended time, protein-digesting enzymes in the muscles turn the meat from mouthwatering to mushy. Spending too much time over the dry heat of the grill can also dry out the tender meat. We like to set up the grill for indirect medium heat and sear the meat over the hot side for a few minutes. Then we flip the lobster, meat side up, and move it to the unheated side of the grill to finish cooking in its juices, protected by the shell.

Baste the shells with fat. Basting lobster not only keeps the meat moist but also extracts fat-soluble flavor compounds from the shell that enhance the flavor of the meat. Baste whole lobsters with oil or clarified butter, or use an oil-based sauce like pesto or Moroccan chermoula (facing page) to help draw more flavor from the shell.

Chermoula is a spicy Moroccan herb sauce that's often served with fish and is perfect on grilled lobster. This recipe calls for two lobsters, but you can double the recipe to serve four as a main course. Just make sure you have space for eight lobster halves on the cool side of your grill after searing them over the hot side.

LOBSTER WITH CHERMOULA

MAKES 4 APPETIZER SERVINGS

1 cup (1 oz/30 g) packed fresh cilantro leaves and small stems

½ cup (½ oz/15 g) packed fresh flat-leaf parsley leaves and small stems

4 cloves garlic

½ cup (4 fl oz/125 ml) olive oil

Juice of 1 lemon

1 teaspoon ground cumin

1 teaspoon smoked paprika

½ teaspoon salt

¼ teaspoon cayenne pepper

2 live lobsters, about 1 lb (500 g) each

1 To make the chermoula, bring a pot of water to a boil. Ready a large bowl of ice water. Add the cilantro and parsley to the boiling water and blanch until bright green, about 30 seconds. Using a slotted spoon, scoop the herbs out of the boiling water and transfer them to the ice water to stop the cooking. When the herbs have cooled, drain them and transfer them to a food processor. Add the garlic, oil, lemon juice, cumin, paprika, salt, and cayenne and process until a coarse puree forms. Use immediately, or transfer to an airtight container and refrigerate for up to 1 week. Set aside ½ cup (4 fl oz/125 ml) of the chermoula for serving.

2 Heat the grill for medium indirect heat (about 325°F/165°C). Split the lobsters in half, discarding the sand sac, tomalley, and roe sac (if present; see below for more details). Collect the lobster juices and mix them into the remaining chermoula. Brush a few tablespoons of the mixture over the cut sides of the lobsters. Spoon some into the cracked claws, as well.

3 Brush the grill grate and coat with oil. Put the lobsters, cut side down, directly over the fire and cook until just starting to brown on the edges, 3–4 minutes. Flip the lobsters over and move them away from the fire. Brush them with the remaining chermoula–lobster juice mixture. Cover the grill and cool until the lobster meat just turns opaque and an instant-read thermometer inserted into the center of the meat registers 140°F (60°C), 8–10 minutes. Transfer to a platter and serve with chermoula.

SPLITTING A LOBSTER

Refrigerate the lobster for 30 minutes to help sedate it. Hold the lobster by its back shell and place it on its belly on a cutting board with a groove or on a rimmed baking sheet. Uncurl the tail and lay it out flat. Insert a sharp knife just behind the head and cut the shell of the thorax (its back) in half lengthwise through the head, killing the lobster. Turn the lobster onto its back and insert the knife into the abdomen right where the tail meets the thorax, with the edge of the blade facing the head. In one motion, bring the knife down the center line of the body, splitting the front end of the lobster in half. Now reverse direction and split the back end the same way. Separate the halves by pressing lightly on them. Remove and discard the sand sac from behind the head. Remove the light green tomalley from the body cavity and, if present, the long sac of dark green roe. Crack the claws by whacking them across the crest of their bulge with the back of a heavy knife. Collect the lobster juices to flavor a sauce.

8

VEGETABLES

156 LESSON 1: ROOTS

157 COAL-BAKED SWEET POTATOES WITH BACON BOURBON BUTTER

158 HONEY-SMOKED BEETS

160 LESSON 2: STEMS

161 GRILLED ASPARAGUS WITH LEMON OIL

162 GRILL-WOKED BROCCOLI & CAULIFLOWER FLORETS WITH TOM KHA GAI GLAZE

164 GRILLED FENNEL BASTED WITH ROSEMARY ABSINTHE

165 GRILLED COLESLAW

166 LESSON 3: LEAVES

167 GRILL-CARAMELIZED ONIONS

168 GRILLED ROMAINE SALAD WITH ANCHOVY-MUSTARD VINAIGRETTE

171 ROASTED SESAME BRUSSELS SPROUTS

172 LESSON 4: SOFT VEGETABLES

173 GRILLED ZUCCHINI WITH CAPERS, PINE NUTS & ORANGE VINAIGRETTE

174 GRILLED EGGPLANT WITH TAHINI SAUCE & POMEGRANATE SEEDS

176 LESSON 5: MUSHROOMS

177 LESSON 6: CORN

179 GRILLED SHIITAKES WITH SHICHIMI TOGARASHI

180 OAXACAN GRILLED CORN

ROOTS

Roots are hard. That's because they have a botanical job to do. A root holds its plant in the ground, so it needs to be strong and rigid. Roots are built of hard fibers, and those fibers pose some challenges for grilling. Hard plant fibers need a long time and a lot of moisture to become tender, and the dry intense heat of an open fire isn't the best way to accomplish the task. But several techniques can help.

Regardless of the type of root being grilled—beet, carrot, parsnip, potato, turnip, or yam—the first thing you have to do is determine how tough the root is. As a plant matures, its root gets bigger and harder. It also gets packed full with nutrients like sugar, starch, minerals, and vitamins. The best way to determine the characteristics of a particular root vegetable is to judge by size. Small roots tend to be mild and tender, medium-size specimens are sweet and crunchy, and large roots are tough and flavorful. Potatoes and yams are an exception because they are not technically roots. Their hardness does not increase with size.

Small roots are usually tender enough to be grilled without any special preparation. Medium-size roots will need some help to soften their tough fibers before or during grilling. For example, you can blanch carrots briefly before grilling to soften the connections between their fibers, or you can slowly grill medium-size roots over low indirect heat near a water pan to create steam. Large roots are not good candidates for grilling whole, though they can be cut into smaller pieces and grilled as you would a medium-size root.

METHODS & TIMING FOR GRILLING ROOT VEGETABLES

ROOT	PREPARATION	GRILLING
Beets, small	Whole, oiled	Indirect, 10–15 min
	Sliced, oiled, seasoned	Direct, 10 min, turned often
Beets, medium	Sliced or quartered, oiled, seasoned	Indirect, 15 min
	Whole, oiled	Indirect, 1 hour
Beets, large	Sliced, oiled, seasoned	Indirect, 15–20 min
Carrots, baby or thin	Whole, oiled, seasoned	Direct, 8–10 min
Carrots, medium	Sliced lengthwise, oiled, seasoned	Direct, 8–10 min, turned often
Jerusalem artichokes	Halved, oiled, seasoned	Direct, 10–15 min
Parsnips, medium	Sliced lengthwise, oiled, seasoned	Direct, 8–10 min
Potatoes, round	Sliced, oiled, seasoned	Direct, 15–20 min
Potatoes, russet	Whole, oiled	Indirect, 60–80 min
Turnips, medium	Sliced or quartered, oiled, seasoned	Indirect, 15–20 min
Yams	Whole, oiled	Indirect, 1 hour

Any food that can be eaten out of its skin makes a good candidate for grilling directly in the coals of a charcoal or wood fire. The skin is usually left uneaten anyway, so who cares if it gets charred? Plus, the close proximity to the coals infuses the food with a smoky flavor. The toppings are up to you, but we like to pair sweet potatoes with a rich combo of honey, bacon, and bourbon.

MAKES 6 SERVINGS

4 orange-fleshed sweet potatoes, 3–3½ lb (1.5–1.75 kg) total weight

⅓ cup (3 oz/90 g) Bacon Bourbon Butter (page 227)

COAL-BAKED SWEET POTATOES WITH BACON BOURBON BUTTER

1 Heat a charcoal grill for medium-high direct heat (400°–450°F/200°–230°C). You will need an even bed of ash-covered red-hot coals. Leave the grill grate off the grill so the coals are accessible.

2 Nestle the sweet potatoes directly in the coals, raking extra coals around each sweet potato. Cook, turning once or twice, until a skewer slides easily in and out of the center of a sweet potato, about 45 minutes.

3 When the sweet potatoes are done, brush off any loose ash and then, using tongs, transfer to individual plates or a platter. Let cool for a few minutes. Cut each sweet potato in half lengthwise and mash the flesh of each half with a fork. Drizzle evenly with the bacon butter. Invite diners to scoop the sweet potatoes from the jackets.

 EXTRA CREDIT

To cook these sweet potatoes on a gas grill, cook the sweet potatoes directly over medium-high heat, turning them a few times, until blackened all over, 45–55 minutes. The grill should be covered.

The same coal-roasting technique is delicious for beets. Use medium size, and cook 15–20 minutes longer.

Change your topping:

- Your favorite BBQ spice blend mixed with butter and a squeeze of tomato paste

- A pile of Grill-Caramelized Onions (page 167) and slices of jalapeño chile.

- Green Chile Queso (page 223)

Beets are fantastic grilled. Like most root vegetables, beets are high in sugar, which melts and caramelizes on the grill and creates complex flavors. We like to grill these roots whole via indirect heat, then slice them, fan out the slices, and drizzle on a sauce.

4 large handfuls wood chips or chunks

4 large beets, about 1 lb (500 g) without greens, hairy roots trimmed and scrubbed but not peeled

2 tablespoons canola oil or other mild vegetable oil

½ teaspoon smoked salt

¼ teaspoon freshly ground black pepper

¼ cup (3 oz/90 g) honey

2 tablespoons mild hot-pepper sauce such as Frank's RedHot

2 tablespoons chopped fresh flat-leaf parsley, or 1 tablespoon coarsely chopped fresh rosemary

HONEY-SMOKED BEETS

1 Heat the grill for medium-high indirect heat (350°–400°F/180°–200°C). Wrap the wood chips in 2 perforated aluminum foil packets and place on the hot coals, or place 2 handfuls of wood chunks directly on the coals. If using a gas grill, wrap the chips in 2 perforated foil packets, and put one packet directly over one of the gas burners under the cooking grate. Or if your grill has a smoker box, use it.

2 Brush the grill grate and coat with oil. Prick the scrubbed beets all over with a fork and rub with the oil. Put the beets on the grate away from the fire, cover the grill, and cook until tender, 40–50 minutes. A skewer should slide very easily in and out of the center of a beet. If your grill has a temperature gauge, it should stay around 375°F (190°C). When the wood stops smoking, about halfway through the cooking, add the remaining foil packet of chips or handfuls of chunks.

3 Transfer the beets to a cutting board and let cool for a few minutes. Peel the beets and then slice them crosswise. Fan out the slices on individual plates or a platter. Season with the salt and pepper.

4 In a small bowl, mix together the honey and hot sauce and then drizzle over the beets. Sprinkle with the parsley.

 **EXTRA CREDIT**

Horseradish Honey: Substitute prepared horseradish for the hot-pepper sauce.

Habanero Orange Honey: Substitute 1 tablespoon fresh orange juice and ¼ teaspoon ground habanero chile for the hot-pepper sauce.

Masala Honey: Warm 1 teaspoon curry powder or garam masala in 1 tablespoon unsalted butter and use in place of the hot-pepper sauce.

Buy beets with the leaves attached for the best flavor. Remove the leaves for this recipe, but don't throw them out! Cut the stems and leaves into 2-inch (5-cm) lengths and sauté them with some garlic, fresh ginger, soy sauce, and a bit of Asian sesame oil for a delicious side dish to an Asian meal.

LESSON 2

STEMS

Stems contain tough, fibrous veins through which nutrients move up to the leaves, fruits, and flowers, and sugars manufactured in the leaves descend back down to the roots for storage. While liquid is moving through the veins, stems have no problem maintaining rigidity, but once they are harvested, they quickly dehydrate and go limp. That makes grilling most stem vegetables easy: expose them to enough heat to steam away some of their moisture and they immediately become tender.

Grilling mature stems like celery and fennel that have pretty thick veins requires a bit of a balance. You need to give the vegetable enough time over heat to soften its fibers without completely dehydrating it. For that reason, it's helpful to grill them by slicing the whole head lengthwise, leaving the ribs attached at the bottom root end, and then basting the slices as they grill to keep replenishing moisture until the tough fibers soften.

It's easier to prep young stems like asparagus for grilling. Trim any hard bottoms or tough stalk portions (see Extra Credit, facing page) and let the direct heat of the grill do its work. Young asparagus grill best. You can tell that asparagus spears are young and tender by looking at their buds, which should be tightly closed. Even young asparagus will be fibrous at their wider ends, however.

Broccoli and cauliflower contain both stem and flower bud. As with asparagus, you need to get rid of the tougher end of the stalk. Simply trim the stems just below the point where the heads join the stalks, creating miniature bouquets or florets. Florets are best grilled on a grill screen or in a grill wok to keep them from falling through the grate.

This simple recipe is the best way we know to cook asparagus—more toothsome than boiling and way more flavorful than steaming. The asparagus spears are tossed with a fragrant oil both before and after grilling. Choose young, thin asparagus for grilling. Freshly harvested young asparagus is noticeably sweet (about 4 percent sugar) and tender and will grill in just minutes. As the stalks age, they become too fibrous to soften during grilling and the flavor changes from sweet to acrid.

MAKES 4–6 SERVINGS

¼ cup extra-virgin olive oil

Grated zest of 1 lemon

1 lb (500 g) asparagus
(40 to 45 thin spears),
tough bottoms
snapped off

½ teaspoon flake sea salt
such as Maldon

GRILLED ASPARAGUS WITH LEMON OIL

1 Heat the grill for medium-high direct heat (400°–450°F/200°–230°C).

2 In a small saucepan, warm the oil and lemon zest over very low heat until the oil is fragrant, about 10 minutes. Do not let the oil get too hot; it should stay lukewarm.

3 On a rimmed baking sheet or in a zippered plastic bag, toss the asparagus with 1 tablespoon of the lemon oil, coating the spears evenly.

4 Brush the grill grate and coat with oil. Lay the asparagus on the grate perpendicular to the bars, cover the grill, and cook the asparagus, rolling the spears once or twice with tongs, until deep green and charred in spots, about 5 minutes.

5 Transfer the asparagus to a platter, drizzle with the remaining lemon oil, and season with the salt.

 **EXTRA CREDIT**

Asparagus, the stalk of a member of the lily family, is unusual because it doesn't bear leaves. Small bracts (leaf-like plates that cover a flower bud) traverse the stalk, gathering at the tip in a pointed crown. These changes progress rapidly within the first 24 hours after harvest, so all commercially purchased asparagus have tough bases that must be trimmed before cooking (see following).

To trim asparagus, hold a spear with one end in each hand. Gradually bend the stalk. It will naturally snap where the stalk becomes tough. Discard the tough end. If the spears are very thick, peel them by laying each spear on a work surface and peeling with a vegetable peeler from the tip to the stem end.

Any fragrant-flavored oil—herb oil, garlic oil, spice oil—can be used in this recipe. Make these oils in the same way you make the lemon oil, using whole dried herbs, whole dried spices, or whole garlic cloves. The exact proportions are not important. Keep in mind, however, that less solid ingredients will need longer to infuse and more solid ingredients will infuse more quickly.

Tom kha gai, the classic chicken coconut soup from Thailand, is the inspiration for this stir-fry. Stir-frying in a grill wok is less active than stir-frying on the stove top, but the perforations in the pan will give you an authentic tasting char, similar to the prized "flavor of the wok" that is so difficult to achieve without a blazing-hot restaurant wok setup.

MAKES 4–6 SERVINGS

½ cup (4 fl oz/125 ml)
Vietnamese Dipping Sauce
(page 222)

1-inch (2.5-cm) piece fresh
ginger, peeled and finely
chopped

2 lemongrass stalks,
cut into 1-inch (2.5-cm)
lengths and crushed

1 cup (8 fl oz/250 ml)
canned coconut milk, can
well shaken before opening

3 cups (6 oz/185 g)
broccoli florets

3 cups (9 oz/270 g)
cauliflower florets

GRILL-WOKED BROCCOLI & CAULIFLOWER FLORETS WITH TOM KHA GAI GLAZE

1 Heat the grill for medium direct heat (350°–400°F/180°–200°C).

2 In a frying pan, combine the dipping sauce, ginger, lemongrass, and coconut milk over medium heat. Bring to a gentle boil and boil until the mixture is reduced by half and lightly thickened to a glaze consistency, about 5 minutes. Strain into a bowl and discard the ginger and lemongrass.

3 Put a grill wok on the grill grate and coat with oil. Put the florets in the wok, cover, and cook, turning and coating with the coconut glaze every 3 minutes, until browned and tender, about 8 minutes. If your grill has a temperature gauge it should stay around 375°F (190°C).

4 Transfer to a serving bowl and serve with any remaining glaze.

 **EXTRA CREDIT**

Grill woking can be done with any vegetable that can be stir-fried. The coconut glaze used with the cauliflower and broccoli is also delicious with green beans, asparagus, mushrooms, or thinly sliced sweet potatoes.

Several of the other glazes in this book can be used for grill woking. Try Ssam Jang (page 222), Chimichurri (page 228), or Spicy Korean Glaze (page 220).

Fennel (sometimes called anise) is a striking vegetable: a white-green broad bulb that tapers into slim celery-like stems, topped with dark green, feathery fronds. The bulb is the only part that is cooked. The stalks are fibrous and should be discarded. For this recipe, the bulb is sliced lengthwise into thick planks, leaving the root end intact so the ribs hold together. Fennel needs to be basted as it browns to help it tenderize. In this recipe, absinthe intensifies the vegetable's natural licorice-like flavor.

MAKES 4 SERVINGS

2 tablespoons extra-virgin olive oil

2 cloves garlic, minced

2 tablespoons coarsely chopped fresh rosemary

2 fennel bulbs, stems and leaves trimmed and root end intact, cut lengthwise into slices ½ inch (12 mm) thick

¼ teaspoon fine sea salt, preferably fleur de sel

¼ teaspoon freshly ground pepper

4 fresh rosemary sprigs, tied together with kitchen string to form a basting brush

¾ cup (6 fl oz/180 ml) absinthe

GRILLED FENNEL BASTED WITH ROSEMARY ABSINTHE

1 Heat the grill for medium indirect heat (300°–350°F/150°–180°C).

2 In a small bowl, combine the oil, garlic, and chopped rosemary and mix well. Coat the fennel slices evenly with the oil mixture. Season with the salt and pepper.

3 Brush the grill grate and coat with oil. Put the fennel on the grate away from the fire, cover the grill, and cook until browned and tender, about 20 minutes. As the fennel cooks, about every 5 minutes, turn the slices and use the rosemary brush to baste them with some of the absinthe. If your grill has a temperature gauge, it should stay around 350°F (180°C).

4 Transfer the fennel to a platter and serve.

 EXTRA CREDIT

Replace the 2 fennel bulbs with 1 large bunch celery, trimmed of leaves and cut lengthwise ½ inch thick. Use sweet or dry vermouth instead of absinthe.

To mitigate the licorice flavor, baste the fennel with a sweet Riesling or Gewürztraminer.

Any citrus is delicious with anise. Add the finely grated zest of an orange or lemon into the oil mixture.

In the summer, substituting mint for rosemary enhances the cooling effect of absinthe.

Coleslaw is boring, not so much because of how it is made but because it is always made the same way. Here, we turn your same old coleslaw on its head by giving it a turn over the fire. As with most leaf grilling, the change is so surprising that the ubiquitous salad is reborn. Instead of a crunchy refreshing foil to grilled meats, it turns into a smoky savory grilled condiment. Serve it with grilled fish or along with half a dozen other grilled vegetables for antipasto.

GRILLED COLESLAW

**MAKES 6 SERVINGS
(1 QT/1 L)**

½ head green cabbage, cut lengthwise into slices ¾ inch (2 cm) thick

½ head red cabbage, cut lengthwise into slices ¾ inch (2 cm) thick

2 carrots, peeled and cut lengthwise into slices ¼ inch (6 mm) thick

¼ pineapple, peeled, cored, and cut crosswise into slices ½ inch (12 mm) thick

¼ cup (2 fl oz/60 ml) plus 1½ tablespoons canola oil or other mild vegetable oil

3 tablespoons cider vinegar

1 tablespoon orange marmalade

1 teaspoon fine sea salt

½ teaspoon freshly ground pepper

1 Heat the grill for medium-high direct heat (425°–450°F/220°–230°C).

2 Brush the grill grate and coat with oil. Coat the cabbage, carrot, and pineapple slices with the 1½ tablespoons oil. Put all of the slices on the grate and cook, turning once, until grill marked and slightly softened, about 1 minute per side for cabbage and 4 minutes per side for the carrots and pineapple. Transfer everything to a cutting board and let cool for 10 minutes.

3 In a serving bowl, whisk together the remaining ¼ cup (2 fl oz/60 ml) oil, the vinegar, marmalade, salt, and pepper to make a dressing.

4 Cut the grilled vegetables and pineapple into julienne strips, making them as thin as possible. Add to the bowl holding the dressing and toss to coat evenly. Set aside for 10 minutes before serving. The coleslaw can be stored in an airtight container in the refrigerator for up to 5 days.

 **EXTRA CREDIT**

Radicchio Slaw: Replace the cabbage with 2 heads radicchio and 1 head napa cabbage, cut into wedges about ½ inch (12 mm) thick, and replace the carrots with 1 beet, peeled and cut into slices ½ inch (12 mm) thick.

If you like, replace the tangy sweet-and-sour dressing with a mayonnaise-based coleslaw dressing of your choice. Or try Sriracha Mayo (page 223) or Real Russian Dressing (page 222).

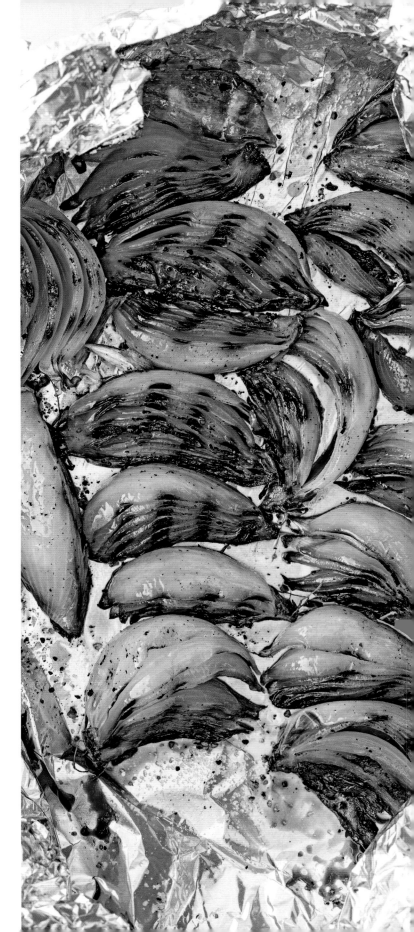

LEAVES

Leaves are filled with air. Expose them to heat and they quickly shrivel to nothing. The trick to grilling them is to keep them together long enough to end up with something edible. The easiest leaves to grill by far are alliums, members of a genus that includes leeks, green onions, bulb onions, and garlic.

ONIONS ARE LEAVES?

We know. It doesn't seem right. But if you think about leeks, which are cousins to onions, it begins to make sense. Unlike leeks and green onions, which are grown for both their leaves and the leaf base (the part that sits just underground), onions and garlic are grown exclusively for the bulbous swollen leaf base that stores energy for the beginning of the next growing season. This leaf base stores energy in the form of fructose sugars, which is why alliums have a delicious balance of sweetness and volatile aromatic molecules. That combo of pungency and sugar is the allure of grilled onions.

THERE IS STRENGTH IN NUMBERS

Individual leaves, like spinach and kale, cannot be grilled. They disintegrate when exposed to high fire. But a bunch of leaves in a head or bundled together take to the open fire quite nicely. That is the principle behind grilled romaine, radicchio, cabbage, and brussels sprouts. Romaine and radicchio are done shortly after hitting the grill, but tightly bunched cabbage heads and brussels sprouts can be cooked through over a direct fire.

To grill leaves, oil them generously, brown them directly over the fire, and if they can tolerate more heat, move them away from the flame to cook quickly to tenderness, which never takes much time. Grilled leaves go well with pungent dressings, including vinaigrettes, creamy-cheesy dressings, and sweet-and-sour glazes.

Even though this is an embarrassingly simple recipe, it is so delicious and so useful that we had to include it. While we normally prefer not to grill in aluminum foil packets, the foil is necessary to trap the onions flavorful juices and keep them moist. We use this preparation all the time for making onion toasts, topping burgers, as a condiment for grilled chicken, and as a stuffing for grilled fish. Feel free to double or triple the volume so that you have enough on hand for spur-of-the-moment grilling inspiration. They keep refrigerated for a week or two.

GRILL-CARAMELIZED ONIONS

MAKES ABOUT 1 CUP
(6½ OZ/200 G)

2 large sweet onions, about 3 lb (1.5 kg), cut into wedges ¼ inch (6 mm) thick

1 tablespoon olive oil

½ teaspoon salt

¼ teaspoon freshly ground pepper

½ teaspoon sugar

1 Heat the grill for high indirect heat (400°–450°F/200°–230°C).

2 Brush the grill grate and coat with oil. Coat the onion wedges with the oil. Put them on the grate directly over the fire and cook, turning once, until deeply grill marked, about 3 minutes per side.

3 Transfer the onion wedges to a large piece of aluminum foil and season with the salt, pepper, and sugar. Fold the foil over the onions, crimp and seal, and put the foil pouch on the grate away from the fire. Cook until tender, 15–20 minutes.

4 Unwrap and use immediately or let cool, transfer to an airtight container, and refrigerate until needed.

 EXTRA CREDIT

Add a splash of balsamic vinegar to the foil packet before sealing and finishing the grilling.

Any sweet onion, such as Vidalia, Maui, Walla Walla, or Sweet Texas 1015, can be used here.

Soy Grilled Shallots: Substitute 12 large shallots for the onions. Peel and cut them in half lengthwise. Use 1 tablespoon soy sauce in place of the salt.

Grill Roasted Garlic: Heat the grill as directed. Cut the pointed end from a head of garlic to expose most of the cloves. Place the head, cut-side up, on a square of foil and drizzle 1 tablespoon oil into the exposed

cloves. Wrap the garlic in the foil and place in the grill away from the fire. Roast until the cloves are very soft, 30–40 minutes. Cool 15 minutes, then unwrap, hold the entire head upside down and squeeze the roasted garlic from the papery skin. Makes about ¼ cup.

If you're multiplying the recipe, it is easier to keep control of the onion wedges by skewering several on a bamboo skewer. Soak the bamboo skewers in water for 30 minutes and drain. Push the skewer through the layers of onions to make sure the wedges will hold together on the grill. Wear grill gloves when turning the skewers.

Leaves are difficult to grill. On their own, they wilt and burn in seconds, but kept in a head, the outside chars slightly while the inner leaves remain juicy, taking on the flavors of smoke and fire quickly and completely. Grilled romaine is dramatically different from its raw counterpart. Instead of tasting like watery refreshment, the lettuce takes on a meaty corpulence that for romaine is a welcome change of pace.

MAKES 4 SERVINGS

1 clove garlic, smashed, peeled, and minced

6 anchovy fillets, minced

1 tablespoon brown mustard

1 large egg yolk

½ cup (4 fl oz/125 ml) plus 2 tablespoons extra-virgin olive oil

Juice of 1 lemon

Fine sea salt and freshly ground pepper

2 heads romaine lettuce, loose leaves removed and each head cut lengthwise into quarters

1 ounce (30 g) Parmigiano-Reggiano cheese, shredded

1 teaspoon flake sea salt such as Maldon

GRILLED ROMAINE SALAD WITH ANCHOVY-MUSTARD VINAIGRETTE

1 Heat the grill to medium indirect heat (300°–350°F/150°–180°C).

2 In a salad bowl, using the back of a fork, mash together the garlic and anchovy fillets into a paste. Whisk in the mustard and egg yolk and then whisk in ½ cup (4 fl oz/125 ml) of the oil a little at a time until a thick sauce forms. Stir in the lemon juice and season to taste with fine sea salt and pepper. Set aside.

3 Brush the grill grate and coat with oil. Coat the romaine quarters with the remaining 2 tablespoons oil. Put them on the grate directly over the fire and grill, turning once, just until grill marked, about 20 seconds per side. Using tongs, transfer the lettuce away from the fire. Paint with half of the vinaigrette, getting the dressing down in between the leaves; sprinkle with half of the cheese. Cover the grill and cook until the cheese just starts to melt and the ends of the lettuce wedges wilt, about 2 minutes.

4 Transfer the romaine to a platter. Dress with the remaining vinaigrette, a scattering of the remaining cheese, and a sprinkle of flake salt.

 EXTRA CREDIT

This is a recipe where the kind of salt you use can make a big difference. Dry, crunchy flake salts are our favorite, but you don't need to stop with Maldon. The sweet, oaky smoke of Halen Môn Gold smoked salt from Scotland is amazing; *sale dolce di Cervia* from Italy gives a lively crunchiness; and deep, dark alder smoked salt from the Pacific Northwest intensifies the flavor of the grill that is at the heart of this preparation.

For a more assertive vegetable and a more dynamic color contrast, substitute a large head of radicchio for one of the romaine heads.

Now that you know the trick to grilling leafy vegetables is to leave them as heads, grilling brussels sprouts should be a no-brainer. These diminutive cabbage heads (they're actually cabbage sprouts) are perfect for grilling, as they brown on the outside and steam on the inside. Brussels sprouts have a tendency to develop distasteful sulfur compounds when cooked on the stove top. But the high-dry heat of the grill keeps the sulfur at bay.

MAKES 4 SERVINGS

16 brussels sprouts, stem end trimmed and halved lengthwise

2 tablespoons Asian sesame oil

½ cup Ssam Jang (page 222)

2 teaspoons sesame seeds, toasted

ROASTED SESAME BRUSSELS SPROUTS

1 Heat the grill for medium-high indirect heat (350°–400°F/180°–200°C). Put a grill screen on the grill grate directly over the fire.

2 In a bowl, toss the brussels sprouts with the sesame oil, coating them evenly. Oil the grill screen. Put the sprouts, cut side down, on the hot screen and cook until browned, about 3 minutes. Wearing grill gloves or using pot holders, move the screen away from the fire. Using tongs, turn the sprouts browned side up, brush with the ssam jang, cover the grill, and roast the sprouts until fork-tender, about 15 minutes.

3 Transfer the sprouts to a serving dish, sprinkle with the toasted sesame seeds, and serve right away.

 **EXTRA CREDIT**

Roast the brussels sprouts on skewers (soak bamboo skewers in water for 30 minutes before using), interspersing them with halved garlic cloves. You won't need the grill screen.

Brussels sprouts are now sometimes available on the stalk. To roast them right on their stalk, look for a stalk of about 2 lb (1 kg). You won't need the screen, and you will not grill directly over the fire. Place the stalk away from the fire, cover the grill, and cook, turning once halfway through, until the sprouts are fork-tender, about 20 minutes. Baste with the ssam jang twice, at the 10- and 15-minute marks.

SOFT VEGETABLES

These vegetables are botanically fruits because they contain the plant's seed. Their bright colors entice animals to eat the fruit and spread the seed, ensuring the plant's survival. Although they are fruits, their sugar content is low, so we treat them like vegetables. The most common soft vegetables for grilling are bell peppers, chiles, cucumbers, eggplants, green beans, okra, summer squashes, tomatillos, and tomatoes. You can also grill soft winter squashes like delicata and sweet dumpling. The benefit of grilling these botanical fruits directly over a hot fire is a complex, grill flavor you can't get from simple pan searing or oven roasting.

HOW DO YOU GRILL SOFT VEGETABLES?

Fire roast them whole. Fire roasting is another method of peeling bell peppers, chile peppers, and tomatoes. Simply grill them whole over a hot fire until the skin is blistered and charred all over. Cover peppers and let them steam, then peel the fire-roasted peppers or tomatoes and use the flesh in salads, sauces, and side dishes. The same can be done with a whole eggplant, scooping the soft flesh from its charred jacket to use in baba ghanoush or other pureed eggplant dishes. Even when peeled, the flesh of grill-roasted vegetables takes on a tantalizing smoky aroma and flavor.

Grill small vegetables whole. Small chiles, okra pods, and green beans can be oiled, seasoned, and grilled directly over a medium-high fire. If they threaten to fall into the flames, use a well-oiled grill screen, grill wok, or grill frying pan.

Halve juicy vegetables. To grill soft and juicy tomatoes, tomatillos, and cucumbers, cut them in half. Cut cucumbers in half lengthwise to expose the greatest surface area to the grill, and cut tomatoes and tomatillos in half. If the tomatoes are especially pulpy, remove and discard the seeds and gel to help them brown on the grill. Then oil, season, and grill over medium-high heat.

Slice other soft vegetables ¼ to ½ inch (6 to 12 mm) thick. Cut yellow squashes, zucchini, eggplants, and thin-skinned winter squashes like delicata ¼ to ½ inch (6 to 12 mm) thick, then oil, season, and grill over medium-high heat just until tender. The flesh of bell peppers is already this thickness, so simply cut the flesh off the core, oil, season, and grill the pieces. You can even grill denser winter squashes like butternut squash and pumpkin: peel them, cut them into slabs ½ inch (12 mm) thick, and use a fire with two heat levels, searing the squash over the hot side and finishing it over the low-heat side.

Weight them for a deep sear. Many soft vegetables are somewhat rounded. To help them make contact with the grill grate, weight them down with a heavy pan, such as cast-iron frying pan, or top them with an aluminum foil–wrapped brick or rock. This technique works especially well with vegetables such as zucchini and Japanese eggplants that can be sliced lengthwise but left attached to the stem and then fanned out on the grill.

A quick sojourn on a medium-hot grill is all that's needed to bump up the bland of zucchini. Here, we serve it with the summery aromas of basil, orange, and raspberry vinegar in a simple vinaigrette with a few capers for spark and pine nuts for texture.

MAKES 4 SERVINGS

2 zucchini, about ¾ lb (375 g) total weight

1 tablespoon olive oil

1 teaspoon fine sea salt

½ teaspoon freshly ground pepper

1 tablespoon small capers

1 tablespoon pine nuts, preferably toasted

½ cup (4 fl oz/125 ml) Orange Vinaigrette (page 227)

GRILLED ZUCCHINI WITH CAPERS, PINE NUTS & ORANGE VINAIGRETTE

1 Heat the grill for medium direct heat (350°–400°F/180°–200°C).

2 Trim the ends from the zucchini and then slice lengthwise into slabs ¼–½ inch (6–12 mm) thick. Coat the slabs all over with the oil, salt, and pepper.

3 Brush the grill grate and coat with oil. Put the zucchini on the grate and cook, turning once, until lightly grilled marked, 2–3 minutes per side.

4 Transfer to a platter and scatter the capers and nuts over the top. Drizzle with the vinaigrette and serve.

 EXTRA CREDIT

For a bigger hit of orange, cut a navel orange or a Moro blood orange into "supremes" (segments free of membrane) and then chop the segments coarsely and scatter over the top when serving.

For even more citrus flavor, replace the salt and pepper with ⅓ cup (1 oz/30 g) Citrus Rub (page 215).

If you like Middle Eastern food, try this easy grilled eggplant dish. Fanning out the eggplants on the serving plate makes a stunning presentation. Tahini gives the dish some creaminess, and pomegranate seeds bring sweet crunch and color.

MAKES 4 SERVINGS

½ cup (4 oz/125 g) tahini

½ cup (4 fl oz/125 ml) lukewarm water, plus more as needed

1 large clove garlic

3 tablespoons fresh lemon juice, plus more as needed

2 tablespoons extra-virgin olive oil

1 teaspoon fine sea salt

¼ teaspoon ground cumin

4 Japanese eggplants

¼ cup (1½ oz/45 g) pomegranate seeds

GRILLED EGGPLANTS WITH TAHINI & POMEGRANATE SEEDS

1 Heat the grill for medium-high direct heat (400°–450°F/200°–230°C).

2 In a food processor, combine the tahini, water, garlic, lemon juice, 1 tablespoon of the oil, ½ teaspoon of the salt, and the cumin and process until a very smooth puree forms, 1–2 minutes, stopping to scrape down the sides of the bowl as needed. Add more water and/or lemon juice 1 tablespoon at a time if needed to make a thick, yet pourable sauce.

3 Starting at the blossom end, cut each eggplant lengthwise into slices ¼–½ inch (6–12 mm) thick, cutting all the way down into the stem end but not through it, so the slices can be fanned out from the stem. Place the eggplants on a rimmed baking sheet. Brush all of the cut sides and the outsides with the remaining 1 tablespoon oil and then sprinkle all of the cut sides and the outsides with the remaining ½ teaspoon salt.

4 Brush the grill grate and coat with oil. Using tongs, fan out the eggplants on the grate and cook, turning once, until tender and grill marked, 3–4 minutes per side (see Extra Credit). The eggplants will fan out more easily as they cook and soften. Remove the eggplants from the grill.

5 Spread a generous amount of the tahini sauce on the bottom of a platter. Arrange the fanned eggplants over the sauce and drizzle with a little more sauce. Garnish with the pomegranate seeds and serve with the remaining sauce.

 EXTRA CREDIT

For deeper grill marks, top the fanned-out eggplants with a heavy cast-iron or other heavy pan as they cook.

If you like it spicy, dust the grilled eggplant with ground Aleppo pepper or cayenne pepper.

For even more flavor, sprinkle the grilled eggplants with za'atar.

Za'atar: Mix together 2 tablespoons toasted sesame seeds, 1 teaspoon ground sumac, ¾ teaspoon dried lemon peel, ¾ teaspoon dried thyme, ½ teaspoon dried oregano, ½ teaspoon dried savory, ½ teaspoon dried marjoram, and ½ teaspoon coarse sea salt.

The tahini sauce can be made ahead and refrigerated in an airtight container for up to 1 week. Drizzle any extra sauce on grilled fish, lamb, or vegetables.

LESSON
5

MUSHROOMS

Mushrooms are the meatiest of plant foods. These edible fungi are high in amino acids like glutamic acid, the same savory (umami) compound found in meat. Some mushrooms such as shiitakes also get meaty aromas from sulfur compounds. The grill enhances the meaty taste of mushrooms by evaporating their water and concentrating their flavor.

HOW DO YOU PREP MUSHROOMS FOR GRILLING?

Clean and trim. Brush off any loose dirt, picking out any tough bits from dense, craggy types, like lobster mushrooms. If necessary, give the mushrooms a brief rinse to clean them. Trim off the bottom of the stem if dirty.

Leave large caps whole. Mushrooms with large caps, like portobellos and shiitakes, can be grilled whole. Just pull or trim off the stems. You can also grill portobello stems by cutting them in half lengthwise.

Slice thick mushrooms ½ inch (12 mm) thick. Cut long, thick mushrooms, like king trumpets, lengthwise ½ inch thick right through the thick stem and cap to expose more surface area to the grill. Cut dense, rounded mushrooms, like lion's manes, into "steaks" ½ to 1 inch (12 mm to 2.5 cm) thick.

Skewer small mushrooms. Small button or cremini mushrooms can be skewered to keep them from falling into the fire. To make the skewers as flat as possible, skewer the mushrooms through the cap instead of through the stem. If you like, get creative and use rosemary sprigs as skewers. You can also use a grill wok or grill frying pan for smaller mushrooms, but you won't get as much grill flavor.

Bundle thinner mushrooms. Cut or tie thin and tender mushrooms, like enoki, into bundles about 1 inch (2.5 cm) thick.

Marinate. Mushrooms are, on average, about 90 percent water, much of which evaporates on the grill. Marinating helps to keep mushrooms moist. Soak delicate species, like oyster mushrooms, up to 1 hour, or give denser mushrooms, like portobellos, a longer soak, up to 24 hours.

Or oil and season. If you choose not to marinate, you can oil and season the mushrooms before grilling.

WHAT'S THE BEST WAY TO GRILL MUSHROOMS?

Use direct high or medium heat. Small mushrooms that will cook through quickly, such as button and cremini, can go directly over a hot fire. They'll also work fine over medium-high heat if you skewer them with other vegetables. Dense yet thin mushrooms, like shiitake caps, work best over medium-high heat. Thicker mushrooms, like portobello caps, grill best over medium heat to ensure they don't burn before they are cooked through. As always, start with a clean, well-oiled grill grate. Mushrooms will be tender and grill marked in 4 to 8 minutes per side, depending on thickness.

Baste. A hot grill can easily dry out mushrooms. Marinating helps, but basting them during grilling makes them even juicier. Use some kind of fat. Peanut oil, Asian sesame oil, and melted clarified butter all work well. Or go with a mixture of fat and flavorful liquid, such as butter and soy sauce or olive oil and balsamic vinegar.

Toss with sauce. If your mushrooms have dried a bit too much on the grill, toss them with sauce after cooking. You can use leftover marinade or basting liquid as the sauce, or you can mix up some combination of umami-rich liquid (soy sauce, fish sauce, tomato juice), a bit of fat (mushrooms love butter and cream), and some acid (rice vinegar, sherry vinegar, lemon juice, yuzu juice).

LESSON

6

CORN

We see all kinds of crazy tips for grilling corn: soaking, shucking, foil-wrapping, or even peeling back the husks, pulling out the silk, and then putting the husks back on. Our favorite method is the simplest: grill corn right in the husk.

WHAT CORN IS BEST FOR GRILLING?

Go with traditional sweet corn. These types contain about 16 percent sugar and 23 percent polysaccharides, which are long-chain carbohydrates that give corn its wonderfully creamy texture. New high-sugar hybrids have been developed to help corn stay sweet during long shipping and storage. These hybrids contain up to 40 percent sugar but only about 5 percent polysaccharides, so they taste watery instead of creamy. Sadly, high-sugar hybrids account for most of today's supermarket corn. Instead, shop farmers' markets to find traditional varieties like Golden Bantam, Silver Queen, and Butter & Sugar.

Buy fresh. As soon as corn is picked, enzymes convert its sweet, juicy sugars to bland, mealy-tasting starches. In only 3 days, fresh corn can lose up to 50 percent of its sweetness. Try to buy fresh corn that was picked that day. A few undeveloped kernels at the top are okay. They indicate that the corn is slightly immature and will taste sweeter than fully matured corn.

Keep it cold. Refrigeration slows down the enzyme activity that converts sugars to starch. Wrapping corn in wet paper towels or standing the cut ears in water like flowers also helps to keep the kernels moist.

HOW DO YOU PREP CORN FOR GRILLING?

Husk if you like. If you plan to grill the corn naked (out of its husk), remove and discard the husk and silk. When grilling corn this way, we prefer to keep the peeled back husk on the cob, using it as a handle. Tie the husk with a piece of husk or kitchen string or, for a nice presentation, braid the husk strips. Either way, slip some foil or a grill tray under the husks during grilling to prevent them from burning.

Lube naked corn. Rub the kernels with oil or melted butter (preferably clarified). Use just enough to lacquer the surface so the fat doesn't create flare-ups.

Season at the table. Some evidence exists that salt toughens the outer skin of corn kernels and keeps them from softening during cooking.

WHAT'S THE BEST WAY TO GRILL CORN?

In the husk. Our preferred method is to just toss the ears of corn over a medium-high fire—husk, silk, and all. When the husk is deeply browned all over—15 to 20 minutes later—the corn is done. This grilling method keeps the kernels nice and juicy. To get some caramelization on the kernels, peel back the husk (along with the silk), baste with oil or butter, and grill the kernels until lightly browned all over.

In the embers. A similar method is to toss whole ears of unhusked corn right onto the embers of a charcoal or wood fire. The husk will char all over and the corn will steam inside, picking up a whiff of smoke and becoming tender and juicy in about 15 minutes.

Husked for deep browning. This is our second favorite method, but it risks burning the corn and drying it out. Discard the husk and silk, oil the kernels judiciously (or use clarified butter), and grill the corn naked directly over a medium-high fire, watching carefully and turning the ears often to prevent burning. The corn should be nicely browned all over in 8 to 10 minutes.

Parallel to the grill grate. Corn won't fall through the grill grate, so there's no need to put it perpendicular to the bars. In fact, setting corn parallel to the grate helps to keep the cobs from rolling and exposes more of the corn to the fire for better browning.

VEGETABLES **177**

Mushrooms take to the grill like no other vegetable, developing a meaty taste as their water evaporates and their flavor concentrates. *Shichimi togarashi,* the classic Japanese table condiment of orange peel, sesame seeds, and chiles, amplifies the effect. So does a quick dip in soy sauce and sesame oil.

MAKES 4 SERVINGS

2 tablespoons tamari or Japanese soy sauce

2 teaspoons Asian sesame oil

2 teaspoons peeled and minced fresh ginger

1 teaspoon rice vinegar

1 teaspoon chile garlic paste

1 lb (500 g) large-cap shiitake mushrooms, stems removed

2 tablespoons Shichimi Togarashi (page 217)

1 yuzu or grapefruit, cut into wedges (optional)

GRILLED SHIITAKES WITH SHICHIMI TOGARASHI

1 In a bowl, combine the tamari, sesame oil, ginger, vinegar, and chile garlic paste and mix well. Add the shiitakes and massage the dressing into them. Let stand at room temperature while the grill heats.

2 Heat the grill for medium-high direct heat (about 400°F/200°C).

3 Brush the grill grate and coat with oil. Remove the shiitakes from the dressing, reserving the dressing. Put the shiitakes, gill side down, on the grate and cook, turning once, just until nicely browned and starting to soften, 1–2 minutes per side. After flipping, drizzle any remaining dressing into the gill side.

4 Transfer the mushrooms to individual plates and scatter the shichimi togarashi over the top. Serve with the yuzu for squeezing, if using.

Mexican street vendors sell tons of grilled ears of corn, called *elotes*. In Oaxaca, the preferred seasoning is a mixture of Mexican sour cream, crumbled aged cheese, chile powder, cilantro, and lime juice. Just grill the corn, husks and all, and then peel back the husks and use them as a handle. That way, you can enjoy this satisfying snack while walking around in the late-summer sunshine.

MAKES 4 SERVINGS

½ cup (4 oz/125 g) Mexican crema, sour cream, or crème fraîche

¼ cup (2 fl oz/60 ml) mayonnaise

⅓ cup (1⅓ oz/40 g) plus 2½ tablespoons finely crumbled Cotija or grated pecorino romano cheese

1 tablespoon ancho chile powder, plus more for garnish

½ teaspoon coarse sea salt, preferably sel gris

4 ears corn in the husk

1 tablespoon finely chopped fresh cilantro (optional)

4 lime wedges for serving

OAXACAN GRILLED CORN

1 Heat the grill for medium-high direct heat (about 425°F/220°C).

2 In a small bowl, combine the crema, mayonnaise, ⅓ cup (1⅓ oz/40 g) of the cheese, the chile powder, and the salt and mix well.

3 Brush the grill grate and coat with oil. Put the corn on the grate and cook, turning every 5 minutes or so, until the husks are charred all over, 15–18 minutes. During the last 5 minutes, put on some grill gloves, pull back the husks to expose the corn kernels, and pull off and discard the silks. Grill the ears, turning them frequently, just until the kernels are lightly browned all over, about 5 minutes. Transfer the ears to a platter. Tie back the husks with kitchen string, if you like, or leave them loose.

4 Brush the corn kernels all over with the crema mixture and then sprinkle with the remaining 2½ tablespoons cheese, a little ancho powder, and the cilantro (if using). Serve with the lime wedges for squeezing.

 **EXTRA CREDIT**

If you're not a fan of Mexican flavors on corn, use the same grilling method but skip the crema mixture. Instead, use Fines Herbes Butter or any of the flavored butters shown there as Extra Credit (page 226).

Grilled Corn with Chimichurri: Replace the crema mixture with Chimichurri (page 228).

9
PIZZA

184 LESSON 1: FLATBREADS

185 GRILLED MARGHERITA PIZZA

186 GRILLED PIZZA WITH BLACK GARLIC, ARUGULA & SOPPRESSATA

188 GRILLED WHITE PIZZA WITH HAM, FIGS & GRUYÈRE

189 GRILLED PIZZA WITH FRESH TOMATO, PESTO & GORGONZOLA

191 GRILLED PIZZA WITH PROSCIUTTO & HOT-PEPPER HONEY

FLATBREADS

If you've never tried it, toast a piece of bread on the grill. It lends a lick of char and a wisp of smoke to the bread, something an electric toaster can't do. Grilling pizza and other flatbreads is similar to grill toasting with the important exception that you start with raw dough and cook it completely on the grill.

WHAT TYPES OF RAW DOUGH WORK BEST ON THE GRILL?

Leavened or not. Both unleavened breads like Indian chapati (roti) and leavened breads like Italian pizza can be grilled. Just roll the dough somewhat flat so it cooks through without burning.

Thin without too much sugar. Some flatbreads like Armenian lavash are rolled paper-thin and grilled over a hot fire. Others like pizza and Arabic *khubz* are rolled a bit thicker, ⅛ to ¼ inch (3 to 6 mm). Still others like Indian naan are up to ½ inch thick. Whichever one you are making, keep the sweeteners in the dough to a minimum to prevent burning.

Not too much surface area. Soft raw dough can be difficult to maneuver on a hot grill. Keep round pizzas to less than 12 inches (30 cm) in diameter.

WHAT'S THE BEST WAY TO GRILL FLATBREADS?

Flip it. Many traditional flatbreads like naan and pizza are cooked in a blazing-hot wood-fired tandoor or brick oven. These ovens deliver heat to the top of the dough by convection air currents. The big difference with grilled flatbread is that you flip the dough to expose both sides to the grill's bottom heat.

Set up a fire with two heat areas. If you're grilling an untopped flatbread like naan or pita, you can use a single heat level across the entire grill. But for topped flatbreads like pizza, you need to deliver heat to the top side to melt the cheese while the bottom side grills without burning. Set up one side of the grill for medium heat and the other for medium-low heat. Brown one side of the dough on the hot side, then move the dough to the cooler side and cover the grill to melt the cheese.

Batch as necessary. The size of your grill determines how many flatbreads you can cook at once. On the average 22-inch (55-cm) kettle grill or four-burner gas grill, you can grill four small (10 inches/25 cm in diameter) flatbreads all at once. If using a smaller grill, batch the cooking as necessary.

Oil the dough. For crisp pizza, it's essential to oil the dough to prevent sticking and promote even browning. Of course, the grill itself should also be clean and well oiled to prevent sticking. Both sides of the dough will be grilled, so it's easiest to shape the dough on an oiled piece of aluminum foil, then rub or spray the top side of the raw dough with a thin coating of oil.

Use tongs and a spatula. To keep soft, thin dough from folding up, locate a good spot on the grill for the dough, then put your hand under the foil and invert it, slapping the dough onto the grill in one quick motion. After a few seconds, use tongs and a spatula to peel off the foil slowly, keeping the dough in place. Save the foil. After the dough is grill marked (about 1 minute), use the tongs and spatula to rotate the dough 90 degrees for even browning. When the dough is evenly browned on the bottom and dry on top, it will be firm enough to grab with tongs and flip. For pizza, flip the dough back onto the foil or a cutting board so the grilled side is face up.

Top pizzas and cover the grill. Spread your toppings on the grilled side of the dough, then return the pizza to the grill grate directly over the fire on the cooler side of the grill. Cover the grill to help melt the cheese. Rotate the dough 90 degrees halfway through cooking for even browning. When the bottom is crisp and the toppings are hot and melted, use a pizza peel or a large spatula and tongs to transfer the pizza to a cutting board.

Margherita is the simplest of pizzas with only tomato sauce, fresh mozzarella, and basil leaves. In Italy, a true Margherita must be made by hand on a disk of dough that has been stretched to no more than 3 millimeters thick (about ⅛ inch). The pizza must also be cooked in a wood-burning brick oven at 905°F (485°C). Grilling the dough is certainly not permitted. But does it taste great grilled? It certainly does.

MAKES 4 PIZZAS

Cooking spray for aluminum foil and dough

1 lb (500 g) Pizza Dough (page 230), thawed if frozen

1 cup (8 fl oz/250 ml) Thick Marinara Sauce (page 220), pureed

1 lb (500 g) fresh mozzarella cheese, thinly sliced

Large handful of fresh basil leaves

GRILLED MARGHERITA PIZZA

1 Heat the grill for medium direct heat (about 350°F/180°C) on one side and medium-low direct heat (about 300°F/150°C) on the other side. Let the grill grate heat up for at least 15 minutes.

2 Coat four 12-inch (30-cm) squares of aluminum foil on one side with cooking spray. Cut the dough into 4 equal pieces. Put a piece of the dough on the center of a piece of foil and press and stretch the dough into a 10-inch (25-cm) round about ⅛ inch (3 mm) thick. Coat the top of the dough with cooking spray. Repeat with the remaining dough and foil squares, spraying the top of each round.

3 Brush the grill grate and coat with oil. Invert each round of dough directly onto the hotter side of the grill, using tongs and a spatula to remove the foil carefully as if peeling off a sticker. Grill until the dough is nicely browned on the bottom and almost dry on top, 1–2 minutes. After about 1 minute, use the tongs and the spatula to rotate the dough 90 degrees to prevent burning.

4 Invert the grilled dough rounds onto a cutting board so the grilled sides are up. Spread ¼ cup (2 fl oz/60 ml) of the marinara over the grilled side of each round. Arrange the mozzarella slices over the sauce, dividing them evenly. One at a time, lift the pizzas and place them back on the grill over the cooler side. Cover the grill and cook, rotating each round about 90 degrees halfway through the cooking, until the bottoms brown and the cheese melts, about 5 minutes. Top with the basil leaves during the last few minutes.

5 Using a large spatula and tongs, transfer the pizzas to the cutting board, cut each pizza into 4 wedges, and serve.

Black garlic is a traditional Asian ingredient made by slowly heating and steaming an entire head of garlic. Weeks later, the garlic darkens and caramelizes, developing incredibly rich flavors and aromas. It's like roasted garlic taken to the extreme. Black garlic makes the perfect flavor bomb for a pizza topped with cured sausage and a few fresh arugula leaves. Look for it in specialty stores or order it online.

GRILLED PIZZA WITH BLACK GARLIC, ARUGULA & SOPPRESSATA

MAKES 4 PIZZAS

Cooking spray for aluminum foil and dough

1 lb (500 g) Pizza Dough (page 230), thawed if frozen

1 cup Thick Marinara Sauce (page 220), pureed

6 cloves black garlic, finely chopped

¾ lb (375 g) fresh mozzarella cheese, thinly sliced

¼ lb (125 g) soppressata, thinly sliced

2 oz (60 g) baby arugula leaves

1 Heat the grill for medium direct heat (about 350°F/180°C) on one side and medium-low direct heat (about 300°F/150°C) on the other side. Let the grill grate heat up for at least 15 minutes.

2 Coat four 12-inch (30-cm) squares of aluminum foil on one side with cooking spray. Cut the dough into 4 equal pieces. Put a piece of the dough on the center of a piece of foil and press and stretch the dough into a 10-inch (25-cm) round about ⅛ inch (3 mm) thick. Coat the top of the dough with cooking spray. Repeat with the remaining dough and foil squares, spraying the top of each round.

3 Brush the grill grate and coat with oil. Invert each round of dough directly onto the hotter side of the grill, using tongs and a spatula to remove the foil carefully as if peeling off a sticker. Grill until the dough is nicely browned on the bottom and almost dry on top, 1–2 minutes. After about 1 minute, use the tongs and the spatula to rotate the dough 90 degrees to prevent burning.

4 Invert the grilled dough rounds onto a cutting board so the grilled sides are up. Spread ¼ cup (2 fl oz/60 ml) of the marinara over the grilled side of each round. Scatter the black garlic evenly over the rounds. Arrange the mozzarella and soppressata slices over the top, dividing them evenly. One at a time, lift the pizzas and place them back on the grill over the cooler side. Cover the grill and cook, rotating each round about 90 degrees halfway through the cooking, until the bottoms brown and the cheese melts, about 5 minutes.

5 Using a large spatula and tongs, transfer the pizzas to the cutting board and top with the arugula. Cut each pizza into 4 wedges and serve.

These days, it seems like you can put anything from pineapple to shrimp on a pizza. It is just flatbread after all—almost like an open-faced sandwich. We love ham, figs, and Gruyère cheese in griddled sandwiches, so why not on pizza? The combination of sweet, salty, and savory works every time.

MAKES 4 PIZZAS

1½ cups (12 oz/375 g) whole milk ricotta cheese

¾ cup (3 oz/90 g) shredded Gruyère cheese

1 teaspoon dried oregano

½ teaspoon salt

¼ teaspoon freshly ground pepper

Cooking spray for aluminum foil and dough

1 lb (500 g) Pizza Dough (page 230), thawed if frozen

¼ lb (125 g) country ham, thinly sliced

8 small, ripe figs, stems trimmed and sliced lengthwise about ¼ inch (6 mm) thick

GRILLED WHITE PIZZA WITH HAM, FIGS & GRUYÈRE

1 Heat the grill for medium direct heat (about 350°F/180°C) on one side and medium-low direct heat (about 300°F/150°C) on the other side. Let the grill grate heat up for at least 15 minutes.

2 In a small bowl, stir together the ricotta, Gruyère, oregano, salt, and pepper, mixing well.

3 Coat four 12-inch (30-cm) squares of aluminum foil on one side with cooking spray. Cut the dough into 4 equal pieces. Put a piece of the dough on the center of a piece of the foil and press and stretch the dough into a 10-inch (25-cm) round about ⅛ inch (3 mm) thick. Coat the top of the dough with cooking spray. Repeat with the remaining dough and foil squares, spraying the top of each round.

4 Brush the grill grate and coat with oil. Invert each round of dough directly onto the hotter side of the grill, using tongs and a spatula to remove the foil carefully as if peeling off a sticker. Cook until the dough is nicely browned on the bottom and almost dry on top, 1–2 minutes. After about 1 minute, use the tongs and the spatula to rotate the dough 90 degrees to prevent burning.

5 Invert the grilled dough rounds onto a cutting board so the grilled sides are up. Spread the ricotta mixture over the grilled side of each round, dividing it evenly. Arrange the ham and fig slices evenly over the ricotta mixture. One at a time, lift the pizzas and place them back on the grill over the cooler side. Cover the grill and cook, rotating each round about 90 degrees halfway through the cooking, until the bottoms brown and the cheese begins to melt, about 5 minutes.

6 Using a large spatula and tongs, transfer the pizzas to the cutting board, cut each pizza into 4 wedges, and serve.

The key to a well-topped pizza is restraint. You want bursts of bold flavor but not so many toppings that the pizza is too heavy to lift. If the crust buckles under the weight of all the toppings, try adding fewer next time. This flavor combination epitomizes the minimalist approach and features the red, white, and green colors of the Italian flag.

MAKES 4 PIZZAS

Cooking spray for aluminum foil and dough

1 lb (500 g) Pizza Dough (page 230), thawed if frozen

½ cup (4 oz/125 g) basil pesto

6 oz (185 g) Gorgonzola cheese, crumbled

2 cups (12 oz/375 g) grape or pear tomatoes, halved or quartered

¼ cup (1¼ oz/37 g) pine nuts

GRILLED PIZZA WITH FRESH TOMATO, PESTO & GORGONZOLA

1 Heat the grill for medium direct heat (about 350°F/180°C) on one side and medium-low direct heat (about 300°F/150°C) on the other side. Let the grill grate heat up for at least 15 minutes.

2 Coat four 12-inch (30-cm) squares of aluminum foil on one side with cooking spray. Cut the dough into 4 equal pieces. Put a piece of the dough on the center of a piece of foil and press and stretch the dough into a 10-inch (25-cm) round about ⅛ inch (3 mm) thick. Coat the top of the dough with cooking spray. Repeat with the remaining dough and foil squares, spraying the top of each round.

3 Brush the grill grate and coat with oil. Invert each round of dough directly onto the hotter side of the grill, using tongs and a spatula to remove the foil carefully as if peeling off a sticker. Grill until the dough is nicely browned on the bottom and almost dry on top, 1–2 minutes. After about 1 minute, use the tongs and the spatula to rotate the dough 90 degrees to prevent burning.

4 Invert the grilled dough rounds onto a cutting board so the grilled sides are up. Spread 2 tablespoons of the pesto over the grilled side of each round. Scatter the cheese, tomatoes, and pine nuts over the pesto, dividing them evenly. One at a time, lift the pizzas and place them back on the grill over the cooler side. Cover the grill and cook, rotating each round about 90 degrees halfway through the cooking, until the bottoms brown and the cheese begins to melt, about 5 minutes.

5 Using a large spatula and tongs, transfer the pizzas to the cutting board, cut each pizza into 4 wedges, and serve.

If you're a fan of spicy-sweet flavor combinations, give this pizza a whirl. Prosciutto gives it meaty, salty satisfaction while the spicy honey arouses your senses. For extra crunch, sprinkle some crushed hazelnuts on the pizza along with the prosciutto.

MAKES 4 PIZZAS

¼ cup (3 oz/90 g) honey

2 teaspoons hot-pepper sauce

¼ teaspoon red pepper flakes

Cooking spray for aluminum foil and dough

1 lb (500 g) Pizza Dough (page 230), thawed if frozen

1 cup (8 fl oz/250 ml) Thick Marinara Sauce (page 220), pureed

¾ lb (375 g) fresh mozzarella cheese, thinly sliced

2 oz (60 g) prosciutto, sliced paper-thin

GRILLED PIZZA WITH PROSCIUTTO & HOT-PEPPER HONEY

1 Heat the grill for medium direct heat (about 350°F/180°C) on one side and medium-low direct heat (about 300°F/150°C) on the other side. Let the grill grate heat up for at least 15 minutes.

2 In a small bowl, stir together the honey, hot sauce, and pepper flakes.

3 Coat four 12-inch (30-cm) squares of aluminum foil on one side with cooking spray. Cut the dough into 4 equal pieces. Put a piece of the dough on the center of a piece of foil and press and stretch the dough into a 10-inch (25-cm) round about ⅛ inch (3 mm) thick. Coat the top of the dough with cooking spray. Repeat with the remaining dough and foil squares, spraying the top of each round.

4 Brush the grill grate and coat with oil. Invert each round of dough directly onto the hotter side of the grill, using tongs and a spatula to remove the foil carefully as if peeling off a sticker. Grill until the dough is nicely browned on the bottom and almost dry on top, 1–2 minutes. After about 1 minute, use the tongs and the spatula to rotate the dough 90 degrees to prevent burning.

5 Invert the grilled dough rounds onto a cutting board so the grilled sides are up. Spread ¼ cup (2 fl oz/60 ml) of the marinara over the grilled side of each round. Arrange the mozzarella and then the prosciutto over the sauce, dividing them evenly. One at a time, lift the pizzas and place them back on the grill over the cooler side. Cover the grill and cook, rotating each round about 90 degrees halfway through the cooking, until the bottoms brown and the cheese melts, about 5 minutes.

6 Using a large spatula and tongs, transfer the pizzas to the cutting board and drizzle the hot-pepper honey evenly over the tops. Cut each pizza into 4 wedges and serve.

10
DESSERTS

194 LESSON 1: FRUIT

195 BARELY BURNT HONEY-GLAZED PEARS WITH ORANGE & ROSEMARY

196 CHAI-SMOKED PINEAPPLE

199 GRILLED PEACHES WITH SALTED CARAMEL SAUCE

200 GRILLED BANANAS WITH COFFEE-CINNAMON HOT FUDGE SAUCE

201 GRILLED QUESO-STUFFED FIGS WITH MOLE-SPICED CHOCOLATE

202 LESSON 2: CAKE

203 GRILLED LEMON POUND CAKE WITH LEMON-GINGER GLAZE & CANDIED LEMON

204 GRILLED POLENTA CAKE WITH FENNEL, RAISINS & ORANGES

207 GRILLED S'MORES DOUGHNUTS

FRUIT

Ripe fruits are naturally soft and sweet, needing no embellishment, and yet a brief sojourn over a flickering fire can do wonders for a bourbon-soaked peach or a honey-glazed banana.

Not all fruits are prime for grilling. Superjuicy fruits like berries and melons are devastated by flame, but as long as a fruit contains a modicum of fiber and is not overly wet, its transformation by fire can be revelatory. And it's never a lot of work. Perhaps because we are so accustomed to eating sweet fruits raw, the experience of charring them tastes revolutionary, and in most cases, there is little more to it than that.

GRILLING FRESH FRUIT IS A SNAP

- For drupe fruits (stone fruits) like peaches, apricots, and plums: halve the fruit and discard the pit. Coat the cut side with glaze and brown directly over a high fire.

- For firm orchard fruits like apples and pears: coat with a flavorful glaze and cook over indirect heat until tender. These fruits can be grilled halved or whole. If halved, they are frequently grill marked directly over the heat before cooking through away from the fire.

- For pulpy, low-moisture fruits like bananas and figs: halve the fruit and grill until lightly charred and fragrant. You cannot use tenderness to judge the doneness of these fruits because they yield easily to touch even when raw.

- For meaty tropical fruits like pineapples, mangoes, and guavas: simply char for flavor. The tangy tutti-frutti flavor of these fruits makes a great pairing with the flavor of smoke.

Pears and apples lend themselves equally well to grilling. Because these fruits are dense and fibrous, they can be started directly over the fire to develop a grilled patina and caramelized flavor, but they must be finished away from the heat to give their fibers time to tenderize. Here, rosemary-skewered pears are basted with honey and orange juice. The vision of rosemary leaves sprouting from the crown of a caramelized pear is both disarming and charming.

MAKES 4 SERVINGS

¼ cup (3 oz/90 g) honey

¼ cup (2 fl oz/60 ml) fresh orange juice

1 tablespoon cider vinegar

1 teaspoon pure vanilla extract

Leaves of 1 small rosemary sprig, finely chopped

Pinch of fine sea salt

8 fresh sturdy rosemary sprigs (optional)

4 barely ripe Bartlett pears, halved lengthwise and cored

2 tablespoons extra-virgin olive oil

BARELY BURNT HONEY-GLAZED PEARS WITH ORANGE & ROSEMARY

1 Heat the grill for medium-high indirect heat (350°–400°F/180°–200°C).

2 In a small bowl, combine the honey, orange juice, vinegar, vanilla, finely chopped rosemary, and salt and mix well to create a glaze. Set aside.

3 Skewer each pear half lengthwise with a rosemary sprig.

4 Coat the pear halves with the oil.

5 Brush the grill grate and coat with oil. Put the pear halves, cut side down, on the grate and cook, turning once, until grill marked, 3–4 minutes per side. Brush the pear halves on both sides with some of the glaze and move them away from the fire. Cover the grill and cook the pears, turning them and brushing them with the glaze every 5 minutes, until they are easily pierced with a fork, about 20 minutes.

6 Transfer the pear halves to individual plates, placing 2 halves on each plate. Drizzle with any remaining glaze and serve.

This highly aromatic concoction borrows its spicy persona from *masala chai,* the Indian blend of black tea, cardamom, cloves, allspice, anise, and cinnamon. To up the ante, we use these spices two ways: ground together as a rub and scattered whole over hot coals to create fragrant smoke. They all come together, invading the flesh of the pineapple, a natural grill fruit if there ever was one.

MAKES 4 SERVINGS

6 green cardamom pods

6 allspice berries

6 whole cloves

6 star anise pods

3 cinnamon sticks, broken into large pieces

⅓ cup (4 oz/125 g) honey

¼ cup (2 fl oz/60 ml) dark rum

Juice of ½ lime

2 teaspoons Chai Spice Blend (facing page)

3 tablespoons unsalted butter, cut into 3 or 4 pieces

1 small pineapple

CHAI-SMOKED PINEAPPLE

1 Wrap the cardamom, allspice, cloves, star anise, and cinnamon in foil to make a flat packet, then poke holes in the foil.

2 In a small saucepan, combine the honey, rum, lime juice, and spice blend and bring to a boil over high heat. Reduce the heat to medium-high and cook until reduced to about ⅓ cup (4 oz/125 g) to create a glaze. Remove from the heat and whisk in the butter. Set aside.

3 Trim, peel, and quarter the pineapple lengthwise. Core, then cut each quarter crosswise into wedges about 1 inch (2.5 cm) thick.

4 Heat the grill for high indirect heat (400°–450°F/200°–230°C). Put the foil packet of spices on the hot coals. If using a gas grill, put the packet directly over one of the gas burners under the cooking grate. Or if your grill has a smoker box, use it. Cover the grill and wait a few minutes for the spices to start smoking.

5 Brush the grill grate and coat with oil. Put the pineapple on the grate over the fire, cover the grill, and cook, turning once, until nicely grill marked, about 3 minutes per side. Brush with some of the glaze and move the fruit away from the fire. Cover the grill and smoke until the pineapple is browned and smoky, about 10 minutes. Transfer the pineapple to plates, drizzle with the remaining glaze, and serve.

 EXTRA CREDIT

Grilled Honey Habanero Pineapple: Replace the glaze ingredients with a mixture of 1 cup (12 oz/375 g) honey (preferably orange blossom), 2 teaspoons grated orange zest, ⅓ cup orange juice, and 2 habanero chiles, seeded and chopped. Bring to a boil, add 3 tablespoons butter, whisk until melted, then strain.

To make pineapple rings instead of wedges, peel the pineapple. Cut the whole pineapple crosswise into slices 1 inch (2.5 cm) thick. Lay the slices on the cutting board and use the large side of a melon baller to remove the tough core from each slice. Grill the slices as directed. You can also purchase an already peeled and cored pineapple and cut it crosswise into slices.

For crosshatch marks, use high heat and rotate the pineapple 45 degrees halfway through cooking on each side.

Serve the pineapple with coconut ice cream and caramel sauce.

CHAI SPICE BLEND

MAKES 3 TABLESPOONS

1 teaspoon cardamom seeds
1 teaspoon allspice berries
½ teaspoon whole cloves
1 star anise, broken into pieces
½ teaspoon peppercorns
1 tablespoon ground ginger
2 teaspoons ground cinnamon

In a spice grinder, combine the cardamom, allspice, cloves, star anise, and peppercorns and grind to a fine powder. Transfer to a small bowl and stir in the ginger and cinnamon.

Store in an airtight container at room temperature for up to 1 month.

This salted caramel sauce is so good that you can put it on anything. But we are talking grill school, so let's give the peaches their due. Peaches love to be grilled. The loss of moisture makes them meaty, the slight char gives their natural floral scent gravitas, and the heat softens the fruit, causing the juices to swell in the flesh, rather than gushing and squirting with each bite. Be sure to use freestone peaches so the halves will separate easily from the stone when cut and twisted.

MAKES 4 SERVINGS

1¼ cups (10 oz/315 g) sugar

¼ cup (2 fl oz/60 ml) heavy cream

1 tablespoon bourbon

4 large, ripe peaches

2 pinches of smoked flake salt such as Halen Môn Gold or smoked Maldon

GRILLED PEACHES WITH SALTED CARAMEL SAUCE

1 In a heavy saucepan, combine the sugar and 3 tablespoons water over medium heat and stir until the sugar dissolves. Bring the mixture to a boil, stirring occasionally to make sure the caramel cooks evenly, until the syrup turns dark amber, about 5 minutes. Immediately pour in the cream, stepping back as there will be a lot of steam and splatter. When the steam subsides, stir the mixture until smooth. Stir in the bourbon, transfer to a heatproof container, and let cool.

2 Heat the grill for medium-high direct heat (400°–450°F/200°–230°C).

3 Brush the grill grate and coat with oil. Halve the peaches from the stem end to the blossom end and twist the halves in opposite directions to separate. Remove and discard the pits. Brush the peach halves all over with some of the caramel. Put the halves, cut side down, on the grate and cook, turning once, until nicely grilled marked on both sides, 2–3 minutes per side.

4 Transfer the peach halves, cut side up, to individual plates, placing 2 halves on each plate. Drizzle with the remaining caramel and top with a generous sprinkle of smoked salt.

 EXTRA CREDIT

Feel free to substitute another stone fruit. Nectarines, apricots, and plums will all work great.

Flavor your caramel with liqueur (St-Germain, Cointreau, Frangelico), other booze (Scotch, añejo tequila, brandy), or fruit juice (orange, peach, cherry).

Substitute strong brewed coffee for the cream for a dairy-free, reduced-calorie, richly dark caramel.

Serve grilled peaches solo or team them with slices of grilled pound cake or gingerbread, or a big scoop of salted caramel ice cream.

Cooks like to combine coffee, chocolate, and cinnamon—the dark flavors of the tropics. Put that combination over a tropical fruit like bananas and you have paradise. Ripe bananas are a natural for grilling. Their lack of moisture makes them caramelize readily, and their creamy consistency means that once they have browned and heated through, they're done. Serve these richly spiced bananas with ice cream or pound cake.

GRILLED BANANAS WITH COFFEE-CINNAMON HOT FUDGE SAUCE

MAKES 4 SERVINGS

4 large just-ripe bananas
(see Extra Credit)

2 teaspoons golden
brown sugar

1 teaspoon finely ground
espresso roast coffee

1 teaspoon unsweetened
cocoa powder

1 teaspoon ground
cinnamon

1 cup (8 fl oz/250 ml)
Hot Fudge Sauce
(page 228)

1 Heat the grill for medium direct heat (350°–400°F/180°–200°C).

2 Cut the bananas in half lengthwise through the peel, following the arc of the curve so the halves will lie flat on the grill.

3 In a small bowl, combine the brown sugar, coffee, cocoa powder, and ½ teaspoon of the cinnamon and mix well. Sprinkle the mixture evenly over the cut side of each banana half, pressing it in gently with your fingertips.

4 Put the fudge sauce in a small saucepan, stir in the remaining ½ teaspoon cinnamon, and warm over low heat.

5 Brush the grill grate and coat with oil. Put the banana halves, cut side down, on the grill and cook until nicely grill marked, 3–4 minutes.

6 Transfer the banana halves, in their peels, cut side up, to individual plates, placing 2 halves on each plate. Serve drizzled with the warm fudge sauce.

 EXTRA CREDIT

Ripeness is always a factor when choosing bananas for grilling. The skin of the banana should be fully yellow, which indicates that the fruit has made the transition from starchy to sweet. But it should not have much brown running through the yellow, a sign the banana has converted so much starch that it will no longer hold its shape during grilling.

Serve the banana halves cut side up in their skins, if you like. Or loosen the banana flesh from the skin and slip it, cut side up, onto a plate.

Serve with ice cream for a grilled banana split. Feel free to gild with the salted caramel sauce from the grilled peaches recipe on page 199.

There are hundreds of fig varieties, from green-skinned Smyrna and Calimyrna to purple-skinned Mission. All have an abundance of edible crunchy seeds and, when ripe, a hefty dose of sugar (55 percent by weight). When ripe figs are sliced, they ooze with nectar that browns deliciously on the grill. In this recipe, we stuff them with Mexican queso fresco (creamy, soft, mild fresh cheese) and honey and serve them with a mole-spiced chocolate sauce, fragrant with chiles and baking spices.

MAKES 6 SERVINGS

18 large fresh figs, stems trimmed

3 oz (90 g) queso fresco (about ¾ cup crumbled), at room temperature

1 tablespoon honey

1 teaspoon finely chopped fresh oregano

1 tablespoon olive oil

½ cup (4 fl oz/125 ml) Hot Fudge Sauce (page 228)

2 teaspoons Chai Spice Blend (page 197)

2 teaspoons ancho chile powder

½ teaspoon chipotle chile powder

¼ teaspoon ground cumin

GRILLED QUESO-STUFFED FIGS WITH MOLE-SPICED CHOCOLATE

1 Heat the grill for medium-low direct heat (300°–350F/150°–180°C).

2 Cut a narrow slit into the bottom of end of each fig. Stick your pinky finger into the slit and use it to press indentations into both sides of the slit, creating a small cavity in the center of each fig.

3 In a small bowl, mash the queso with a fork and then mix in the honey and oregano. Using a small spoon and your fingertips, stuff about 1 teaspoon of the cheese mixture into each fig cavity. Gently squeeze together the bottom to enclose the filling.

4 Have ready 6 metal skewers. Skewer 3 figs crosswise onto each skewer (the stem end should be perpendicular to the skewer). Brush the figs with the oil, coating evenly.

5 Put the fudge sauce in a small saucepan, stir in the spice blend, chile powders, and cumin, and warm over low heat.

6 Brush the grill grate and coat with oil. Put the fig skewers on the grate and cook, turning once or twice, until nicely grill marked, 5–8 minutes.

7 Transfer the skewers to individual plates, placing 1 skewer on each plate. Serve with a small pool of spiced fudge sauce as a dip.

 EXTRA CREDIT

For a hint of spice, add ⅛ teaspoon chile powder, such as guajillo or ancho, to the cheese stuffing.

To make this recipe with dried figs, put the figs in a heatproof bowl, add boiling water to cover, and let soak until plump, 10–15 minutes. Drain the figs and proceed as directed. It won't be as mind-blowing as it is with fresh figs, but it will still make you smile.

CAKE

We are all for stretching our grilling chops by figuring out ever more new fangled ways to cook things over fire, but we have learned through countless burnt, raw-in the center, bitter encounters that few cakes are improved by being baked over an open flame. The main problem is that, unlike pizza and other flatbread doughs, cake batters are wet. They need lots of time and extremely gentle heat to dehydrate as they rise and set. You can fiddle with your grill and get it to work, but an oven is so much easier and does a fine job. Cornmeal cakes that benefit from a hefty crust and a bit of smoke are the exception.

For all other cakes, the best technique is to grill toast slices of already-baked cake. Cakes tend to be sweet and because of that, they scorch easily. Use medium-low to medium heat to keep them from burning. It's also helpful to use a grill screen for toasting pound cake, pastries, and other delicate cakes to keep them from crumbling and falling into the flames. Scones and biscuits, which are naturally lower in sugar, and less fragile, toast particularly well.

Grilled doughnuts are a complete revelation. In general, we tend to make nearly everything from scratch, but in the case of doughnuts, we have found that a glazed doughnut from Krispy Kreme or Dunkin' Donuts is just as mind-blowing as any homemade doughnut fresh from the fryer.

The delicate chemistry of traditional pound cake means it can't be baked over an open flame. It would rise irregularly and burn on the edges long before it is done. But that doesn't mean that the buttery crumb and dense sweetness of an oven-baked pound cake can't be embellished by toasting for a few minutes over a fire. This lemon pound cake is enhanced with grilled candied lemon slices and a fragrant lemon syrup.

MAKES 8 SERVINGS

3 large lemons, cut into rounds ⅛ inch (3 mm) thick

3-inch (7.5-cm) piece fresh ginger, peeled and cut into rounds ⅛ inch (3 mm) thick

2 cups (16 oz/500 g) sugar

8 slices (each 1 inch/ 2.5 cm thick) Lemon Pound Cake (page 231) or store-bought

GRILLED LEMON POUND CAKE WITH LEMON-GINGER GLAZE & CANDIED LEMON

1 Bring a pot of water to a boil. Add the lemon slices and blanch for 10 minutes. Drain.

2 In a deep frying pan, combine the ginger, 3 cups (24 fl oz/750 ml) water, and the sugar over medium-high heat and warm, stirring often, until the sugar dissolves. Add the lemon slices, reduce the heat to low, and simmer gently until the lemon slices are sugar soaked, tender, and translucent, about 1 hour. While the lemon slices are cooking, set a large wire rack on a rimmed baking sheet or a piece of aluminum foil. When the lemon slices are ready, using tongs, transfer them in a single layer to the rack on the pan or foil and let cool completely. Scoop out and discard the ginger slices from the syrup and reserve the syrup. To make the lemon slices in advance, let the slices cool in the syrup, transfer the syrup and slices to an airtight container, and refrigerate for up to 2 days.

3 Heat the grill for medium direct heat (350°–400°F/180°–200°C).

4 Brush the grill grate. Put a grill screen on the grate and coat with oil. Put the lemon slices on the screen and cook, turning once, until browned in spots, about 2 minutes per side. Transfer the lemon slices to a plate and remove the grill screen. Coat the grate with oil. Put the pound cake slices on the grate and cook, turning once, until toasted and grill marked, about 3 minutes per side.

5 Transfer the cake slices to a platter and arrange the lemon slices on top. Drizzle with some of the reserved syrup and serve.

 EXTRA CREDIT

Switch out the lemon for any citrus: grapefruit, lime, Meyer lemon, or orange.

Any firm loaf cake can be grilled using the same method as we use for this pound cake.

Baking a cake on a grill isn't easy. The outcome is hard to control even when using indirect grilling techniques to keep the cake away from direct flame. We find that cakes with a minimum of sugar work best, especially when the cake is improved by heavy crusting. Cornmeal cake is a natural. In the Italian style, this polenta pound cake is baked in a frying pan to increase the surface area, so the cake bakes through faster than it would in a loaf pan. Sweetness comes mostly in the form of a sweet orange syrup poured over the cake after it leaves the grill, another Italian innovation.

GRILLED POLENTA CAKE WITH FENNEL, RAISINS & ORANGES

MAKES 6–8 SERVINGS

Baking spray for cake pan

2 cups (7 oz/220 g) almond meal

¾ cup (4¼ oz/130 g) fine polenta or stone-ground cornmeal

1½ teaspoons baking powder

1 tablespoon ground fennel seed

1 cup (6 oz/185 g) golden raisins

¾ cup plus 2 tablespoons (7 oz/220) unsalted butter, at room temperature

1 cup (8 oz/250 g) sugar

3 large eggs

Grated zest and juice of 2 oranges

1 cup (4 oz/125 g) confectioners' sugar

1 Heat the grill for medium indirect heat (300°–350°F/150°–180°C), trying to keep the temperature near the middle of the range. Spray a 10-inch (25-cm) cast-iron frying pan with baking spray.

2 In a bowl, whisk together the almond meal, polenta, baking powder, and fennel. Add the raisins and toss to coat with the dry ingredients.

3 In a bowl, using a handheld mixer or a wooden spoon, beat together the butter and sugar until creamy. Beat in a few spoonfuls of the dry ingredients, followed by 1 egg, beating after each addition until incorporated. Add half of the remaining dry ingredients, followed by the remaining 2 eggs, and then the remaining dry ingredients, again beating after each addition until incorporated. Beat in the orange zest. Pour and scrape the batter into the prepared pan.

4 Put the pan on the grill grate away from the fire, cover the grill, and bake the cake until browned and a cake tester inserted into the center comes out with just a few moist crumbs clinging to it, about 70 minutes. Transfer the pan to wire rack and let the cake cool.

5 While the cake is cooling but is still warm, in a small frying pan, combine the orange juice and confectioners' sugar, place over medium heat, and cook, stirring often, until a syrup forms, about 3 minutes.

6 Prick the top of the still-warm cake all over with a skewer or cake tester and pour the hot syrup evenly over the top. Let the cake cool completely in the pan. Cut into wedges to serve.

Freshly made doughnuts are one of the easy extravagances of modern life. Warm doughnuts, slightly charred and lightly caramelized on a grill, escalates the extravagance exponentially. Fill a doughnut with melted marshmallows and dunk it into creamy milk chocolate and the ecstasy quotient is incalculable.

1½ cups (4½ oz/ 140 g) unsweetened cocoa powder

1½ cups (10½ oz/330 g) firmly packed brown sugar

Pinch of salt

2 cups (16 fl oz/500 ml) half-and-half

1½ teaspoons unsalted butter

8 marshmallows or 32 mini marshmallows

½ teaspoon pure vanilla extract

6 glazed doughnuts, split horizontally

Cooking spray for doughnuts

GRILLED S'MORES DOUGHNUTS

1 Heat the grill for medium-low direct heat (300°–350°F/150°–180°C).

2 In a large, heavy saucepan, stir together the cocoa powder, brown sugar, and salt. Add the half-and-half and whisk until the mixture is smooth. Place over medium heat and cook, stirring constantly with a wooden spoon or a heat-resistant spatula, until the sauce comes to a boil. Reduce the heat to a gentle simmer and cook, stirring, until lightly thickened and very smooth, about 2 minutes. Keep warm.

3 In a small saucepan, combine the butter and marshmallows over medium heat and cook, stirring constantly, until smooth. Stir in the vanilla and remove from the heat.

4 Sandwich a heaping spoonful of the marshmallow goo between the halves of each doughnut. Coat the doughnuts on both sides with cooking spray.

5 Brush the grill grate and coat with oil. Put the doughnuts on the grate and cook, turning once, until the doughnuts are browned, about 40 seconds per side.

6 Transfer the doughnuts to individual plates. Serve with the chocolate sauce for dunking.

11

BRINES, RUBS
& SAUCES

210 LESSON 1: BRINES & MARINADES

212 CUMIN & CORIANDER BRINE

212 SPICY CITRUS MARINADE

212 MEXICAN SOUR ORANGE MARINADE

212 BEER MOP

214 LESSON 2: RUBS

215 BASIC BARBECUE RUB

215 ANCHO CHILE RUB

215 BEDOUIN SPICE RUB

215 ESPRESSO RUB

215 MOLE RUB

215 CITRUS RUB

215 CHINESE FIVE-SPICE RUB

217 RAS EL HANOUT

217 SHICHIMI TOGARASHI

217 BERBERE

217 VADOUVAN

218 LESSON 3: SAUCES

219 BASIC BARBECUE SAUCE

219 ALABAMA WHITE BARBECUE SAUCE

219 WESTERN CAROLINA BARBECUE SAUCE

219 ANCHO CHOCOLATE BBQ SAUCE

220 MARINARA SAUCE

220 HOMEMADE STEAK SAUCE

220 SPICY KOREAN GLAZE

222 SSAM JANG (KOREAN WRAP PASTE)

222 VIETNAMESE DIPPING SAUCE

222 REAL RUSSIAN DRESSING

222 ROASTED TOMATO FRENCH DRESSING

222 BLUE CHEESE DRESSING

222 RANCH DRESSING

223 SRIRACHA MAYO

223 GREEN CHILE QUESO

223 PICKLED SALSA

223 GRILLED TOMATO JAM

225 QUICK PICKLES

225 PORT KETCHUP

225 HARISSA

225 ZA'ATAR TZATZIKI

226 PRESERVED LEMONS

226 PRESERVED LEMON YOGURT

226 ANCHOVY BUTTER

226 FINES HERBES BUTTER

227 GORGONZOLA BUTTER

227 BACON BOURBON BUTTER

227 WILD MUSHROOM MOSTARDA

227 BUFFALO SAUCE

227 ORANGE VINAIGRETTE

228 CHIMICHURRI

228 ROMESCO

228 HOT FUDGE SAUCE

BRINES & MARINADES

Brines are salted mixtures (wet or dry) that increase the juiciness of foods. Marinades, on the other hand, are seasoned liquids that serve primarily to flavor the surface of food. We mostly use dry brines these days because they are easier than wet brines. As for marinating, we do it only on occasion because rubs and sauces are simply more effective seasoning methods.

HOW DO BRINES & MARINADES WORK?

Brines make food juicier. In both wet and dry brines, the active ingredient is salt. Like the acid in a marinade, the salt in a brine diffuses into the food and denatures or unwinds the food's tightly coiled proteins. By loosening the structure of protein, salt allows the food to hang onto more water as it cooks. Meat naturally loses about 20 percent of its moisture when it cooks—even more so in the dry heat of a grill. But brined meat loses only about 10 percent of its moisture. The result: brined meat tastes juicier even after grilling. Brining also helps bring the flavor-amplifying effect of salt deeper into the food.

Marinades flavor the surface. These liquid mixtures typically include oil, seasonings, and some kind of acidic ingredient such as vinegar, citrus juice, wine, buttermilk, yogurt, tea, coffee, or a soft drink. The acid denatures or breaks apart the structure of the protein in the marinated food by disrupting its chemical bonds. This helps to "tenderize" the food by making the protein at the surface easier to chew. The seasonings in the marinade also flavor the food. However, marinades penetrate only $\frac{1}{16}$ to $\frac{1}{8}$ inch (2 to 3 mm) into the surface of the food, so the tenderizing and seasoning effects are minimal. Plus, when you discard the marinade (as you should), you throw away most of the flavor.

WHAT'S THE BEST WAY TO USE BRINES & MARINADES?

Use brines with lean foods. Because pork loin, poultry, and fish lack fat, they tend to dry out on the grill. These lean foods benefit most from the moisture-enhancing effect of brining. A little sugar in the brine also helps to brown the surface. But go easy on other sources of salt because brines essentially presalt the food. Skip the salt in rubs and sauces, using only spices and herbs for flavor. Do not brine kosher meats or those labeled "flavor enhanced" or "self-basting," as these meats have already been salted with a dry or wet brine. If you plan to use the drippings from brined meat to make a sauce, taste them before adding salt. For skin-on poultry, we prefer dry brines to help create a crisp skin. Wet brines work well with smaller pieces of skinless chicken and turkey and with pork chops and ribs. The denser the food, the more time it needs to brine. As with marinades, if the food is done brining before you're ready to grill it, remove it from the brine and refrigerate it until you are ready. See the chart on page 211 for brining times and basic wet and dry brine formulas.

Use marinades for small, thin, and soft foods. Since marinades only work at the surface, they're most effective on thin and porous foods like shrimp, fish fillets, and vegetables. These foods will absorb the flavor of a marinade in as little as an hour. To help marinades penetrate thicker foods, score the surface. Even so, bone-in poultry pieces and pork chops may take up to 8 hours to see an effect, depending on how much acid is in the marinade. If the food is done marinating before you're ready to grill it, remove it from the marinade and refrigerate it until you are ready. Although most marinades are discarded, you can use them for basting or as the base for a sauce. You must boil them first, however, to kill any pathogens that have migrated from the raw food into the marinade. See the chart on page 211 for a basic marinade formula and marinating times.

BASIC BRINES & MARINADES

To make a basic wet brine, dissolve 2 tablespoons salt and 1 tablespoon sugar in 2½ cups (20 fl oz/ 625 ml) water. That's enough to brine 1 pound (500 g) of meat, seafood, or poultry. For a basic dry brine, combine 1 teaspoon coarse salt (or ½ teaspoon table salt) and ⅛ teaspoon sugar and sprinkle it evenly over 1 pound (500 g) of meat, seafood, or poultry. For a basic marinade, combine 1 cup (8 fl oz/250 ml) oil, ⅓ cup (3 fl oz/80 ml) vinegar, and 1 teaspoon coarse salt (or ½ teaspoon table salt), adding spices, herbs, and other flavorings as desired. That's enough to marinate ½ pound (250 g) of meat, seafood, or poultry.

FOOD	BRINING	MARINATING
Small seafood and thin fish (less than 1 inch/2.5 cm)	about 30 minutes	about 1 hour
Vegetables and thick fish (more than 1 inch/ 2.5 cm)	about 1 hour	2–4 hours
Boneless poultry, chops, and steaks	1–3 hours	3–6 hours
Bone-in poultry, chops, and steaks	3–6 hours	6–8 hours
Ribs and roasts (less than 3 lb/ 1.5 kg)	4–6 hours	8–12 hours
Large roasts and whole birds (3–6 lb/1.5–3 kg)	6–8 hours	12–16 hours

MEASURING SALT

Weight is the most accurate way to measure salt. That's because volume measures vary according to the size and shape of the crystals of different types of salt. Here are equivalent volumes and weights for the most common salts used in cooking.

MORTON'S KOSHER	DIAMOND CRYSTAL KOSHER	TABLE OR FINE SEA SALT	GRAMS
¾ tsp	1 tsp	½ tsp	3
1½ tsp	2 tsp	1 tsp	6
1 Tbsp	4 tsp	2 tsp	12
2 Tbsp	8 tsp	4 tsp	24
2½ Tbsp	10 tsp	4¾ tsp	30
¼ cup	⅓ cup	8 tsp	48

CUMIN & CORIANDER BRINE

MAKES ABOUT 1½ CUPS (12 FL OZ/375 ML)

2 tablespoons kosher salt

1 tablespoon honey

2 cloves garlic, pressed or minced

1 tablespoon ground cumin

1 tablespoon ground coriander

4 ice cubes

In a microwave-safe bowl, combine 1 cup (8 fl oz/
250 ml) water, the salt, honey, garlic, cumin,
and coriander and microwave until warm, about
2 minutes. Stir to dissolve the salt and honey.
(Alternatively, warm the same ingredients in a
small saucepan on the stove top and stir to dissolve
the salt and honey.) Add the ice cubes to cool down
the mixture.

SPICY CITRUS MARINADE

MAKES ABOUT 1⅓ CUPS (11 FL OZ/340 ML)

¼ cup (2 fl oz/60 ml) extra-virgin olive oil

1 yellow onion, thinly sliced

2 cloves garlic, minced

1–2 serrano chiles, seeded and thinly sliced

¼ cup (2 fl oz/60 ml) blanco tequila

Grated zest and juice of 1 lemon

Grated zest and juice of 1 lime

Grated zest and juice of 1 orange

1 teaspoon dried basil

1 teaspoon fine sea salt

In a frying pan, heat the oil over medium heat. Add
the onion, garlic, and chiles and sauté until tender
and translucent, about 5 minutes. Add the tequila,
bring to a boil, and boil for 1 minute. Remove from
the heat and stir in all of the citrus zests and juices,
the basil, and the salt. Let cool to room temperature.

Use immediately, or store in an airtight container in
the refrigerator for up to 4 days.

MEXICAN SOUR ORANGE MARINADE

MAKES ABOUT 1¾ CUPS (14 FL OZ/430 ML)

5 tablespoons (1¾ oz/50 g) annatto seeds

1 tablespoon peppercorns

1 tablespoon dried oregano, preferably Mexican

1½ teaspoons cumin seeds

8 allspice berries

½ teaspoon whole cloves

1½ cups (12 fl oz/375 ml) fresh sour orange juice

8 cloves garlic, coarsely chopped

1 tablespoon coarse sea salt

In a spice grinder, combine the annatto seeds,
peppercorns, oregano, cumin seeds, allspice, and
cloves and grind to a fine powder.

In a blender, combine the orange juice, garlic, salt,
and ground spice mixture and process until as
smooth as possible.

Use immediately, or transfer to an airtight container
and store in the refrigerator for up to 1 week.

BEER MOP

MAKES ABOUT 2½ CUPS (20 FL OZ/590 ML)

¾ cup (6 fl oz/180 ml) dark beer

¾ cup (6 fl oz/180 ml) strong brewed coffee, at room
temperature

½ cup (4 fl oz/125 ml) canola oil or other mild vegetable oil

¼ cup (2 fl oz/60 ml) malt vinegar

¼ cup (2 fl oz/60 ml) apple cider

2 tablespoons Worcestershire sauce

In a bowl, whisk together all of the ingredients,
mixing well. Use immediately, or store in an airtight
container in the refrigerator for up to 1 month.

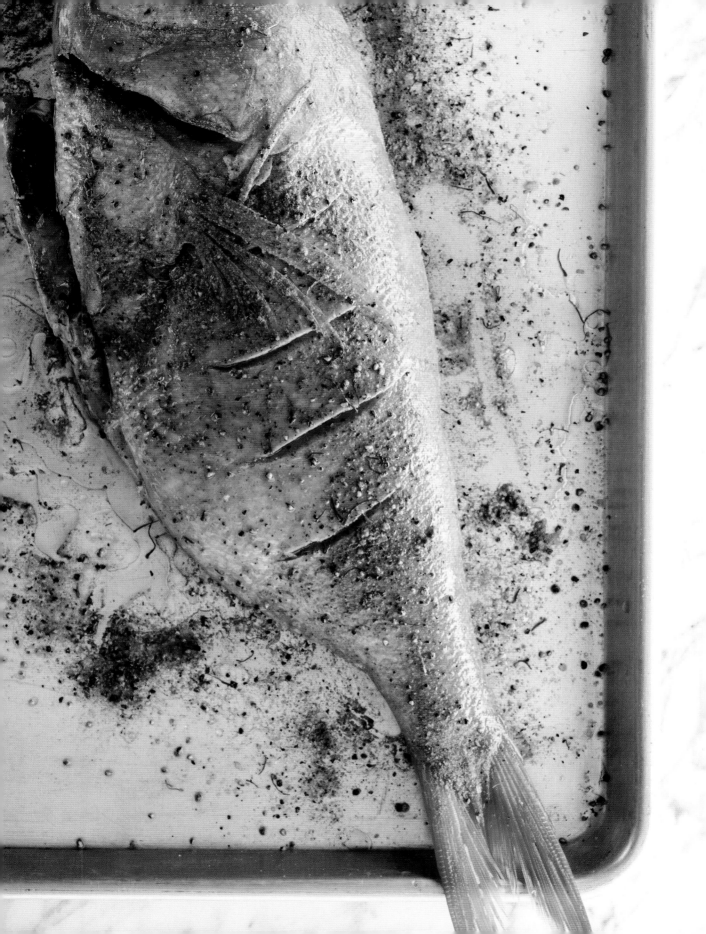

LESSON
2

RUBS

Spice rubs are the quickest way to flavor grilled food. When exposed to fire, rubs form an intensely flavored crust on the food's surface. They are the first thing to hit the palate, and they ignite a dynamic interplay between the relatively untouched moist interior and the slightly charred, somewhat salty, wonderfully spicy surface.

Most rubs contain a significant amount of salt and sugar. The salt attacks the protein in meats, opening up the structure of the amino acids so they are better able to absorb the flavors in the rub. At the same time, the sugar mixes with the protein and forms a weak chemical structure that quickly breaks down into hundreds of flavorful compounds when it hits heat. This reaction of sugars and proteins, known as the Maillard reactions (after a French chemist who discovered them; see page 22), is why browned meat tastes so good.

Allowing a food coated with a rub to rest while the grill is heating helps the salt and sugar to do their jobs. Sometimes we refrigerate rub-coated foods for 24 hours or more to allow the salt and sugar reactions to go a bit deeper and develop the thickest crust possible. Even with that extra time, do not

expect the effects of a rub to go much deeper than the surface, which is not a bad thing. Because we perceive flavors in layers, it is possible to concoct highly sophisticated flavor juxtapositions, such as infusing a steak with a savory brine, rubbing it with a spicy rub, grilling it until a nice spicy crust forms, and then enhancing the work of the rub and the brine with a tangy dipping sauce at the table.

Rubs made from all dry ingredients, called dry rubs, can usually be stored in a tightly closed zippered plastic bag or jar in a cabinet for a couple of weeks or up to a month. Fresh rubs, which are rubs that contain such moist or fresh ingredients as chopped garlic and herbs, should be refrigerated in airtight containers and will keep from a few days up to a week, depending on the shelf life of their most perishable ingredient.

BASIC BARBECUE RUB

MAKES ABOUT ½ CUP (1¾ OZ/50 G)

2 tablespoons sweet paprika, preferably smoked
2 tablespoons golden brown sugar
1 tablespoon fine sea salt
2 teaspoons freshly ground black pepper
2 teaspoons onion powder
2 teaspoons dry mustard
1 teaspoon cayenne pepper

In a small bowl, stir together all of the ingredients, mixing well. Use immediately, or store in an airtight container at room temperature for up to 6 months.

ANCHO CHILE RUB

MAKES ⅓ CUP (1½ OZ/45 G)

2 tablespoons ancho chile powder
1 tablespoon guajillo chile powder
1 tablespoon hot paprika
1 tablespoon dried oregano, preferably Mexican
1 tablespoon coarse sea salt
1 tablespoon coarsely ground black pepper
2 teaspoons onion powder
1 teaspoon cayenne pepper
1 teaspoon sugar

In a small bowl, stir together all of the ingredients, mixing well. Use immediately, or store in an airtight container at room temperature for up to 1 month.

BEDOUIN SPICE RUB

MAKES ABOUT ⅓ CUP (1¾ OZ/50 G)

2 tablespoons coarsely ground black pepper
1 tablespoon coarsely ground caraway
2 teaspoons ground coriander
2 teaspoons turbinado or Demerara sugar
2 teaspoons coarse sea salt
1 teaspoon ground cardamom
1 teaspoon ground turmeric
½ teaspoon saffron threads
⅛ teaspoon cayenne pepper

In a small bowl, stir together all of the ingredients, mixing well. Use immediately, or store in an airtight container at room temperature for up to 1 month.

ESPRESSO RUB

MAKES ⅓ CUP (1¾ OZ/50 G)

1 tablespoon finely ground dark roasted coffee
1 tablespoon dark brown sugar

1 tablespoon coarse sea salt
2 teaspoons sweet paprika, preferably smoked
1½ teaspoons freshly ground black pepper
1 teaspoon chipotle chile powder
1 teaspoon chili powder
1 teaspoon grated lemon zest

In a small bowl, stir together all of the ingredients, mixing well. Use immediately, or store in an airtight container at room temperature for up to 2 weeks.

MOLE RUB

MAKES ABOUT 1 CUP (4½ OZ/140 G)

¼ cup (¾ oz/20 g) unsweetened cocoa powder
2 tablespoons ancho chile powder
2 tablespoons guajillo chile powder
2 tablespoons sesame seeds, toasted
2 tablespoons kosher salt
2 tablespoons dark brown sugar
2 teaspoons ground cinnamon
1 tablespoon chipotle chile powder
1 teaspoon ground anise
1 teaspoon garlic powder
1 teaspoon onion powder
1 teaspoon freshly ground black pepper
1 teaspoon dried thyme leaves
1 teaspoon ground oregano
Pinch of ground cloves

In a small bowl, stir together all of the ingredients, mixing well. Use immediately, or store in an airtight container at room temperature for up to 1 month.

CITRUS RUB

Grated zest of 2 lemons
Grated zest of 2 limes
Grated zest of 1 orange
2 teaspoons ground coriander
1 teaspoon fine sea salt such as fleur de sel
½ teaspoon freshly ground black pepper
Pinch of crushed red pepper flakes

In a small bowl, stir together all of the ingredients, mixing well. Use immediately, or store in an airtight container in the refrigerator for up to 4 days.

CHINESE FIVE-SPICE RUB

MAKES ABOUT ½ CUP (2¼ OZ/70 G)

18 star anise pods (with seeds)
2 tablespoons fennel seeds
2 teaspoons Sichuan peppercorns

1 teaspoon whole cloves

1 tablespoon ground cinnamon

2 teaspoons fine sea salt

2 teaspoons light brown sugar

In a spice grinder, combine the star anise, fennel seeds, Sichuan peppercorns, and cloves and grind to a fine powder. Transfer to a small bowl and stir in the cinnamon, salt, and sugar. Use immediately, or store in an airtight container at room temperature for up to 6 months.

RAS EL HANOUT

MAKES ABOUT ¼ CUP (1¼ OZ/37 G)

2 teaspoons each ground cumin, ground ginger, and freshly ground pepper

1½ teaspoons fine sea salt

1½ teaspoons ground cinnamon

1 teaspoon each ground coriander and ground allspice

1 teaspoon ground Aleppo or cayenne pepper

1 teaspoon saffron threads, crushed

½ teaspoon ground cloves

¼ teaspoon freshly grated nutmeg

In a small bowl, stir together all of the ingredients, mixing well. Use immediately, or store in an airtight container at room temperature for up to 1 month.

SHICHIMI TOGARASHI

MAKES ABOUT 3 TABLESPOONS

1 tablespoon dried granulated orange peel

2 teaspoons garlic powder

1 teaspoon sesame seeds, toasted

1 teaspoon black sesame seeds

1 teaspoon freshly ground black pepper

¾ teaspoon fine sea salt

½ teaspoon red pepper flakes

In a small bowl, stir together all of the ingredients, mixing well. Use immediately, or store in an airtight container at cool room temperature for up to 6 months.

BERBERE

MAKES ABOUT 6 TABLESPOONS (1½ OZ/45 G)

2 teaspoons coriander seeds

1 teaspoon fenugreek seeds

½ teaspoon each cumin seeds and peppercorns

4 allspice berries

4 whole cloves

Seeds from 4 green cardamom pods

4 or 5 dried red chiles (cayenne type)

3 tablespoons sweet paprika

1½ teaspoons fine sea salt

½ teaspoon ground ginger

¼ teaspoon each ground cinnamon and freshly grated nutmeg

In a small, heavy frying pan, toast the coriander, fenugreek, cumin, peppercorns, allspice, cloves, and cardamom over medium-high heat, shaking the pan to prevent burning. When the spices smell fragrant, after 4–5 minutes, transfer them to a bowl and let cool slightly. Transfer the toasted spices to a spice grinder. Break open the chiles and discard the seeds and stems. Add the chiles to the spice grinder and grind everything to a fine powder. Transfer to a bowl and stir in the paprika, salt, ginger, cinnamon, and nutmeg. Store in an airtight container at cool room temperature for up to 6 months.

VADOUVAN

MAKES ABOUT ¾ CUP (5 OZ/155 G)

2 tablespoons unsalted butter, preferably clarified

2 tablespoons canola oil or other mild vegetable oil

2 yellow onions, finely chopped

1 large shallot, finely chopped

½ teaspoon fine sea salt

4 cloves garlic, minced

1 teaspoon ground cumin

½ teaspoon each ground cardamom, ground fenugreek, brown mustard seeds, and ground turmeric

¼ teaspoon ground coriander

⅛ teaspoon each freshly grated nutmeg and ground cloves

⅛–¼ teaspoon cayenne pepper

Preheat the oven to 300°F (150°C). Line a rimmed baking sheet with parchment paper. In a large frying pan, melt the butter with the oil over medium heat. Add the onions, shallot, and salt and cook, stirring frequently to prevent burning, until soft and golden brown, about 30 minutes. Add the garlic, spices, and cayenne and cook, continuing to stir, until golden brown, 5–10 minutes. Transfer the onion mixture to the prepared baking sheet and spread it in a thin layer. Bake until deeply browned and only slightly moist, 45–60 minutes.

Let cool completely. Use immediately, or transfer to an airtight container and refrigerate for up to 1 week or freeze for up to 3 months.

SAUCES

The indiscriminate slathering of barbecue sauce over anything grilled is more common than we like to see. Most flavoring and saucing of grilled food is better accomplished by rubs, brines, mops, and marinades. Sauces are better used après grill at the table as counterpoints to the more important fire-infused flavors that you worked so hard to develop on the grill.

The biggest problem with most barbecue sauce is the dominance of sugar. When a thin sauce contains enough sugar to melt across the surface of an ingredient on the grill, it forms a lustrous, lacquered glaze. Unfortunately, the sugar that makes a shiny and delicious glaze also makes the surface burn easily. To prevent burning, brush on glazes only during the last few minutes of grilling. Keep in mind that the flavors of a glaze don't have enough time to penetrate the interior of an ingredient. Glazes are most effective for providing a new flavor or textural contrast to the base flavor developed with a rub, brine, or marinade.

Vinaigrettes, on the other hand, can be very effective brushed repeatedly on the surface of grilling fish, poultry, or lean meats to add deep, bright flavor. Plus, a vinaigrette does not scorch nearly as easily as a barbecue sauce.

Condiments, like flavored mustards, pickles, salsas, and chutneys, are best used as table accompaniments to grilled meats, poultry, or seafood. When paired with the right marinade or rub, they can increase the enjoyment of a grilled meal. If you must cook with any of them, use them like a glaze, that is, only during the last few minutes of cooking, and then pass more at the table. With something chunky, like a salsa or a chutney, we like to puree some of the condiment to brush on as a glaze and then serve the reserved chunky portion at the table.

BASIC BARBECUE SAUCE

MAKES ABOUT 3 CUPS (24 FL OZ/750 ML)

2 cups (16 oz/500 g) tomato ketchup

3 tablespoons dark brown sugar

3 tablespoons cider vinegar

2 tablespoons yellow mustard

2 tablespoons Worcestershire sauce

2 teaspoons smoked paprika

1½ teaspoons fine sea salt

1 teaspoon garlic powder

½ teaspoon onion powder

½ teaspoon freshly ground black pepper

In a saucepan, combine all of the ingredients and bring to a boil over high heat. Reduce the heat to medium-low and simmer until slightly thickened, about 20 minutes. Use immediately, or let cool, transfer to an airtight container, and refrigerate for up to 1 month.

If the sauce has been refrigerated, reheat over low heat before using. Always brush warm sauce onto meats as they are cooking. Brushing cold sauce onto hot meat lowers the meat temperature slightly and slows down the cooking.

EXTRA CREDIT

Sweet, Rich & Smoky Barbecue Sauce: Add 4 tablespoons (2 oz/60 g) unsalted butter, 2 tablespoons dark (not blackstrap) molasses, 1 tablespoon honey, and 2 teaspoons liquid smoke with the other ingredients.

Chipotle Rye Barbecue Sauce: Follow the directions for Sweet, Rich, and Smoky Barbecue Sauce (above), adding ½ cup (4 fl oz/125 ml) rye whiskey and 2–3 teaspoons chipotle chile powder with the other ingredients.

Maple Bourbon Barbecue Sauce: Add ½ cup (4 fl oz/125 ml) bourbon, 4 tablespoons (2 oz/60 g) unsalted butter, and 3 tablespoons maple syrup with the other ingredients.

Peach Bourbon Barbecue Sauce: Add 1 cup (8 fl oz/250 ml) peach nectar, ½ cup (4 fl oz/125 ml) bourbon, 4 tablespoons (2 oz/60 g) unsalted butter, and 2 tablespoons dark (not blackstrap) molasses with the other ingredients.

Rich and Smoky Texas Barbecue Sauce: Increase the cider vinegar to ½ cup (4 fl oz/125 ml) and add 4 tablespoons (2 oz/60 g) unsalted butter, 2 teaspoons liquid smoke, 1 tablespoon ancho or other chile powder, and 1 teaspoon cayenne pepper, or more to taste, with the other ingredients.

Creamy Stout Barbecue Sauce: Add ½ cup (4 fl oz/125 ml) stout beer, 4 tablespoons (2 oz/60 g) unsalted butter, and ¼ cup (2 fl oz/60 ml) heavy cream with the other ingredients.

ALABAMA WHITE BARBECUE SAUCE

MAKES ABOUT 2 CUPS (16 FL OZ/500 ML)

1½ cups (12 fl oz/375 ml) mayonnaise, preferably Duke's

½ cup (4 fl oz/125 ml) cider vinegar

Juice of ½ lemon

2 teaspoons prepared horseradish

2 teaspoons freshly ground black pepper

1 teaspoon fine sea salt

1 teaspoon sugar

2 cloves garlic, pressed or crushed

½ teaspoon garlic powder

¼ teaspoon cayenne pepper

In a bowl, combine all of the ingredients and mix well. Use immediately, or transfer to an airtight container and refrigerate for up to 1 week.

WESTERN CAROLINA BARBECUE SAUCE

MAKES ABOUT 3¼ CUPS (26 FL OZ/810 ML)

2 cups (16 fl oz/500 ml) cider vinegar

¾ cup (6 oz/185 g) tomato ketchup

½ cup (4 fl oz/125 ml) water

2 tablespoons sugar

1 tablespoon mild hot-pepper sauce such as Frank's RedHot

2 teaspoons kosher salt

1 teaspoon red pepper flakes

½ teaspoon freshly ground black pepper

In a saucepan, combine all of the ingredients and bring to a simmer over medium heat, stirring often. Remove from the heat and use immediately, or let cool, transfer to an airtight container, and refrigerate for up to 1 month.

ANCHO CHOCOLATE BBQ SAUCE

MAKES ABOUT 3 CUPS (24 FL OZ/750 ML)

3 dried ancho chiles, stemmed and seeded

2 dried guajillo chiles, stemmed and seeded

2 large, ripe plum tomatoes

2 cloves garlic, unpeeled

½ oz (15 g) bittersweet chocolate, finely chopped

¼ cup (1½ oz/45 g) raisins

½ teaspoon dried oregano, preferably Mexican

¼ teaspoon ground cumin

¼ teaspoon ground cinnamon

¼ teaspoon freshly ground pepper

1 cup (8 fl oz/250 ml) beef broth

¼ cup (2 fl oz/60 ml) sherry vinegar

¼ cup (2 oz/60 g) firmly packed dark brown sugar

One at a time, grasp the chiles with tongs, hold directly over the high flame of a gas burner or a grill, and toast for about 30 seconds per side. Char the skins of the tomatoes in the same way and then the garlic clove. Put the chiles in a bowl, add hot water to cover, and set aside to soak until soft, about 20 minutes.

When the tomatoes and garlic are cool enough to handle, peel them with your fingers and place in a blender. Pluck the chiles from their soaking liquid and add to the blender along with the chocolate, raisins, oregano, cumin, cinnamon, pepper, broth, vinegar, sugar and ½ cup (4 fl oz/125 ml) of the chile soaking liquid. Blend until completely smooth.

Pour the sauce in a frying pan, place over high heat, and bring to a boil. Boil vigorously until the sauce thickens to the consistency of tomato ketchup. Let cool. Store in an airtight container in the refrigerator for up to 1 month.

MARINARA SAUCE

MAKES ABOUT 3 CUPS (24 FL OZ/750 ML)

¼ cup (2 fl oz/60 ml) extra-virgin olive oil

4 cloves garlic, minced

1 can (28 oz/875 g) plum tomatoes in puree

3 tablespoons chopped fresh basil or flat-leaf parsley, or 1 teaspoon dried basil or oregano

Fine sea salt and freshly ground pepper

In a large frying pan, heat the oil over medium heat. Add the garlic and cook, stirring often, until light golden brown, 3–5 minutes.

Working near the frying pan, pluck the tomatoes from the can one by one. For each tomato, grab the firm stem end and pinch and pull out the core from the tomato flesh. Discard the core and tear the flesh with your fingers, dropping the pieces into the pan. Pour half of the liquid from the can into the pan and add 2 tablespoons of the fresh basil or all of the dried basil. Bring the mixture to a boil, reduce the heat to medium-low, and cook until the tomatoes begin to break down, 10–15 minutes. For a thicker sauce, crush the tomatoes with a wooden spoon as they

cook. Taste the sauce, then season to taste with salt and pepper. Stir in the remaining 1 tablespoon fresh basil, if using. Use immediately, or let cool, transfer to an airtight container, and store in the refrigerator for up to 2 days or freeze for up to 2 months.

EXTRA CREDIT

Marinara Sauce with Red Wine: Add ½ cup (4 fl oz/ 125 ml) red wine after cooking the garlic and simmer until the liquid reduces in volume by about half.

Thick Marinara Sauce: Stir in 2 tablespoons tomato paste along with the tomatoes.

Spicy Marinara Sauce (Arrabbiata): Add ¼–½ teaspoon crushed red pepper flakes along with the garlic.

HOMEMADE STEAK SAUCE

MAKES ½ CUP (4 FL OZ/125 ML)

4 tablespoons (2 oz/60 g) unsalted butter

1 tablespoon brown mustard

1 tablespoon tomato paste

2 tablespoons Worcestershire sauce

In a small saucepan, melt the butter over low heat. Whisk in the mustard and tomato paste and then slowly whisk in the Worcestershire sauce. Remove from the heat and use immediately or transfer to an airtight container and refrigerator for up to 1 week.

EXTRA CREDIT

Espresso Steak Sauce: Replace 1 tablespoon of the Worcestershire sauce with 1 tablespoon brewed espresso.

SPICY KOREAN GLAZE

MAKES ABOUT ¾ CUP (6 FL OZ/180 ML)

6 cloves garlic, minced

4 green onions, white and pale green parts, thinly sliced

⅓ cup (2½ oz/75 g) firmly packed dark brown sugar

⅓ cup (3 fl oz/80 ml) tamari or Japanese soy sauce

2 tablespoons gochujang (Korean red chile paste)

1 tablespoon cider vinegar

1 teaspoon Asian sesame oil

½ teaspoon freshly ground pepper

½-inch (12-mm) piece fresh ginger, peeled and minced

In a small saucepan, combine all of the ingredients and bring to a boil over high heat, stirring constantly. Reduce the heat to a simmer and cook until lightly thickened, about 3 minutes. Let cool before using or transfer to an airtight container and store in the refrigerator for up to 1 month.

SSAM JANG

MAKES ABOUT ½ CUP (3½ OZ/105 G)

¼ cup (2¼ oz/70 g) doenjang (Korean fermented soybean paste)

1–2 teaspoons gochujang (Korean red chile paste)

1 clove garlic, minced

1 green onion, white and pale green parts, chopped

2 teaspoons honey

2 teaspoons Asian sesame oil

1 teaspoon sesame seeds, toasted

In a small bowl, combine all of the ingredients and mix well. Use immediately, or store in an airtight container in the refrigerator for up to 1 week.

VIETNAMESE DIPPING SAUCE

MAKES ABOUT ¾ CUP (6 FL OZ/180 ML)

¼ cup (2 fl oz/60 ml) fresh lime juice

¼ cup (2 fl oz/60 ml) fish sauce

¼ cup (2 fl oz/60 ml) water

1 tablespoon rice vinegar

1 clove garlic, minced

1 fresh hot chile such as bird's eye or habanero, seeded and minced

In a small bowl, combine all of the ingredients and mix well. Use immediately, or store in an airtight container in the refrigerator for up to 2 weeks.

REAL RUSSIAN DRESSING

MAKES ABOUT ¾ CUP (6 FL OZ/180 ML)

¼ cup (2 fl oz/60 ml) mayonnaise

¼ cup (2 oz/60 g) sour cream

1 tablespoon tomato paste

3 tablespoons fresh lemon juice

2 tablespoons red or black caviar

In a small bowl, combine the mayonnaise, sour cream, tomato paste, and lemon juice and mix well. Fold in the caviar. Use immediately, or store in an airtight container in the refrigerator for up to 2 weeks.

ROASTED TOMATO FRENCH DRESSING

MAKES ABOUT 1 CUP (8 FL OZ/250 ML)

1 lb (500 g) ripe plum tomatoes, cored and quartered lengthwise

2 cloves garlic, finely chopped

5 tablespoons (2½ fl oz/75 ml) olive oil

Pinch of coarse sea salt

¼ cup (2 fl oz/60 ml) red wine vinegar

1 tablespoon sweet paprika

1 tablespoon mayonnaise

Preheat the oven to 400°F (200°C). On a rimmed baking sheet, combine the tomatoes and garlic, drizzle with 1 tablespoon of oil, and toss to coat evenly. Spread the tomatoes in a single layer on the pan and sprinkle with the salt. Roast the tomatoes until softened and slightly shriveled, about 30 minutes.

Let the tomatoes cool completely and then transfer to a food processor. Add the vinegar, paprika, mayonnaise, and the remaining 4 tablespoons (2 fl oz/60 ml) oil and process until smooth. Use immediately, or transfer to an airtight container and store in the refrigerator for up to 2 weeks.

BLUE CHEESE DRESSING

MAKES ABOUT 2½ CUPS (20 FL OZ/625 ML)

1 cup (4½ oz/140 g) crumbled blue cheese

¾ cup (6 oz/185 g) sour cream

¾ cup (6 fl oz/180 ml) mayonnaise

2 tablespoons minced yellow onion

1 tablespoon white wine vinegar

½ teaspoon salt

¼ teaspoon freshly ground pepper

1 small clove garlic, minced

In a bowl, combine all of the ingredients and mix well. Use immediately, or store in an airtight container in the refrigerator for up 4 days.

RANCH DRESSING

MAKES 1 CUP (8 FL OZ/250 ML)

½ clove garlic, minced

½ teaspoon fine sea salt

¼ cup (2 fl oz/60 ml) mayonnaise

Juice of ½ lemon

3 tablespoons buttermilk

½ teaspoon Worcestershire sauce or soy sauce

1 teaspoon hot-pepper sauce

1 tablespoon chopped fresh flat-leaf parsley

1 tablespoon chopped fresh cilantro

½ teaspoon freshly ground pepper

In a bowl, using the back of fork, mash together the garlic and salt into a paste. Add the mayonnaise, lemon juice, buttermilk, Worcestershire sauce, hot sauce, parsley, cilantro, and pepper and mix well. Use immediately, or transfer to an airtight container and store in the refrigerator for up to 1 week.

SRIRACHA MAYO

MAKES 1 CUP (8 FL OZ/250 ML)

¾ cup (6 fl oz/180 ml) mayonnaise
¼ cup (2 fl oz/60 ml) Sriracha sauce
Grated zest and juice of 1 lime

In a bowl, combine all of the ingredients and mix well. Use immediately, or transfer to an airtight container and store in the refrigerator for up to 2 weeks.

GREEN CHILE QUESO

MAKES ABOUT 2 CUPS (32 OZ/907 G)

1 tablespoon canola oil or other mild vegetable oil
½ pound (250 g) ground beef
½ yellow onion, chopped
1 lb (500 g) Velveeta cheese, cut into 1-inch (25-cm) cubes
½ cup (3 oz/90 g) canned diced tomatoes with green chiles, such as Rotel, drained
1 can (4 oz/125 g) diced green chiles, drained
1 jalapeño chile, finely diced

In a large frying pan, heat the canola oil over medium-high heat. Add the beef and onion and cook, breaking up the meat with a wooden spoon and stirring often, until the meat is cooked through and the onion is tender, about 10 minutes.

Pour off as much of the fat from the pan as possible, then return the pan to medium-low heat. Add the cheese, diced tomatoes and chiles, and diced chiles and stir until the cheese melts and the mixture is bubbling. Stir in the jalapeño chile and serve.

PICKLED SALSA

MAKES 2 CUPS (16 OZ/500 G)

⅓ cup (3 fl oz/80 ml) olive oil
1 tablespoon peeled and grated fresh ginger
3 cloves garlic, minced
1 tablespoon ground pickling spice
½ cup (4 fl oz/125 ml) white vinegar
2 tablespoons sugar
2 teaspoons fine sea salt
1 lb (500 g) tomatoes, diced
½ red onion, diced
3 serrano chiles, seeded and finely diced

In a saucepan, heat the oil, ginger, and garlic over medium heat until the ginger and garlic bubble vigorously, about 2 minutes. Add the pickling spice, vinegar, sugar, and salt and bring to a boil, stirring often. Remove from the heat and stir in the tomatoes, onion, and chiles.

Set the salsa aside for 2 hours before serving. Or transfer the cooled salsa to an airtight container and store in the refrigerator for up to 2 weeks.

GRILLED TOMATO JAM

MAKES ABOUT 2 CUPS (20 OZ/625 G)

2 lb (1 kg) plum tomatoes, halved lengthwise
1 tablespoon olive oil
¾ teaspoon fine sea salt
¼ teaspoon freshly ground pepper
½ cup (4 oz/125 g) sugar
¼ cup (2 fl oz/60 ml) apple juice

Heat the grill for medium-high direct heat (400°–450°F/200°–230°C).

Scoop out and discard the seeds from the tomato halves, coat with the oil, and season with the salt and pepper. Brush the grill grate and coat with oil. Put the tomatoes on the grate, cover the grill, and cook, turning once, until browned, about 4 minutes per side.

Transfer the tomatoes to a cutting board and let cool for a few minutes. Peel away the skin and discard. Chop the tomato flesh finely, transfer to a saucepan, and stir in the sugar and apple juice. Place over medium heat, bring to a simmer, and cook, stirring often, until the mixture thickens, about 20 minutes.

Taste and adjust the seasoning with salt and pepper if needed. Let cool. To store, transfer to an airtight container and refrigerate for up to 2 weeks.

QUICK PICKLES

MAKES ABOUT 1 PT (16 FL OZ/500 ML)

½ cup (4 fl oz/125 ml) white or cider vinegar

1 tablespoon sugar

1 teaspoon mustard seeds, any color

1 teaspoon pickling spices

1 teaspoon fine sea salt

2 cloves garlic, smashed

1 bay leaf

4 Kirby cucumbers, sliced; 1 small head cauliflower, broken into small florets; 8 small white onions, peeled and quartered; or 12 okra pods, sliced

In a small saucepan, combine the vinegar, sugar, mustard seeds, pickling spice, and salt and bring to a boil over high heat. Remove from the heat.

Put the garlic, bay leaf, and vegetable of choice in a pint (16 fl oz/500 ml) heatproof jar or liquid measuring cup. Pour the hot brine into the jar or cup, making sure the vegetables are submerged.

Let cool for at least 3 hours before serving. To store, cap the jar tightly (or, if using the measuring cup, transfer to an airtight container) and refrigerate for up to 1 month.

PORT KETCHUP

MAKES ABOUT ⅔ CUP (5 OZ/155 G)

½ cup (4 fl oz/125 ml) port wine

½ cup (4 oz/125 g) tomato ketchup

In a small frying pan, bring the port to a boil over medium heat and boil, stirring frequently (especially near the end), until lightly thickened. When finished, you should have 2–3 tablespoons port wine syrup. Let cool completely, then add the ketchup and mix well. Use immediately, or transfer to an airtight container and store in the refrigerator for up to 1 month.

HARISSA

MAKES ABOUT ½ CUP (4 OZ/125 G)

2 oz (60 g) dried ancho or guajillo chiles (about 2 large chiles)

¼ oz (7 g) dried African bird chiles (about 3 chiles)

½ teaspoon coriander seeds

½ teaspoon caraway seeds

2 cloves garlic

½ teaspoon fine sea salt

1 tablespoon smoked paprika

1 tablespoon double concentrated tomato paste

2 tablespoons olive oil

Put all of the chiles in a heatproof bowl and add boiling water to cover. Let soak for 30 minutes.

While the chiles are soaking, heat a small frying pan over high heat until smoking hot. Add the coriander and caraway, remove from the heat, and stir until the spices are toasted, about 30 seconds. Dump the contents of the pan into a mortar or spice grinder and grind finely.

Drain the chiles, reserving the soaking water. Discard the stems and seeds from the chiles.

Put the chiles, ground spices, and garlic in a food processor and pulse until finely chopped. Add the salt, paprika, tomato paste, and 2 tablespoons of the chile-soaking water and process until a thick paste forms, adding more soaking water if needed. With the processor running, slowly drizzle in the oil and then thin to the consistency of ketchup with some of the reserved chile soaking water. Use immediately, or transfer to an airtight container and refrigerate for up to 1 month.

ZA'ATAR TZATZIKI

MAKES ABOUT 1¾ CUPS (14 FL OZ/430 ML)

1 large cucumber, halved lengthwise and seeded, unpeeled

2 teaspoons fine sea salt

1 cup plain Greek yogurt or drained regular yogurt

1 tablespoon extra-virgin olive oil

1 tablespoon white wine vinegar

1 large clove garlic, crushed or pressed

2 teaspoons Za'atar (page 174)

¼ preserved lemon (page 226), finely chopped (optional)

Place a colander over a shallow bowl. Using the large holes of a box grater, grate the cucumber and transfer to the colander. Scatter on the salt, toss gently, and let stand for 15 minutes.

Press on the cucumber to extract as much liquid as possible and discard the liquid. Transfer the cucumber to a small bowl and stir in the yogurt. Add the oil, vinegar, garlic, za'atar, and the lemon (if using) and mix well. (The lemon is particularly delicious.) Use immediately, or transfer to an airtight container and store in the refrigerator for up to 2 days.

PRESERVED LEMONS

MAKES 4 PRESERVED LEMONS

4 lemons
3/4 cup (9 1/2 oz/295 g) coarse sea salt
1/2 cup (4 fl oz/125 ml) fresh lemon juice

Cut the tips off the ends of the lemons. Cut each lemon lengthwise into eighths, leaving them attached at the stem end. Pack the lemons and salt into a widemouthed pint (16 fl oz/500 ml) container, gently rubbing the salt into the lemons and releasing some lemon juice. Pour in the fresh lemon juice. The lemons should be covered with liquid.

Cap the container tightly and leave at room temperature for 2–3 weeks, shaking the jar every day to distribute the salt. Store in the refrigerator for up to 1 month. Rinse well before using.

EXTRA CREDIT

To store the preserved lemons for months, rinse them and place them in a container just big enough to hold them. Add olive oil to cover and refrigerate.

PRESERVED LEMON YOGURT

MAKES ABOUT 2 CUPS (16 FL OZ/500 ML)

2 preserved lemons (above), seeded and coarsely chopped
1/2 cup (1/2 oz/15 g) fresh cilantro and/or flat-leaf parsley leaves and small stems
4 cloves garlic, coarsely chopped
1/4 cup (2 fl oz/60 ml) extra-virgin olive oil
1 cup (8 oz/250 g) plain yogurt

In a food processor, combine the lemons, cilantro, and garlic and pulse until finely chopped. Add the oil and yogurt and process until creamy, or transfer to an airtight container and store in the refrigerator for up to 2 weeks.

ANCHOVY BUTTER

MAKES ABOUT 1/4 CUP (2 OZ/60 G)

6 anchovy fillets (about 1 oz/30 g)
2 cloves garlic, pressed or minced
3 tablespoons minced fresh flat-leaf parsley
2 tablespoons unsalted butter, at room temperature
Pinch of crushed red pepper flakes
Pinch of fine sea salt

In a small bowl, using the back of a fork, mash together all of the ingredients until well mixed.

Use immediately, or transfer to an airtight container and store in the refrigerator for up to 4 days.

FINES HERBES BUTTER

MAKES 1 CUP (8 OZ/250 G)

1 cup (8 oz/250 g) unsalted butter, at room temperature
1/4 cup (1/3 oz/10 g) chopped fresh flat-leaf parsley
1/4 cup (1/3 oz/10 g) chopped fresh chervil
1/4 cup (1/3 oz/10 g) chopped fresh tarragon
1/4 cup (1/3 oz/10 g) chopped fresh chives
1 small clove garlic, pressed or crushed
1/2 teaspoon anchovy paste (optional)
1/2 teaspoon fine sea salt
1/8 teaspoon freshly ground pepper

In a bowl, using a fork, stir together all of the ingredients, mixing well, or, combine all of the ingredients in a food processor and use brief pulses to mix thoroughly. Transfer to a sheet of plastic wrap and, using a rubber spatula and the plastic wrap, shape the butter into a log about 1 1/2 inches (3.8 cm) in diameter. Wrap the log in the plastic wrap and refrigerate until firm, about 30 minutes, before using, or store in the refrigerator for or up to 1 week.

EXTRA CREDIT

Forest Herb Butter: Replace the chervil, tarragon, and chives with fresh rosemary, thyme, and sage.

Tomato Basil Butter: Omit all of the seasonings. Flavor the butter with 1/2 cup (3/4 oz/20 g) chopped fresh basil, 2 tablespoons tomato paste, 1/2 teaspoon salt, and 1/4 teaspoon freshly ground pepper.

Citrus Butter: Omit all of the seasonings. Flavor the butter with the grated zest and juice of 1 lemon or lime (or 1/2 orange or yuzu), 1/2 teaspoon salt, and 1/4 teaspoon freshly ground pepper.

Roasted Garlic Butter: Omit all of the seasonings. Flavor the butter with 1 tablespoon roasted garlic paste, 1/2 teaspoon salt, and 1/4 teaspoon freshly ground pepper.

Hazelnut Butter: Omit all of the seasonings. Combine 1 cup (5 oz/155 g) peeled hazelnuts and 4 teaspoons fresh lemon juice in a food processor and process until the nuts are finely ground. Flavor the butter with the ground nut mixture, 1/2 teaspoon salt, and 1/4 teaspoon freshly ground pepper.

GORGONZOLA BUTTER

MAKES ½ CUP (4 OZ/125 G)

1 small clove garlic, minced
3 oz (90 g) Gorgonzola cheese, without rind
2 tablespoons unsalted butter, at room temperature
2 tablespoons extra-virgin olive oil
Fine sea salt and freshly ground pepper

In a small bowl, using a fork, mix together the garlic, cheese, butter, and oil until light and fluffy. Season with salt and pepper. Use immediately, or transfer to an airtight container and refrigerate for up to 1 week. Bring to room temperature before serving.

BACON BOURBON BUTTER

MAKES ⅓ CUP (3 OZ/90 G)

2 thick-cut bacon slices, finely chopped
½ cup (4 fl oz/125 ml) bourbon
½ teaspoon pumpkin pie spice
3 tablespoons honey
3 tablespoons unsalted butter, softened

In a frying pan, cook the bacon over medium heat until most of its fat has rendered and the bacon pieces are cooked but not yet crisp, about 4 minutes. Scrape the bacon and its rendered fat into a small bowl.

Add the bourbon to the frying pan over medium-high heat. Add the spice blend and boil until reduced to 3 tablespoons, about one-third of its original volume. Add the spiced bourbon to the bacon and stir in the honey. Let cool to room temperature.

Mix in the butter, 1 tablespoon at a time, until thoroughly blended. Use immediately, or transfer to an airtight container and store in the refrigerator for up to 4 days.

WILD MUSHROOM MOSTARDA

MAKES 2½ CUPS (30 OZ/850 G)

1 oz (30 g) dried porcini mushrooms, about ⅔ cup
1 cup (8 fl oz/250 ml) dry red wine
1 tablespoon extra-virgin olive oil
1 tablespoon peeled and minced or grated fresh ginger
1 large shallot, minced (about ¼ cup/1½ oz/45 g)
1 teaspoon truffle salt
1 tablespoon fresh rosemary leaves, finely chopped
2 cloves garlic, minced
1 lb (500 g) mixed fresh wild mushrooms, trimmed and coarsely chopped
1 tablespoon tomato paste

1 tablespoon yellow mustard seeds, cracked with a mortar and pestle
1 teaspoon coriander seeds, cracked with a mortar and pestle
1 teaspoon black peppercorns, cracked with a mortar and pestle
½ teaspoon red pepper flakes
2 tablespoons honey
2 tablespoons prepared spicy brown mustard
2 tablespoons red wine vinegar
1 teaspoon balsamic vinegar
1 teaspoon fresh thyme leaves

In a bowl, combine the porcini and the wine and let the mushrooms soak until softened, about 15 minutes. Scoop out the mushrooms, chop coarsely, and return them to the wine.

In a large frying pan, heat the oil over medium-high heat. Add the ginger and shallot, truffle salt, black pepper, rosemary, and garlic and sauté until the shallot loses its raw look, about 1 minute. Add the fresh mushrooms and sauté until they lose their raw look, about 5 minutes. Add the tomato paste, mustard seeds, coriander, black peppercorns, red pepper flakes, and the soaked porcini and their soaking liquid. Bring to a boil, reduce the heat to a simmer, and cook until all of the mushrooms are tender, about 5 minutes. Remove from the heat and stir in the honey, prepared mustard, red wine and balsamic vinegars, and thyme leaves.

BUFFALO SAUCE

MAKES 1¾ CUPS (14 FL OZ/430 ML)

¾ cup (6 oz/185 g) unsalted butter
1 cup mild hot-pepper sauce such as Frank's RedHot
¼ teaspoon salt

In a small saucepan, combine the butter, hot sauce, and salt and heat over low heat, stirring occasionally, until the butter melts and the sauce is well blended. Alternatively, combine the same ingredients in a microwave-safe bowl and microwave until the butter melts, then stir to mix. Use immediately or transfer to an airtight container and refrigerate for up to 1 week.

ORANGE VINAIGRETTE

MAKES ABOUT ¾ CUP (6 FL OZ/180 ML)

2 tablespoons raspberry vinegar or red wine vinegar
¼ cup (2 fl oz/60 ml) walnut oil or extra-virgin olive oil
½ cup (5 oz/155 g) orange marmalade
½ teaspoon Dijon mustard
½ clove garlic, minced

½ teaspoon kosher salt

¼ teaspoon freshly ground pepper

1 tablespoon chopped fresh basil

Put the vinegar into a small bowl. Add the oil in a thin, steady stream while whisking constantly until emulsified. Whisk in the marmalade, mustard, garlic, salt, pepper, and basil. Use immediately, or transfer to an airtight container and store in the refrigerator for up to 2 weeks.

CHIMICHURRI

MAKES ABOUT 1 CUP (8 FL OZ/250 ML)

1 cup (1 oz/30 g) packed fresh flat-leaf parsley leaves and small stems

1 cup (1 oz/30 g) packed fresh cilantro leaves and small stems

⅓ cup (3 fl oz/80 ml) extra-virgin olive oil

¼ small red bell pepper, seeded and coarsely chopped

3 cloves garlic, coarsely chopped

2 tablespoons coarsely chopped yellow onion

½ teaspoon dried oregano

¼ to ½ teaspoon red pepper flakes

1 teaspoon salt

3 tablespoons sherry vinegar

In a food processor, combine the parsley, cilantro, oil, ¼ cup (2 fl oz/60 ml) water, bell pepper, garlic, onion, oregano, red pepper flakes, and salt and process until finely chopped but not completely pureed, stopping to scrape down the sides of the bowl once. Use immediately, or transfer to an airtight container and store in the refrigerator for up to 2 days. Stir in the vinegar just before serving.

EXTRA CREDIT

If you make the chimichurri in advance, blanch and shock the herbs to keep them bright green. Just plunge the herbs in boiling water for 30 seconds and then transfer them to ice water to stop the cooking. Drain and proceed with the recipe.

ROMESCO

MAKES ABOUT 1½ CUPS (12 FL OZ/375 ML)

1 red bell pepper, roasted, peeled, and seeded

½ cup (3 oz/90 g) diced roasted tomatoes, drained if canned

2 tablespoons blanched almonds

2 tablespoons blanched hazelnuts

⅓ cup (3 fl oz/80 ml) olive oil

1 tablespoon roasted garlic paste

1 tablespoon ancho chile powder

2 teaspoons red wine vinegar

½ teaspoon smoked paprika

½ teaspoon salt

1 thin slice country-style bread, torn into pieces

Tomato juice or water, as needed to thin

In a food processor, combine the bell pepper, tomatoes, nuts, oil, garlic paste, chile powder, vinegar, paprika, salt, and bread and process until a coarse puree forms. The sauce should be thick yet pourable. If it isn't, add tomato juice until you achieve a pourable consistency. Use immediately, or transfer to an airtight container and store in the refrigerator for up to 1 week.

HOT FUDGE SAUCE

MAKES 1 CUP (8 FL OZ/250 ML)

1 cup (3 oz/90 g) unsweetened cocoa powder

¾ cup (6 oz/185 g) sugar

Pinch of fine sea salt

¾ cup (6 fl oz/180 ml) strong brewed coffee

1 tablespoon unsalted butter

¼ teaspoon pure vanilla extract

In a small, heavy saucepan, stir together the cocoa, sugar, and salt. Add the coffee and whisk until the mixture is smooth. Place the pan over medium-high heat and bring to a boil, stirring often. Remove from the heat and stir in the butter and vanilla until the butter melts. Let cool slightly, then serve warm. Or let cool completely, transfer to an airtight container, and store in the refrigerator for up to 1 week. Just before serving, reheat over low heat until warm.

BASIC RECIPES

PIZZA DOUGH

MAKES ENOUGH FOR FOUR 10-INCH (25-CM) PIZZAS
(ABOUT 1 LB/500 G)

1 cup (8 fl oz/250 ml) warm water (110°–115°F/43°–46°C)
2 teaspoons active dry yeast
1 teaspoon sugar
4 tablespoons (2 fl oz/60 ml) olive oil
1½ teaspoons fine sea salt
2¾ cups (11 oz/345 g) bread flour, plus more for kneading

In a large bowl, stir together the water, yeast, and sugar. Let stand until foamy, about 5 minutes. Stir in 3 tablespoons of the oil, the salt, and the flour until the dough comes together.

Turn the dough out onto a lightly floured work surface and knead until the dough is smooth and elastic, about 5 minutes. Add more flour as needed to keep the dough from sticking to your hands or the work surface, but try to add as little flour as possible. Shape the dough into a ball.

Coat a large bowl with the remaining 1 tablespoon oil. Put the dough in the bowl and then turn the dough to coat it with oil. Cover the bowl with plastic wrap and let the dough rise in a warm spot (about 90°F/32°C) until doubled in bulk, about 1 hour. Or, for more complex flavor, place the bowl in the refrigerator and let the dough rise overnight, then bring the dough back to room temperature before rolling it out. To freeze the dough, cut it into 4 pieces and shape each piece into a somewhat flat disk. Place each disk in a zippered plastic bag, press out the air, and freeze for up to 1 month. To use, thaw in a bowl of cold water for a few hours or thaw in the refrigerator overnight. Bring the dough to room temperature before rolling it out.

SESAME SLAW

MAKES 6 SERVINGS

1 lb (500 g) napa cabbage (about ½ head), finely sliced
2 teaspoons coarse sea salt
2 tablespoons soy sauce, such as Japanese white soy sauce
1 tablespoon rice vinegar
½ teaspoon honey
4 teaspoons Asian sesame oil
4 red radishes, halved lengthwise and thinly sliced crosswise
½ avocado, peeled and cut into small pieces
3 tablespoons sesame seeds
¼ cup (2 fl oz/60 ml) Sriracha Mayo (page 223)

To make the slaw, in a large bowl, mix together the cabbage and sea salt. Let stand for 20 minutes. During that time, the cabbage will soften and leach out much of its water. Using your hands, pick up the cabbage and put it on a clean, flat-weave kitchen towel. Wrap the towel around the cabbage, hold it over a sink, and squeeze hard to rid the cabbage of most of its water. Rinse out the bowl and return the cabbage to it. Add the soy sauce, vinegar, honey, sesame oil, radishes, avocado, and sesame seeds and toss to combine evenly. Cover and refrigerate until needed.

LEMON POUND CAKE

MAKES 1 LOAF CAKE

1 cup (8 oz/250 g) unsalted butter,
at room temperature, plus more for the pan
Grated zest and juice of 1 large lemon
1¾ cups (14 oz/440 g) sugar
1 teaspoon pure vanilla extract
½ teaspoon freshly grated nutmeg
¼ teaspoon salt
5 large eggs
1¾ cups (7 oz/220 g) cake flour or
(9 oz/280 g) all-purpose flour

Preheat the oven to 350°F (180°C). Butter a 9-by-5-inch (23-by-13-cm) loaf pan, preferably nonstick.

In a small bowl, mix together the lemon zest and juice.

Using a handheld mixer or stand mixer on medium speed, beat the butter until creamy. Add the sugar, vanilla, nutmeg, and salt and beat until light and fluffy, stopping to scrape down the sides once or twice.

On medium speed, beat in the eggs one at a time, beating after each addition until incorporated. Add the lemon zest and juice mixture and beat until combined. On very low speed or with a wooden spoon, mix in the flour just until incorporated.

Pour and scrape the batter into the prepared pan and smooth the top. Cover the pan with aluminum foil. Bake for 30 minutes, then remove the foil and continue to bake until well browned on the top and a cake tester inserted into the center comes out clean, about 1 hour longer.

Let the cake cool in the pan on a wire rack for about 15 minutes. Invert a second rack on top of the cake, invert the cake onto the rack, and then carefully lift off the pan. Cover the cake with the first rack and invert again onto the rack to finish cooling the cake right side up.

INDEX

A

Agrodolce Sauce, 118
Alabama White Barbecue Sauce, 219
Almonds
 Grilled Polenta Cake with Fennel, Raisins & Oranges, 204
 Salmon Stuffed with Cilantro Pesto, 125
Aluminum foil pans, 17–18
Ancho Chile Rub, 215
Ancho Chocolate BBQ Sauce, 219–20
Anchovies
 Anchovy Butter, 226
 Grilled Romaine Salad with Anchovy Mustard Vinaigrette, 168
Apple, Grilled, Horseradish & Grilled Onion Toasts, Grill-Roasted Rib Roast with, 63
Apricots
 Grilled Quail with Apricot-Sage Sauce, 102
 preparing mostarda with, 60
Artichokes
 Artichoke-Pecorino Slather, 103
 Planked Salmon with Citrus Rub & Artichoke Relish, 131
Arugula, Black Garlic & Soppressata, Grilled Pizza with, 186
Asparagus
 about, 161
 Grilled Asparagus with Lemon Oil, 161
 Steak, Potatoes & Asparagus, 54

B

Bacon
 Bacon Bourbon Butter, 227
 Bacon Burgers, 40
 Bacon Burgers with Caramelized Onions & Roasted Tomato Dressing, 41
 Bacon-Wrapped Pork Tenderloin with Chipotle Rye Barbecue Sauce, 94
 Breakfast Burgers, 41
 Jalapeño Cheddar Bacon Explosion, 88–93
 Mustard-Sage Pork Tenderloin Wrapped in Pancetta, 94
 Taleggio Pancetta Burgers, 41
Bananas, Grilled, with Coffee Cinnamon Hot Fudge Sauce, 200
Barbecue Butter, 157
Barbecued Chicken with Alabama White Barbecue Sauce, 101
Barbecue Rub, Basic, 215
Barbecue sauces
 Alabama White Barbecue Sauce, 219
 Ancho Chocolate BBQ Sauce, 219–20
 Basic Barbecue Sauce, 219
 Chipotle Rye Barbecue Sauce, 219
 Creamy Stout Barbecue Sauce, 219
 Maple Bourbon Barbecue Sauce, 219
 Peach Bourbon Barbecue Sauce, 219
 Rich and Smoky Texas Barbecue Sauce, 219
 Sweet, Rich & Smoky Barbecue Sauce, 219
 Western Carolina Barbecue Sauce, 219
 working with, 76, 218
Barbecuing on a grill, 27–30
Barely Burnt Honey-Glazed Pears with Orange & Rosemary, 195
Basic Barbecue Rub, 215
Basil
 Grilled Margherita Pizza, 185
 Tomato Basil Butter, 226
Basting brushes, 17
BBQ Brisket with Ancho Chocolate BBQ Sauce, 67
Bean, Black, Burgers with Sriracha Mayo & Sesame Slaw, 48
Bedouin-Spiced Snapper with Lime Butter, 128
Bedouin Spice Rub, 215
Beef
 Bacon Burgers, 40
 BBQ Brisket with Ancho Chocolate BBQ Sauce, 67
 Classic Beef Burgers with Lots of Toppings, 39–41
 Espresso-Buzzed Rib-Eye Steaks, 53
 flank steaks, about, 52
 flat-iron steaks, about, 52, 54
 Garlic-Crusted T-Bone with Gorgonzola Butter, 57
 Green Chile Queso, 223
 Grill-Roasted Rib Roast with Grilled Onion Toasts & Grilled Apple Horseradish, 63
 Grill-Roasted Tenderloin with Wild Mushroom Mostarda, 60
 Grill-Roasted Tri-Tip with Spicy Korean Glaze, 59
 hanger steaks, about, 52
 porterhouse steaks, about, 52
 rib eye steaks, about, 52, 53
 roasts, grilling, 58
 sirloin steaks, about, 52
 skirt steaks, about, 52
 Steak, Potatoes & Asparagus, 54
 steaks, grilling, 52
 strip steaks, about, 52
 T-bone steaks, about, 52, 57
 tenderloin roasts, about, 60
 tenderloin steaks, about, 52
 testing for doneness, 32
 tough cuts, grilling, 64
 tri-tip roasts, about, 59
Beer
 Beer Mop, 212
 Classic Grilled Brats in Beer, 85
 Creamy Stout Barbecue Sauce, 219
 Beer Can Chicken with Barbecue Rub, 107
Beets
 Black Bean Burgers with Sriracha Mayo & Sesame Slaw, 48
 cooking leaves of, 158
 Honey Smoked Beets, 158
Berbere, 217
Berbere Sauce, 113
Black Bean Burgers with Sriracha Mayo & Sesame Slaw, 48
Blue Cheese Dressing, 222
Bourbon
 Bacon Bourbon Butter, 227
 Maple Bourbon Barbecue Sauce, 219

Peach Bourbon Barbecue
  Sauce, 219
Brined Pork Chops with Chipotle
  Rye Barbecue Sauce, 73
Brined Pork Chops with Fennel and
  Juniper Rub, 73
Brined Ribs with Cumin, Coriander,
  and Lime Butter, 79
Brines
  basic wet brine, preparing, 211
  Cumin & Coriander Brine, 212
  working with, 210
Broccoli & Cauliflower Florets,
  Grill-Woked, with Tom Kha Gai
  Glaze, 162
Brussels Sprouts, Roasted
  Sesame, 171
BTU ratings, 13
Buffalo Pork Chops, 74
Buffalo Pork Steaks, 74
Buffalo Sauce, 227
Burgers
  Bacon Burgers, 40
  Black Bean Burgers with Sriracha
    Mayo & Sesame Slaw, 48
  Classic Beef Burgers with
    Lots of Toppings, 39–41
  grilling, 36
  Lamb Kofta Burgers with
    Za'atar Tzatziki, 43
  Shrimp or Scallop Burgers, 47
  Sichuan Tuna Burgers with
    Pickled-Ginger Relish, 44–47
  Umami Turkey Burgers with
    Harissa Ketchup, 37
Butterflied Turkey Breast with
  Spicy Peanut Glaze, 119
Butters, flavored
  Anchovy Butter, 226
  Bacon Bourbon Butter, 227
  Barbecue Butter, 157
  Citrus Butter, 226
  Fines Herbes Butter, 226
  Forest Herb Butter, 226
  Gorgonzola Butter, 227
  Hazelnut Butter, 226
  Roasted Garlic Butter, 226
  Tomato Basil Butter, 226

C

Cabbage
  Grilled Coleslaw, 165
  Radicchio Slaw, 165
  Sesame Slaw, 230
Cake
  Grilled Lemon Pound Cake
    with Lemon-Ginger Glaze
    & Candied Lemon, 203
  Grilled Polenta Cake with Fennel,
    Raisins & Oranges, 204
  grilling, 202
  Lemon Pound Cake, 231
Campfire grills, 12
Capers, Pine Nuts & Orange
  Vinaigrette, Grilled Zucchini
  with, 173
Caramel Sauce, Salted, Grilled
  Peaches with, 199
Cauliflower & Broccoli Florets,
  Grill Woked, with Tom Kha Ga
  Glaze, 162
Ceramic grills, 13
Chai-Smoked Pineapple, 196
Chai Spice Blend, 197
Charcoal, 15, 18
Cheese
  Artichoke-Pecorino Slather, 103
  Blue Cheese Dressing, 222
  Classic Beef Burgers with
    Lots of Toppings, 39–41
  Gorgonzola Butter, 227
  Green Chile Queso, 223
  Grilled Margherita Pizza, 185
  Grilled Pizza with Black Garlic,
    Arugula & Soppressata, 186
  Grilled Pizza with Fresh Tomato,
    Pesto & Gorgonzola, 189
  Grilled Pizza with Prosciutto
    & Hot-Pepper Honey, 191
  Grilled Queso-Stuffed Figs with
    Mole-Spiced Chocolate, 201
  Grilled Romaine Salad with
    Anchovy Mustard
    Vinaigrette, 168
  Grilled White Pizza with Ham,
    Figs & Gruyère, 188
  Jalapeño Cheddar Bacon
    Explosion, 88–93
  Mediterranean Tomato Salad, 104
  Oaxacan Grilled Corn, 180

Chicken
  Barbecued Chicken with Alabama
    White Barbecue Sauce, 101
  Beer Can Chicken with Barbecue
    Rub, 107
  boneless breasts and thighs,
    grilling, 112
  Classic Barbecued Chicken, 101
  cutting in half, 103
  cutting up, 100
  free-range, 104
  Grilled Butterflied Chicken
    with Artichoke-Pecorino
    Slather, 103–4
  Grilled Chicken Breasts in
    Berbere Sauce, 113
  Grilled Chicken Thighs
    Agrodolce, 118
  Grilled Chicken Thighs with
    Romesco, 118
  Grilled Chicken Tikka Masala, 114
  Grilled Chimichurri Chicken, 101
  Grilled Citrus Chicken, 101
  Grilled Ranch Chicken, 101
  Grill-Roasted Chicken with
    Shichimi Togarashi, 107
  how to butterfly, 104
  how to truss, 111
  kosher, 104
  organic, 104
  parts, grilling, 98
  pastured, 104
  Spit-Roasted Lemon Tarragon
    Chicken, 106–7
  testing for doneness, 32
  whole and half, grilling, 99
Chiles
  Ancho Chile Rub, 215
  Ancho Chocolate BBQ
    Sauce, 219–20
  Berbere, 217
  Chipotle Rye Barbecue
    Sauce, 219
  Green Chile Queso, 223
  Grill-Braised Chorizo with
    Poblano Chile, Cilantro
    & Lime, 85
  Grilled Honey Habanero
    Pineapple, 196
  Habanero Orange Honey, 158
  Harissa, 225

Jalapeño Cheddar Bacon
Explosion, 88–93
Pickled Salsa, 223
Spicy Citrus Marinade, 212
Chimichurri, 228
Chimichurri Clams on the Grill, 151
Chimney starter, 18
Chinese Five-Spice Rub, 215–17
Chipotle Rye Barbecue Sauce, 219
Chocolate
Ancho Chocolate BBQ
Sauce, 219–20
Grilled Bananas with
Coffee Cinnamon Hot
Fudge Sauce, 200
Grilled Queso-Stuffed Figs with
Mole-Spiced Chocolate, 201
Grilled S'mores Doughnuts, 207
Hot Fudge Sauce, 228
Mole Rub, 215
Cilantro
Chimichurri, 228
Lobster with Chermoula, 153
Preserved Lemon Yogurt, 226
Salmon Stuffed with Cilantro
Pesto, 125
Citrus Butter, 226
Citrus Rub, 215
Clams
Chimichurri Clams on the Grill, 151
grilling, 148
preparing, 148
Classic Barbecued Chicken, 101
Classic Beef Burgers with
Lots of Toppings, 39–41
Classic Grilled Brats in Beer, 85
Classic Grilled Sausage and
Peppers, 85
Coal-Baked Sweet Potatoes with
Bourbon Bacon Butter, 157
Coal poker, 18
Coal rake, 18
Coal shovel, 18
Coconut
Grill-Woked Broccoli & Cauliflower
Florets with Tom Kha Gai
Glaze, 162
Vietnamese Coconut
Swordfish, 137
Coffee. See Espresso
Condiments
Grilled Tomato Jam, 223
Pickled-Ginger Relish, 44
Pickled Salsa, 223

Port Ketchup, 225
Preserved Lemons, 226
Quick Pickles, 225
Wild Mushroom Mostarda, 227
Coriander
Berbere, 217
Brined Ribs with Cumin,
Coriander, and Lime Butter, 79
Cumin and Coriander Pork
Tenderloin with Chimichurri, 94
Cumin & Coriander Brine, 212
Corn
Grilled Corn with Chimichurri, 180
grilling, 177
Oaxacan Grilled Corn, 180
preparing, 177
Creamy Stout Barbecue Sauce, 219
Cucumbers
Cucumber Raita, 143
Quick Pickles, 225
Za'atar Tzatziki, 225
Cumin
Brined Ribs with Cumin,
Coriander, and Lime Butter, 79
Cumin and Coriander Pork
Tenderloin with Chimichurri, 94
Cumin & Coriander Brine, 212

D
Desserts, list of, 193
Direct grilling
best foods for, 22
controlling temperature, 24
description of, 22
heat levels, 24
setting up grill for, 22–24
Dough, pizza, 231
Doughnuts, Grilled S'mores, 207
Duck
boneless breasts, grilling, 112
Grilled Five-Spice Duck Breasts
with Hoisin Glaze, 117
Grilled Ras El Hanout Duck
Breast with Orange Glaze, 117
testing for doneness, 32

E
Eggplant, Grilled, with Tahini Sauce
& Pomegranate Seeds, 174
Eggs
Breakfast Burgers, 41
Electric grills, 12
Equipment. See Fuels; Grills

Espresso
Espresso-Buzzed Rib-Eye
Steaks, 53
Espresso Rub, 215
Espresso-Rubbed Ribs with
Creamy Stout Barbecue
Sauce, 79
Espresso Steak Sauce, 220
Grilled Bananas with Coffee
Cinnamon Hot Fudge
Sauce, 200

F
Fennel
Brined Pork Chops with Fennel
and Juniper Rub, 73
Grilled Fennel Basted with
Rosemary Absinthe, 164
Grilled Polenta Cake with Fennel,
Raisins & Oranges, 204
Figs
Grilled Queso-Stuffed Figs with
Mole-Spiced Chocolate, 201
Grilled White Pizza with Ham,
Figs & Gruyère, 188
Fines Herbes Butter, 226
Fish. See also specific types
brining and marinating times, 211
buying, 122
common types, for grilling, 123
farmed vs. wild caught, 129
fillets, grilling, 130
fillets, removing pin bones, 130
grilling chart, 123
spice or herb blends for, 128
steaks, grilling, 136
testing for doneness, 32
whole, cleaning and grilling, 122
Five-Pepper Ribs with Peach-
Bourbon Barbecue Sauce, 77–79
Flatbreads. See also Pizza
grilling, 184
Forest Herb Butter, 226
Fruit. See also specific fruits
grilling, 194
Fuels, 15

G
Garlic
Garlic-Crusted T-Bone with
Gorgonzola Butter, 57
Grilled Pizza with Black Garlic,
Arugula & Soppressata, 186

Grill Roasted Garlic, 167
Roasted Garlic Butter, 226
Gas fuel, 15, 16–17
Gas grills, 13, 16–17
Ginger
    Berbere Sauce, 113
    Grilled Chicken Tikka Masala, 114
    Grilled Lemon Pound Cake with
        Lemon-Ginger Glaze & Candied
        Lemon, 203
    Grill-Woked Broccoli & Cauliflower
        Florets with Tom Kha Gai
        Glaze, 162
    Masala Sauce, 114
    Pickled-Ginger Relish, 44
Glaze, Spicy Korean, 220
Gorgonzola Butter, 227
Gravy, Turkey, 111
Green Chile Queso, 223
Grill baskets, 18
Grill-Braised Chorizo with Poblano
    Chile, Cilantro & Lime, 85
Grill brushes, scrapers, and
    scrubbers, 17
Grilled Asparagus with
    Lemon Oil, 161
Grilled Bananas with Coffee
    Cinnamon Hot Fudge Sauce, 200
Grilled Butterflied Chicken with
    Artichoke-Pecorino Slather, 103–4
Grilled Caramelized Onions, 167
Grilled Chicken Breasts in
    Berbere Sauce, 113
Grilled Chicken Thighs
    Agrodolce, 118
Grilled Chicken Thighs with
    Romesco, 118
Grilled Chicken Tikka Masala, 114
Grilled Chimichurri Chicken, 101
Grilled Citrus Chicken, 101
Grilled Coleslaw, 165
Grilled Corn with Chimichurri, 180
Grilled Eggplant with Tahini Sauce
    & Pomegranate Seeds, 174
Grilled Fennel Basted with
    Rosemary Absinthe, 164
Grilled Five-Spice Duck Breasts with
    Hoisin Glaze, 117
Grilled Halibut Escabeche, 134
Grilled Honey Habanero
    Pineapple, 196
Grilled Lemon Pound Cake with
    Lemon-Ginger Glaze
    & Candied Lemon, 203
Grilled Margherita Pizza, 185

Grilled Mussels Marinara, 151
Grilled Oysters with Fines Herbes
    Butter, 149
Grilled Peaches with Salted Caramel
    Sauce, 199
Grilled Pizza with Black Garlic,
    Arugula & Soppressata, 186
Grilled Pizza with Fresh Tomato,
    Pesto & Gorgonzola, 189
Grilled Pizza with Prosciutto
    & Hot-Pepper Honey, 191
Grilled Polenta Cake with Fennel,
    Raisins & Oranges, 204
Grilled Pork Belly with Spicy-Sweet
    Korean Glaze, 87
Grilled Quail with Apricot-Sage
    Sauce, 102
Grilled Queso-Stuffed Figs with
    Mole-Spiced Chocolate, 201
Grilled Ranch Chicken, 101
Grilled Ras El Hanout Duck Breast
    with Orange Glaze, 117
Grilled Romaine Salad with Anchovy
    Mustard Vinaigrette, 168
Grilled Scallops with Citrus Rub and
    Fines Herbes Butter, 141
Grilled Shiitakes with Shichimi
    Togarashi, 179
Grilled S'mores Doughnuts, 207
Grilled Squid with Chorizo &
    Romesco, 147
Grilled Squid with Soppressata and
    Spicy Marinara Sauce, 147
Grilled Tilapia Tacos, 133
Grilled Tomato Jam, 223
Grilled White Pizza with Ham,
    Figs & Gruyère, 188
Grilled Zucchini with Capers, Pine
    Nuts & Orange Vinaigrette, 173
Grill forks, 18
Grill frying pans and woks, 18
Grill gloves, 17
Grill lamp, 18
Grill mops, 17
Grill Roasted Chicken with Shichimi
    Togarashi, 107
Grill Roasted Garlic, 167
Grill-Roasted Rib Roast with Grilled
    Onion Toasts & Grilled Apple
    Horseradish, 63
Grill-Roasted Tenderloin with Wild
    Mushroom Mostarda, 60
Grill-Roasted Tri-Tip with Spicy
    Korean Glaze, 59
Grill-Roasted Turkey with Lemon-
    Rosemary Dry Brine, 108–11

Grills
    adding smoke and barbecuing,
        27–30
    BTU ratings, 13
    checking approximate
        temperature, 25
    cleaning, 16
    evaluating, 12
    fuels for, 15
    gas leak testing, 16–17
    grill setups for heat levels, 24
    maintenance, 16–17
    tools and accessories, 17–18
    two basic parts, 12
    types of, 12–13
Grill screens, trays, and grates, 17
Grill-Woked Broccoli & Cauliflower
    Florets with Tom Kha Gai
    Glaze, 162

H

Habanero Orange Honey, 158
Halibut, Grilled, Escabeche, 134
Ham
    Grilled Pizza with Prosciutto
        & Hot-Pepper Honey, 191
    Grilled White Pizza with Ham,
        Figs & Gruyère, 188
Harissa, 225
Hazelnuts
    Grilled Pizza with Prosciutto
        & Hot-Pepper Honey, 191
    Hazelnut Butter, 226
Herbs. *See also specific herbs*
    Fines Herbes Butter, 226
    Forest Herb Butter, 226
    Grilled Oysters with Fines Herbes
        Butter, 149
    Grilled Scallops with Citrus Rub
        and Fines Herbes Butter, 141
    Ranch Dressing, 222–23
Hibachis, 12
Hoisin Glaze, Grilled Five-Spice
    Duck Breasts with, 117
Homemade Steak Sauce, 220
Honey
    Barely Burnt Honey-Glazed Pears
        with Orange & Rosemary, 195
    Chai-Smoked Pineapple, 196
    Grilled Honey Habanero
        Pineapple, 196
    Grilled Pizza with Prosciutto
        & Hot-Pepper Honey, 191
    Habanero Orange Honey, 158

Honey Smoked Beets, 158
Horseradish Honey, 158
Masala Honey, 158
Horseradish
    Grill-Roasted Rib Roast with
        Grilled Onion Toasts & Grilled
        Apple Horseradish, 63
    Horseradish Honey, 158
Hot Fudge Sauce, 228

I

Indirect grilling
    best foods for, 25
    heat levels, 24
    setting up grill for, 25–27
Injectors, 18

J

Jam, Grilled Tomato, 223
Juniper and Fennel Rub, Brined
    Pork Chops with, 73

K

Ketchup, Port, 225
Kettle grills, 12–13

L

Lamb
    Lamb Kofta Burgers with
        Za'atar Tzatziki, 43
    testing for doneness, 32
Lemons
    Citrus Butter, 226
    Citrus Rub, 215
    Grilled Asparagus with
        Lemon Oil, 161
    Grilled Lemon Pound Cake with
        Lemon-Ginger Glaze & Candied
        Lemon, 203
    Grill-Roasted Turkey with Lemon-
        Rosemary Dry Brine, 108–11
    Lemon Pound Cake, 231
    Preserved Lemons, 226
    Preserved Lemon Yogurt, 226
    Spicy Citrus Marinade, 212
    Spit-Roasted Lemon Tarragon
        Chicken, 106–7
Lettuce
    Grilled Pork Belly with Spicy-
        Sweet Korean Glaze, 87
    Grilled Romaine Salad with
        Anchovy Mustard
        Vinaigrette, 168

Vietnamese-Style Octopus
    Lettuce Wraps, 145
Limes
    Bedouin-Spiced Snapper with
        Lime Butter, 128
    Citrus Butter, 226
    Citrus Rub, 215
    Spicy Citrus Marinade, 212
    Vietnamese Dipping Sauce, 222
Lobsters
    grilling, 152
    Lobster with Chermoula, 153
    preparing, 152
    splitting in half, 153
Long-stem lighters, 17

M

Maple Bourbon Barbecue
    Sauce, 219
Maple Bourbon Pork Steaks, 74
Marinades
    basic marinade, preparing, 211
    Beer Mop, 212
    Mexican Sour Orange
        Marinade, 212
    Spicy Citrus Marinade, 212
    working with, 210
Marinara Sauce, 220
Marinara Sauce with Red Wine, 220
Marshmallows
    Grilled S'mores Doughnuts, 207
Masala Honey, 158
Masala Sauce, 114
Mayo, Sriracha, 223
Meat. See also Beef; Lamb; Pork
    brining and marinating times, 211
    tough cuts, about, 64
Mediterranean Tomato Salad, 104
Mexican Roast Pork with
    Sour Orange Marinade
    (Cochinita Pibil), 82
Mexican Sour Orange Marinade, 212
Mole Rub, 215
Mushrooms
    Black Bean Burgers with Sriracha
        Mayo & Sesame Slaw, 48
    Grilled Shiitakes with
        Shichimi Togarashi, 179
    grilling, 176
    Mushroom Burgers with
        Port Ketchup, 41
    preparing, 176
    Wild Mushroom Mostarda, 227

Mussels
    Grilled Mussels Marinara, 151
    grilling, 148
    preparing, 148
Mustard
    Mustard-Sage Pork Tenderloin
        Wrapped in Pancetta, 94
    Wild Mushroom Mostarda, 227

N

North Carolina–Style Pulled Pork
    Barbecue, 81–82
Nuts. See specific nuts

O

Oaxacan Grilled Corn, 180
Octopus
    cleaning, 145
    grilling, 144
    preparing, 144
    Vietnamese-Style Octopus
        Lettuce Wraps, 145
Olives
    Agrodolce Sauce, 118
    Mediterranean Tomato Salad, 104
Onions
    Bacon Burgers with Caramelized
        Onions & Roasted Tomato
        Dressing, 41
    Berbere Sauce, 113
    Grilled Caramelized Onions, 167
    Grill-Roasted Rib Roast with
        Grilled Onion Toasts & Grilled
        Apple Horseradish, 63
    Special Burgers, 41
    Steak House Burgers, 41
    Vadouvan, 217
Oranges
    Agrodolce Sauce, 118
    Barely Burnt Honey-Glazed Pears
        with Orange & Rosemary, 195
    Citrus Rub, 215
    Grilled Polenta Cake with Fennel,
        Raisins & Oranges, 204
    Habanero Orange Honey, 158
    Mexican Sour Orange
        Marinade, 212
    Orange Vinaigrette, 227–28
    Shichimi Togarashi, 217
    Spicy Citrus Marinade, 212
Oysters
    Grilled Oysters with Fines Herbes
        Butter, 149

grilling, 148

preparing, 148

shucking, 149

P

Pancetta

Mustard-Sage Pork Tenderloin Wrapped in Pancetta, 94

Taleggio Pancetta Burgers, 41

Paraffin lighter cubes, 18

Parsley

Chimichurri, 228

Grilled Quail with Apricot-Sage Sauce, 102

Lobster with Chermoula, 153

Preserved Lemon Yogurt, 226

Peaches

Grilled Peaches with Salted Caramel Sauce, 199

Peach Bourbon Barbecue Sauce, 219

preparing mostarda with, 60

Peanut Glaze, Spicy, Butterflied Turkey Breast with, 119

Pears, Barely Burnt Honey-Glazed, with Orange & Rosemary, 195

Peppers. See also Chiles

Classic Grilled Brats in Beer, 85

Classic Grilled Sausage and Peppers, 85

Queso Burgers, 41

Romesco, 228

Pesto

Grilled Pizza with Fresh Tomato, Pesto & Gorgonzola, 189

Salmon Stuffed with Cilantro Pesto, 125

Pickled Salsa, 223

Pickles, Quick, 225

Pineapple

Chai-Smoked Pineapple, 196

Grilled Honey Habanero Pineapple, 196

Pine nuts

Grilled Pizza with Fresh Tomato, Pesto & Gorgonzola, 189

Grilled Zucchini with Capers, Pine Nuts & Orange Vinaigrette, 173

Pit grills or smokers, 13

Pizza

Grilled Margherita Pizza, 185

Grilled Pizza with Black Garlic, Arugula & Soppressata, 186

Grilled Pizza with Fresh Tomato, Pesto & Gorgonzola, 189

Grilled Pizza with Prosciutto & Hot-Pepper Honey, 191

Grilled White Pizza with Ham, Figs & Gruyère, 188

grilling, 184

Pizza Dough, 231

Pizza peels, 18

Plank cooking, 31

Planked Salmon with Citrus Rub & Artichoke Relish, 131

Polenta Cake, Grilled, with Fennel, Raisins & Oranges, 204

Pomegranate Seeds & Tahini Sauce, Grilled Eggplant with, 174

Pork. See also Bacon; Ham; Sausages

baby back ribs, about, 76

Bacon-Wrapped Pork Tenderloin with Chipotle Rye Barbecue Sauce, 94

belly, grilling, 84

blade chops, about, 70

Boston butt, about, 80

Brined Pork Chops with Chipotle Rye Barbecue Sauce, 73

Brined Pork Chops with Fennel and Juniper Rub, 73

Brined Ribs with Cumin, Coriander, and Lime Butter, 79

Buffalo Pork Chops, 74

Buffalo Pork Steaks, 74

chops, grilling, 70

country-style ribs, about, 76

Cumin and Coriander Pork Tenderloin with Chimichurri, 94

Espresso-Rubbed Ribs with Creamy Stout Barbecue Sauce, 79

Five-Pepper Ribs with Peach-Bourbon Barbecue Sauce, 77–79

Grilled Pork Belly with Spicy-Sweet Korean Glaze, 87

Maple Bourbon Pork Steaks, 74

Mexican Roast Pork with Sour Orange Marinade (Cochinita Pibil), 82

Mustard-Sage Pork Tenderloin Wrapped in Pancetta, 94

New York chops, about, 70

North Carolina–Style Pulled Pork Barbecue, 81–82

picnic ham, about, 80

porterhouse chops, about, 70, 73

Pulled Pork Sandwiches, 82

rib-eye chops, about, 70

ribs, grilling, 76

shoulder, grilling, 80

sirloin chops, about, 70

spareribs, about, 76

St. Louis–style ribs, about, 76

testing for doneness, 32

Port Ketchup, 225

Potatoes

Coal-Baked Sweet Potatoes with Bourbon Bacon Butter, 157

Steak, Potatoes & Asparagus, 54

Poultry. See also Chicken; Duck; Quail; Turkey

boneless breasts and thighs, grilling, 112

brining and marinating times, 211

cutting in half, 103

cutting up, 100

how to truss, 111

parts, grilling, 98

production methods, 104

whole and half birds, grilling, 99

Preserved Lemons, 226

Preserved Lemon Yogurt, 226

Prosciutto & Hot-Pepper Honey, Grilled Pizza with, 191

Q

Quail, Grilled, with Apricot-Sage Sauce, 102

Queso Burgers, 41

Quick Pickles, 225

R

Radicchio Slaw, 165

Raisins, Fennel & Oranges, Grilled Polenta Cake with, 204

Ranch Dressing, 222–23

Ras El Hanout, 217

Real Russian Dressing, 222

Relish, Pickled-Ginger, 44

Rib rack, 18

Rich and Smoky Texas Barbecue Sauce, 219

Roasted Garlic Butter, 226

Roasted Sesame Brussels Sprouts, 171

Roasted Tomato French Dressing, 222

Romesco, 228

Rosemary
Agrodolce Sauce, 118
Barely Burnt Honey-Glazed Pears with Orange & Rosemary, 195
Grilled Fennel Basted with Rosemary Absinthe, 164
Grill-Roasted Turkey with Lemon-Rosemary Dry Brine, 108–11
Rotisserie grilling, 30–31
Rye Chipotle Barbecue Sauce, 219

S

Sage-Apricot Sauce, Grilled Quail with, 102
Salads. *See also* Slaws
Grilled Romaine Salad with Anchovy Mustard Vinaigrette, 168
Mediterranean Tomato Salad, 104
Salmon
Planked Salmon with Citrus Rub & Artichoke Relish, 131
Salmon Stuffed with Cilantro Pesto, 125
Salsa, Pickled, 223
Salt, equivalent volumes and weights, 211
Sandwiches. *See also* Burgers
Pulled Pork Sandwiches, 82
Sauces. *See also* Barbecue sauces
Artichoke-Pecorino Slather, 103
Berbere Sauce, 113
Blue Cheese Dressing, 222
Buffalo Sauce, 227
Chimichurri, 228
Cucumber Raita, 143
Espresso Steak Sauce, 220
Green Chile Queso, 223
Grilled Tomato Jam, 223
Harissa, 225
Homemade Steak Sauce, 220
Hot Fudge Sauce, 228
Marinara Sauce, 220
Marinara Sauce with Red Wine, 220
Masala Sauce, 114
Orange Vinaigrette, 227–28
pairing with spice rubs, 53
Pickled Salsa, 223
Port Ketchup, 225
Ranch Dressing, 222–23
Real Russian Dressing, 222

Roasted Tomato French Dressing, 222
Romesco, 228
Spicy Marinara Sauce, 220
Sriracha Mayo, 223
Ssam Jang, 222
Thick Marinara Sauce, 220
Turkey Gravy, 111
Vietnamese Dipping Sauce, 222
Wild Mushroom Mostarda, 227
working with, 218
Za'atar Tzatziki, 225
Sausages
Classic Grilled Brats in Beer, 85
Classic Grilled Sausage and Peppers, 85
Grill-Braised Chorizo with Poblano Chile, Cilantro & Lime, 85
Grilled Pizza with Black Garlic, Arugula & Soppressata, 186
Grilled Squid with Chorizo & Romesco, 147
Grilled Squid with Soppressata and Spicy Marinara Sauce, 147
grilling, 84
Jalapeño Cheddar Bacon Explosion, 88–93
Scallops
buying and preparing, 140
Grilled Scallops with Citrus Rub and Fines Herbes Butter, 141
grilling, 140
Scallops with Ras El Hanout & Preserved Lemon Yogurt, 141
Shrimp or Scallop Burgers, 47
Sesame Brussels Sprouts, Roasted, 171
Sesame Slaw, 231
Shallots
Mushroom Burgers with Port Ketchup, 41
Soy Grilled Shallots, 167
Sriracha Burgers, 41
Shellfish. *See specific types*
Shichimi Togarashi, 217
Shrimp
buying and preparing, 140
grilling, 140
Shrimp or Scallop Burgers, 47
sizes and counts, 142
Vadouvan Grilled Shrimp, 143
Sichuan Tuna Burgers with Pickled-Ginger Relish, 44–47

Skewers, 17
Slaws
Grilled Coleslaw, 165
Grilled Tilapia Tacos, 133
Pulled Pork Sandwiches, 82
Radicchio Slaw, 165
Sesame Slaw, 231
Special Burgers, 41
Smoke flavor, 27–30
Smoke ring, 30
Smokers and pit grills, 13
Snapper, Bedouin-Spiced, with Lime Butter, 128
Soy Grilled Shallots, 167
Spatulas, 17
Special Burgers, 41
Spice rubs and blends
Ancho Chile Rub, 215
Basic Barbecue Rub, 215
Bedouin Spice Rub, 215
Berbere, 217
Chai Spice Blend, 197
Chinese Five-Spice Rub, 215–17
Citrus Rub, 215
Espresso Rub, 215
for fish, 128
Mole Rub, 215
pairing with sauces, 53
Ras El Hanout, 217
Shichimi Togarashi, 217
Vadouvan, 217
working with, 214
za'atar, preparing, 174
Spicy Citrus Marinade, 212
Spicy Korean Glaze, 220
Spicy Marinara Sauce, 220
Spinach
Lamb Kofta Burgers with Za'atar Tzatziki, 43
Spit-Roasted Lemon Tarragon Chicken, 106–7
Spray bottle, 18
Squid
cleaning, 145
Grilled Squid with Chorizo & Romesco, 147
Grilled Squid with Soppressata and Spicy Marinara Sauce, 147
grilling, 144
preparing, 144
Sriracha Burgers, 41
Sriracha Mayo, 223

Ssam Jang, 222

Steak, Potatoes & Asparagus, 54

Steak House Burgers, 41

Sweet, Rich & Smoky Barbecue
Sauce, 219

Sweet Potatoes, Coal-Baked, with
Bourbon Bacon Butter, 157

Swordfish, Vietnamese
Coconut, 137

T

Tacos, Grilled Tilapia, 133

Tahini Sauce & Pomegranate Seeds,
Grilled Eggplant with, 174

Taleggio Pancetta Burgers, 41

Techniques

adding smoke and barbecuing,
27–30

checking grill temperature, 25

controlling temperature, 24

cooking in the coals, 25

deepening smoke ring, 30

direct grilling, 22–24

indirect grilling, 24, 25–27

minimizing gray and black
smoke, 27

plank cooking, 31

rotisserie grilling, 30–31

testing foods for doneness, 32

vertical roasting, 27

wrapping food, 31

Temperature regulator, 18

Thermometers, 17

Thick Marinara Sauce, 220

Tilapia, Grilled, Tacos, 133

Tomatoes

Bacon Burgers with Caramelized
Onions & Roasted Tomato
Dressing, 41

Classic Burgers, 41

Grilled Margherita Pizza, 185

Grilled Pizza with Fresh Tomato,
Pesto & Gorgonzola, 189

Grilled Tomato Jam, 223

making fresh puree with, 114

Marinara Sauce, 220

Marinara Sauce with
Red Wine, 220

Masala Sauce, 114

Mediterranean Tomato Salad, 104

Pickled Salsa, 223

Port Ketchup, 225

Roasted Tomato French
Dressing, 222

Romesco, 228

Spicy Marinara Sauce, 220

Steak House Burgers, 41

Thick Marinara Sauce, 220

Tomato Basil Butter, 226

Tongs, 17

Tuna Burgers, Sichuan, with
Pickled-Ginger Relish, 44–47

Turkey

boneless breasts, grilling, 112

Butterflied Turkey Breast with
Spicy Peanut Glaze, 119

Grill-Roasted Turkey with Lemon-
Rosemary Dry Brine, 108–11

how to truss, 111

London broil, about, 119

testing for doneness, 32

Turkey Gravy, 111

Umami Turkey Burgers with
Harissa Ketchup, 37

whole and half, grilling, 99

U

Umami Turkey Burgers with
Harissa Ketchup, 37

V

Vadouvan, 217

Vadouvan Grilled Shrimp, 143

Veal, testing for doneness, 32

Vegetables. *See also specific
vegetables*

brining and marinating times, 211

leaves, grilling, 166

root, grilling, 156

soft, grilling, 172

stems, grilling, 160

Venison, testing for doneness, 32

Vertical roasting, 27

Vertical roasting rack, 18

Vietnamese Coconut Swordfish, 137

Vietnamese Dipping Sauce, 222

Vietnamese-Style Octopus Lettuce
Wraps, 145

Vinaigrette, Orange, 227–28

W

Walnuts

Black Bean Burgers with Sriracha
Mayo & Sesame Slaw, 48

Grilled Quail with Apricot-Sage
Sauce, 102

Western Carolina Barbecue
Sauce, 219

Wild Mushroom Mostarda, 227

Wine

Marinara Sauce with
Red Wine, 220

Port Ketchup, 225

Wild Mushroom Mostarda, 227

Wood, 15, 18, 27–30

Y

Yogurt

Cucumber Raita, 143

Grilled Chicken Tikka Masala, 114

Preserved Lemon Yogurt, 226

Za'atar Tzatziki, 225

Z

Za'atar, preparing, 174

Za'atar Tzatziki, 225

Zucchini, Grilled, with Capers, Pine
Nuts & Orange Vinaigrette, 173

weldon**owen**

1045 Sansome Street, Suite 100, San Francisco, CA 94111
www.weldonowen.com

Weldon Owen is a division of Bonnier Publishing

WELDON OWEN, INC.

President & Publisher Roger Shaw
SVP, Sales & Marketing Amy Kaneko
Finance Manager Philip Paulick

Associate Publisher Amy Marr
Project Editor Kim Laidlaw
Associate Editor Emma Rudolph

Creative Director Kelly Booth
Art Director Marisa Kwek
Senior Production Designer Rachel Lopez Metzger

Production Director Chris Hemesath
Associate Production Director Michelle Duggan

Director of Enterprise Systems Shawn Macey
Imaging Manager Don Hill

Photographer Ray Kachatorian
Food Stylist Valerie Aikman-Smith
Prop Stylist Jennifer Barguiarena

GRILL SCHOOL

Conceived and produced by Weldon Owen, Inc.
In collaboration with Williams-Sonoma, Inc.
3250 Van Ness Avenue, San Francisco, CA 94109

A WELDON OWEN PRODUCTION
Copyright © 2016 Weldon Owen, Inc.
and Williams-Sonoma, Inc.
All rights reserved, including the right of
reproduction in whole or in part in any form.

Printed and bound in China by 1010 Printing, Ltd.

First printed in 2016
10 9 8 7 6 5 4 3 2 1

Library of Congress Cataloging-in-Publication
data is available.

ISBN 13: 978-1-68188-108-9
ISBN 10: 1-68188-108-X

ACKNOWLEDGMENTS

Weldon Owen wishes to thank the following people for their generous
support in producing this book: Gloria Geller, Ian Hartman,
Elizabeth Parson, Michelle Reiner, Alyse Sakai, Sharon Silva, and Toven Stith.